THE PELICAN FREUD LIBRARY

General Editor: Angela Richards

VOLUME 10

ON PSYCHOPATHOLOGY

INHIBITIONS, SYMPTOMS AND ANXIETY
AND OTHER WORKS

Sigmund Freud

Sigmund Freud was born in 1856 in Moravia; between the ages of four and eighty-two his home was in Vienna: in 1938 Hitler's invasion of Austria forced him to seek asylum in London, where he died in the following year. His career began with several years of brilliant work on the anatomy and physiology of the nervous system. He was almost thirty when after a period of study under Charcot in Paris, his interests first turned to psychology, and another ten years of clinical work in Vienna (at first in collaboration with Breuer, an older colleague) saw the birth of his creation, psychoanalysis. This began simply as a method of treating neurotic patients by investigating their minds, but it quickly grew into an accumulation of knowledge about the workings of the mind in general, whether sick or healthy. Freud was thus able to demonstrate the normal development of the sexual instinct in childhood and, largely on the basis of an examination of dreams, arrived at his fundamental discovery of the unconscious forces that influence our everyday thoughts and actions. Freud's life was uneventful, but his ideas have shaped not only many specialist disciplines, but the whole intellectual climate of the last half century.

THE PELICAN FREUD LIBRARY
VOLUME 10

•

ON PSYCHOPATHOLOGY
INHIBITIONS, SYMPTOMS AND ANXIETY
AND OTHER WORKS

Sigmund Freud

•

*Translated from the German
under the general editorship of James Strachey*

*The present volume
compiled and edited by Angela Richards*

PENGUIN BOOKS

Penguin Books Ltd, Harmondsworth, Middlesex, England
Penguin Books, 625 Madison Avenue, New York, New York 10022, U.S.A.
Penguin Books Australia Ltd, Ringwood, Victoria, Australia
Penguin Books Canada Ltd, 2801 John Street, Markham, Ontario,
Canada L3R 1B4
Penguin Books (N.Z.) Ltd, 182–190 Wairau Road, Auckland 10,
New Zealand

—

Inhibitions, Symptoms and Anxiety
and other works

Present English translations first published in *The Standard Edition of the Complete Psychological Works of Sigmund Freud* by the Hogarth Press and the Institute of Psycho-Analysis, London, as follows: 'On the Grounds for Detaching a Particular Syndrome from Neurasthenia under the Description "Anxiety Neurosis"', Volume III (1962); 'My Views on the Part Played by Sexuality in the Aetiology of the Neuroses', Volume VII (1953); 'Hysterical Phantasies and their Relation to Bisexuality', 'Some General Remarks on Hysterical Attacks', Volume IX (1959); 'The Psycho-Analytic View of Psychogenic Disturbance of Vision', Volume XI (1957); 'Types of Onset of Neurosis', 'The Disposition to Obsessional Neurosis', Volume XII (1958); 'A Case of Paranoia Running Counter to the Psycho-Analytic Theory of the Disease', Volume XIV (1957); '"A Child is Being Beaten"', Volume XVII (1955); 'Some Neurotic Mechanisms in Jealousy, Paranoia and Homosexuality', Volume XVIII (1955); 'Neurosis and Psychosis', 'The Loss of Reality in Neurosis and Psychosis', Volume XIX (1961); *Inhibitions, Symptoms and Anxiety*, Volume XX (1959).

'Sigmund Freud: A Sketch of his Life and Ideas' first published in
Two Short Accounts of Psycho-Analysis in Pelican Books 1962

This collection, *On Psychopathology*, first published in Pelican Books 1979

Translation and Editorial Matter copyright © Angela Richards and the
Institute of Psycho-Analysis, 1953, 1955, 1957, 1958, 1959, 1961, 1962
Additional Editorial Matter copyright © Angela Richards, 1979
All rights reserved

—

Set, printed and bound in Great Britain by
Cox & Wyman Ltd, Reading
Set in Monotype Bembo

CONTENTS

VOLUME 10
ON PSYCHOPATHOLOGY

Addenda:

INTRODUCTION TO
THE PELICAN FREUD LIBRARY

The Pelican Freud Library is intended to meet the needs of the general reader by providing all Freud's major writings in translation together with an appropriate linking commentary. It is the first time that such an edition has been produced in paperback in the English language. It does not supplant *The Standard Edition of the Complete Psychological Works of Sigmund Freud*, translated from the German under the general editorship of James Strachey in collaboration with Anna Freud, assisted by Alix Strachey and Alan Tyson, editorial assistant Angela Richards (Hogarth Press, 24 volumes, 1953–74). The *Standard Edition* remains the fullest and most authoritative collection published in any language. It does, however, provide a large enough selection to meet the requirements of all but the most specialist reader – in particular it aims to cater for students of sociology, anthropology, criminology, medicine, aesthetics and education, all of them fields in which Freud's ideas have established their relevance.

The texts are reprinted unabridged, with corrections, from the *Standard Edition*. The editorial commentary – introductions, footnotes, internal cross-references, bibliographies and indexes – is also based upon the *Standard Edition*, but it has been abridged and where necessary adapted to suit the less specialized scope and purposes of the *Pelican Freud Library*. Some corrections have been made and some new material added.

Selection of Material

This is not a complete edition of Freud's psychological works – still less of his works as a whole, which included important contributions to neurology and neuropathology dating from the early part of his professional life. Of the psychological writings, virtually all the major works have been included. The arrangement is by subject-matter, so that the main contributions to any particular theme will be found in one volume. Within each volume the works are, for the main part, in chronological sequence. The aim has been to cover the whole field of Freud's observations and his theory of psychoanalysis: that is to say, in the first place, the structure and dynamics of human mental activity; secondly, psychopathology and the mechanism of mental disorder; and thirdly, the application of psychoanalytic theory to wider spheres than the disorders of individuals which Freud originally, and indeed for the greater part of his life, investigated – to the psychology of groups, to social institutions and to religion, art and literature.

In his 'Sigmund Freud: A Sketch of his Life and Ideas' (p. 13 ff. below), James Strachey includes an account of Freud's discoveries as well as defining his principal theories and tracing their development.

Writings excluded from the Edition

The works that have been excluded are (1) The neurological writings and most of those very early works from the period before the idea of psychoanalysis had taken form. (2) Writings on the actual technique of treatment. These were written specifically for practitioners of psychoanalysis and for analysts in training and their interest is correspondingly specialized. Freud never in fact produced a complete text on psychoanalytic treatment and the papers on technique only deal with selected points of difficulty or theoretical interest. (3) Writings which cover the same ground as other major works which have been included; for example, since the *Library* includes the *Introductory Lectures on Psychoanalysis* and the *New Lectures*, it was decided to leave out several of the shorter expository works in which Freud surveys the whole subject. Similarly, because the *Interpretation of Dreams* is included, the shorter writings on this topic have been omitted. (4) Freud's private correspondence, much of which has now been published in translation[1]. This is not to imply that such letters are without interest or importance though they have not yet received full critical treatment. (5) The numerous short writings, such as reviews of books, prefaces to other authors' works, obituary notices and little *pièces d'occasion* – all of which lose interest to a large extent when separated from the books or occasions to which they refer and which would often demand long editorial explanations to make them comprehensible.

All of these excluded writings (with the exception of the works on neurology and the private letters) can be found in the *Standard Edition*.

Editorial Commentary

The bibliographical information, included at the beginning of the Editor's Note or Introduction to each work, gives the title of the German (or other) original, the date and place of its first publication and the position, where applicable, of the work in Freud's *Gesammelte Werke*, the most complete edition at present available of the works in German (published by S. Fischer Verlag, Frankfurt am Main). Details of the first translation of each work into English are also included, together with the *Standard Edition* reference. Other editions are listed only if they contain significant changes. (Full details of all German editions published in Freud's lifetime and of all English editions prior to the *Standard Edition* are included in the *Standard Edition*.)

The date of original publication of each work has been added to the half-title page, with the date of composition included in square brackets wherever it is different from the former date.

1. [See the list, p. 26 *n*. below, and the details in the Bibliography, p. 335 ff.]

Further background information is given in introductory notes and in footnotes to the text. Apart from dealing with the time and circumstances of composition, these notes aim to make it possible to follow the inception and development of important psychoanalytic concepts by means of systematic cross-references. Most of these references are to other works included in the *Pelican Freud Library*. A secondary purpose is to date additions and alterations made by Freud in successive revisions of the text and in certain cases to provide the earlier versions. No attempt has been made to do this as comprehensively as in the *Standard Edition*, but variants are given whenever they indicate a definite change of view. Square brackets are used throughout to distinguish editorial additions from Freud's text and his own footnotes.

It will be clear from this account that I owe an overwhelming debt to the late James Strachey, the general editor and chief translator of the *Standard Edition*. He indeed was mainly responsible for the idea of a *Pelican Freud Library*, and for the original plan of contents. I have also had the advantage of discussions with Miss Anna Freud and the late Mrs Alix Strachey, both of whom gave advice of the greatest value. I am grateful to the late Mr Ernst Freud for his support and to the Publications Committee of the Institute of Psycho-Analysis for help in furthering preparations for this edition.

ANGELA RICHARDS, 1979

SIGMUND FREUD

A SKETCH OF HIS LIFE AND IDEAS

SIGMUND FREUD was born on 6 May 1856 in Freiberg, a small town in Moravia, which was at that time a part of Austria-Hungary. In an external sense the eighty-three years of his life were on the whole uneventful and call for no lengthy history.

He came of a middle-class Jewish family and was the eldest child of his father's second wife. His position in the family was a little unusual, for there were already two grown-up sons by his father's first wife. These were more than twenty years older than he was and one of them was already married, with a little boy; so that Freud was in fact born an uncle. This nephew played at least as important a part in his very earliest years as his own younger brothers and sisters, of whom seven were born after him.

His father was a wool-merchant and soon after Freud's birth found himself in increasing commercial difficulties. He therefore decided, when Freud was just three years old, to leave Freiberg, and a year later the whole family settled in Vienna, with the exception of the two elder half-brothers and their children, who established themselves instead in Manchester. At more than one stage in his life Freud played with the idea of joining them in England, but nothing was to come of this for nearly eighty years.

In Vienna during the whole of Freud's childhood the family lived in the most straitened conditions; but it is much to his father's credit that he gave invariable priority to the charge of Freud's education, for the boy was obviously intelligent and was a hard worker as well. The result was that he won a place in the 'Gymnasium' at the early age of nine, and for the last six of the eight years he spent at the school he was regularly top of his class. When at the age of seventeen he passed out of school his career was still undecided; his education so far had been of the most general kind, and, though he seemed in any case destined for the University, several faculties lay open to him.

Freud insisted more than once that at no time in his life did he feel 'any particular predilection for the career of a doctor. I was moved, rather', he says, 'by a sort of curiosity, which was, however, directed more towards human concerns than towards natural objects.'[1] Elsewhere he writes: 'I have no knowledge of having had any craving in my early childhood to help suffering humanity ... In my youth I felt an overpowering need to understand something of the riddles of the world in which we live and perhaps even to contribute something to their solution.'[2] And in yet another passage in which he was discussing the sociological studies of his last years: 'My interest, after making a lifelong *détour* through the natural sciences, medicine, and psychotherapy, returned to the cultural problems which had fascinated me long before, when I was a youth scarcely old enough for thinking.'[3]

What immediately determined Freud's choice of a scientific career was, so he tells us, being present just when he was leaving school at a public reading of an extremely flowery essay on 'Nature', attributed (wrongly, it seems) to Goethe. But if it was to be science, practical considerations narrowed the choice to medicine. And it was as a medical student that Freud enrolled himself at the University in the autumn of 1873 at the age of seventeen. Even so, however, he was in no hurry to obtain a medical degree. For his first year or two he attended lectures on a variety of subjects, but gradually concentrated first on biology and then on physiology. His very first piece of research was in his third year at the University, when he was deputed by the

1. [*An Autobiographical Study* (1925d), near the opening of the work.]
2. ['Postscript to *The Question of Lay Analysis*' (1927a).]
3. ['Postscript (1935) to *An Autobiographical Study*' (1935a).]

Professor of Comparative Anatomy to investigate a detail in the anatomy of the eel, which involved the dissection of some four hundred specimens. Soon afterwards he entered the Physiological Laboratory under Brücke, and worked there happily for six years. It was no doubt from him that he acquired the main outlines of his attitude to physical science in general. During these years Freud worked chiefly on the anatomy of the central nervous system and was already beginning to produce publications. But it was becoming obvious that no livelihood which would be sufficient to meet the needs of the large family at home was to be picked up from these laboratory studies. So at last, in 1881, he decided to take his medical degree, and a year later, most unwillingly, gave up his position under Brücke and began work in the Vienna General Hospital.

What finally determined this change in his life was something more urgent than family considerations: in June 1882 he became engaged to be married, and thenceforward all his efforts were directed towards making marriage possible. His fiancée, Martha Bernays, came of a well-known Jewish family in Hamburg, and though for the moment she was living in Vienna she was very soon obliged to return to her remote North-German home. During the four years that followed, it was only for brief visits that he could have glimpses of her, and the two lovers had to content themselves with an almost daily interchange of letters. Freud now set himself to establishing a position and a reputation in the medical world. He worked in various departments of the hospital, but soon came to concentrate on neuroanatomy and neuropathology. During this period, too, he published the first inquiry into the possible medical uses of cocaine; and it was this that suggested to Koller the drug's employment as a local anaesthetic. He soon formed two immediate plans: one of these was to obtain an appointment as *Privatdozent*, a post not unlike that of a university lecturer in England, the other was to gain a travelling bursary which would enable him to spend some time in Paris where the reigning figure was the great Charcot. Both of these aims, if they were realized, would, he felt, bring him real advantages, and in 1885, after a hard struggle, he achieved them both.

The months which Freud spent under Charcot at the Salpêtrière (the famous Paris hospital for nervous diseases) brought another change in the course of his life and this time a revolutionary one. So far his work had been concerned entirely with physical science and he was still carrying out histological studies on the brain while he was in Paris. Charcot's interests were at that period concentrated mainly on hysteria and hypnotism. In the world from which Freud came these subjects were regarded as barely respectable, but he became absorbed in them, and, though Charcot himself looked at them purely as branches of neuropathology, for Freud they meant the first beginnings of the investigation of the mind.

On his return to Vienna in the spring of 1886 Freud set up in private practice as a consultant in nervous diseases, and his long-delayed marriage followed soon afterwards. He did not, however, at once abandon all his neuropathological work: for several more years he studied in particular the cerebral palsies of children, on which he became a leading authority. At this period, too, he produced an important monograph on aphasia. But he was becoming more and more engaged in the treatment of the neuroses. After experimenting in vain with electrotherapy, he turned to hypnotic suggestion, and in 1888 visited Nancy to learn the technique used with such apparent success there by Liébeault and Bernheim. This still proved unsatisfactory and he was driven to yet another line of approach. He knew that a friend of his, Dr Josef Breuer, a Vienna consultant considerably his senior, had some ten years earlier cured a girl suffering from hysteria by a quite new procedure. He now persuaded Breuer to take up the method once more, and he himself applied it to several fresh cases with promising results. The method was based on the assumption that hysteria was the product of a psychical trauma which had been forgotten by the patient; and the treatment consisted in inducing her in a hypnotic state to recall the forgotten trauma to the accompaniment of appropriate emotions. Before very long Freud began to make changes both in the procedure and in the underlying theory; this led eventually to a breach with Breuer, and to the ultimate development by Freud of the whole system of ideas to which he soon gave the name of psychoanalysis.

From this moment onwards – from 1895, perhaps – to the very end of his life, the whole of Freud's intellectual existence revolved around this development, its far-reaching implications, and its theoretical and practical repercussions. It would, of course, be impossible to give in a few sentences any consecutive account of Freud's discoveries and ideas, but an attempt will be made presently to indicate in a disconnected fashion some of the main changes he has brought about in our habits of thought. Meanwhile we may continue to follow the course of his external life.

His domestic existence in Vienna was essentially devoid of episode: his home and his consulting rooms were in the same house from 1891 till his departure for London forty-seven years later. His happy marriage and his growing family – three sons and three daughters – provided a solid counterweight to the difficulties which, to begin with at least, surrounded his professional career. It was not only the nature of his discoveries that created prejudice against him in medical circles; just as great, perhaps, was the effect of the intense anti-semitic feeling which dominated the official world of Vienna: his appointment to a university professorship was constantly held back by political influence.

One particular feature of these early years calls for mention on account of its consequences. This was Freud's friendship with Wilhelm Fliess, a brilliant but unbalanced Berlin physician, who specialized in the ear and throat, but whose wider interests extended over human biology and the effects of periodic phenomena in vital processes. For fifteen years, from 1887 to 1902, Freud corresponded with him regularly, reported the development of his ideas, forwarded him long drafts outlining his future writings, and, most important of all, sent him an essay of some forty thousand words which has been given the name of a 'Project for a Scientific Psychology'. This essay was composed in 1895, at what might be described as the watershed of Freud's career, when he was reluctantly moving from physiology to psychology; it is an attempt to state the facts of psychology in purely neurological terms. This paper and all the rest of Freud's communications to Fliess have, by a lucky chance, survived: they throw a fascinating light on the development of Freud's ideas and show how much of the later findings of psychoanalysis were already present in his mind at this early stage.

Apart from his relations with Fliess, Freud had little outside support to begin with. He gradually gathered a few pupils round him in Vienna, but it was only after some ten years, in about 1906, that a change was inaugurated by the adhesion of a number of Swiss psychiatrists to his views. Chief among these were Bleuler, the head of the Zurich mental hospital, and his assistant Jung. This proved to be the beginning of the first spread of psychoanalysis. An international meeting of psychoanalysts gathered at Salzburg in 1908, and in 1909 Freud and Jung were invited to give a number of lectures in the United States. Freud's writings began to be translated into many languages, and groups of practising analysts sprang up all over the world. But the progress of psychoanalysis was not without its set-backs: the currents which its subject-matter stirred up in the mind ran too deep for its easy acceptance. In 1911 one of Freud's prominent Viennese supporters, Alfred Adler, broke away from him, and two or three years later Jung's differences from Freud led to their separation. Almost immediately after this came the First World War and an interruption of the international spread of psychoanalysis. Soon afterwards, too, came the gravest personal tragedies – the death of a daughter and of a favourite grandchild, and the onset of the malignant illness which was to pursue him relentlessly for the last sixteen years of his life. None of these troubles, however, brought any interruption to the development of Freud's observations and inferences. The structure of his ideas continued to expand and to find ever wider applications – particularly in the sociological field. By now he had become generally recognized as a figure of world celebrity, and no honour pleased him more than his election in 1936, the year of his eightieth birthday, as a Corresponding Member of the Royal Society. It was no doubt this fame, supported by the efforts of influential admirers, including, it is said, President Roosevelt, that protected him from the worst excesses of the National Socialists when Hitler invaded Austria in 1938, though they seized and destroyed his publications. Freud's departure from Vienna was nevertheless essential, and in June of that year, accompanied by some of his family, he made the journey to London, and it was there, a year later, on 23 September 1939, that he died.

It has become a journalistic cliché to speak of Freud as one of the revolutionary founders of modern thought and to couple his name with that of Einstein. Most people would however find it almost as hard to summarize the changes introduced by the one as by the other.

Freud's discoveries may be grouped under three headings – an instrument of research, the findings produced by the instrument, and the theoretical hypotheses inferred from the findings – though the three groups were of course mutually interrelated. Behind all of Freud's work, however, we should posit his belief in the universal validity of the law of determinism. As regards physical phenomena this belief was perhaps derived from his experience in Brücke's laboratory and so, ultimately, from the school of Helmholtz; but Freud extended the belief uncompromisingly to the field of mental phenomena, and here he may have been influenced by his teacher, the psychiatrist Meynert, and indirectly by the philosophy of Herbart.

First and foremost, Freud was the discoverer of the first instrument for the scientific examination of the human mind. Creative writers of genius had had fragmentary insight into mental processes, but no systematic method of investigation existed before Freud. It was only gradually that he perfected the instrument, since it was only gradually that the difficulties in the way of such an investigation became apparent. The forgotten trauma in Breuer's explanation of hysteria provided the earliest problem and perhaps the most fundamental of all, for it showed conclusively that there were active parts of the mind not immediately open to inspection either by an on-looker or by the subject himself. These parts of the mind were described by Freud, without regard for metaphysical or ter-minological disputes, as the unconscious. Their existence was equally demonstrated by the fact of post-hypnotic suggestion, where a person in a fully waking state performs an action which had been suggested to him some time earlier, though he had totally forgotten the suggestion itself. No examination of the mind could thus be considered complete unless it included this unconscious part of it in its scope. How was this to be accom-plished? The obvious answer seemed to be: by means of hyp-notic suggestion; and this was the instrument used by Breuer and, to begin with, by Freud. But it soon turned out to be an imperfect one, acting irregularly and uncertainly and sometimes not at all. Little by little, accordingly, Freud abandoned the use of suggestion and replaced it by an entirely fresh instrument, which was later known as 'free association'. He adopted the unheard-of plan of simply asking the person whose mind he was investigating to say whatever came into his head. This crucial decision led at once to the most startling results; even in this primitive form Freud's instrument produced fresh insight. For, though things went along swimmingly for a while, sooner or later the flow of associations dried up: the subject would not or could not think of anything more to say. There thus came to light the fact of 'resistance', of a force, separate from the subject's conscious will, which was refusing to collaborate with the investigation. Here was one basis for a very fundamental piece of theory, for a hypothesis of the mind as something dynamic, as consisting in a number of mental forces, some conscious and some unconscious, operating now in harmony now in opposition with one another.

Though these phenomena eventually turned out to be of universal occurrence, they were first observed and studied in neurotic patients, and the earlier years of Freud's work were largely concerned with discovering means by which the 'resistance' of these patients could be overcome and what lay behind it could be brought to light. The solution was only made possible by an extraordinary piece of self-observation on Freud's part – what we should now describe as his self-analysis. We are fortunate in having a contemporary first-hand description of this event in his letters to Fliess which have already been mentioned. This analysis enabled him to discover the nature of the unconscious processes at work in the mind and to understand why there is such a strong resistance to their becoming conscious; it enabled him to devise techniques for overcoming or evading the resistance in his patients; and, most important of all, it enabled him to realize the very great difference between the mode of functioning of these unconscious processes and that of our familiar conscious ones. A word may be said on each of these three points, for in fact they constitute the core of Freud's contributions to our knowledge of the mind.

The unconscious contents of the mind were found to consist wholly in the activity of conative trends – desires or wishes – which derive their energy directly from the primary physical instincts. They function quite regardless of any consideration other than that of obtaining immediate satisfaction, and are thus liable to be out of step with those more conscious elements in the mind which are concerned with adaptation to reality and the avoidance of external dangers. Since, moreover, these primitive trends are to a great extent of a sexual or of a destructive nature, they are bound to come in conflict with the more social and civilized mental forces. Investigations along this path were what led Freud to his discoveries of the long-disguised secrets of the sexual life of children and of the Oedipus complex.

In the second place, his self-analysis led him to an inquiry into the nature of dreams. These turned out to be, like neurotic symptoms, the product of a conflict and a compromise between the primary unconscious impulses and the secondary conscious ones. By analysing them into their elements it was therefore possible to infer their hidden unconscious contents; and, since dreams are common phenomena of almost universal occurrence, their interpretation turned out to be one of the most useful technical contrivances for penetrating the resistances of neurotic patients.

Finally, the painstaking examination of dreams enabled Freud to classify the remarkable differences between what he termed the primary and secondary processes of thought, between events in the unconscious and conscious regions of the mind. In the unconscious, it was found, there is no sort of organization or coordination: each separate impulse seeks satisfaction independently of all the rest; they proceed uninfluenced by one another; contradictions are completely inoperative, and the most opposite impulses flourish side by side. So, too, in the unconscious, associations of ideas proceed along lines without any regard to logic: similarities are treated as identities, negatives are equated with positives. Again, the objects to which the conative trends are attached in the unconscious are extraordinarily changeable – one may be replaced by another along a whole chain of associations that have no rational basis. Freud perceived that the intrusion into conscious thinking of mechanisms that belong properly to the primary process accounts for the oddity not only of dreams but of many other normal and pathological mental events.

It is not much of an exaggeration to say that all the later part of Freud's work lay in an immense extension and elaboration of these early ideas. They were applied to an elucidation of the mechanisms not only of the psychoneuroses and psychoses but also of such normal processes as slips of the tongue, making jokes, artistic creation, political institutions, and religions; they played a part in throwing fresh light on many applied sciences – archaeology, anthropology, criminology, education; they also served to account for the effectiveness of psychoanalytic therapy. Lastly, too, Freud erected on the basis of these elementary observations a theoretical superstructure, what he named a 'metapsychology', of more general concepts. These, however, fascinating as many people will find them, he always insisted were in the nature of provisional hypotheses. Quite late in his life, indeed, influenced by the ambiguity of the term 'unconscious' and its many conflicting uses, he proposed a new structural account of the mind in which the uncoordinated instinctual trends were called the 'id', the organized realistic part the 'ego', and the critical and moralizing function the 'super-ego' – a new account which has certainly made for a clarification of many issues.

This, then, will have given the reader an outline of the external events of Freud's life and some notion of the scope of his discoveries. Is it legitimate to ask for more? to try to penetrate a little further and to inquire what sort of person Freud was? Possibly not. But human curiosity about great men is insatiable, and if it is not gratified with true accounts it will inevitably clutch at mythological ones. In two of Freud's early books (*The Interpretation of Dreams* and *The Psychopathology of Everyday Life*) the presentation of his thesis had forced on him the necessity of bringing up an unusual amount of personal material. Nevertheless, or perhaps for that very reason, he intensely objected to any intrusion into his private life, and he was correspondingly the subject of a wealth of myths. According to the first and most naïve rumours, for instance, he was an abandoned profligate, devoted to the corruption of public morals. Later fantasies have tended in the opposite direction: he has been represented as a harsh moralist, a ruthless disciplinarian, an autocrat, egocentric and unsmiling, and an essentially unhappy man. To anyone who was acquainted with him, even slightly, both these pictures must seem equally preposterous. The second of them was no doubt partly derived from a knowledge of his physical sufferings during his last years; but partly too it may have been due to the unfortunate impression produced by some of his most widespread portraits. He disliked being photographed, at least by professional photographers, and his features on occasion expressed the fact; artists too seem always to have been overwhelmed by the necessity for representing the inventor of psychoanalysis as a ferocious and terrifying figure. Fortunately, however, alternative versions exist of a more amiable and truer kind – snapshots, for instance, taken on a holiday or with his children, such as will be found in his eldest son's memoir of his father (*Glory Reflected*, by Martin Freud [1957]). In many ways, indeed, this delightful and amusing book serves to redress the balance from more official biographies, invaluable as they are, and reveals something of Freud as he was in ordinary life. Some of these portraits show us that in his earlier days he had well-filled features, but in later life, at any rate after the First World War and even before his illness, this was no longer so, and his features, as well as his whole figure (which was of medium height), were chiefly remarkable for the impression they gave of tense energy and alert observation. He was serious but kindly and considerate in his more formal manners, but in other circumstances could be an entertaining talker with a pleasantly ironical sense of humour. It was easy to discover his devoted fondness for his family and to recognize a man who would inspire affection. He had many miscellaneous interests – he was fond of travelling abroad, of country holidays, of mountain walks – and there

were other, more engrossing subjects, art, archaeology, literature. Freud was a very well read man in many languages, not
only in German. He read English and French fluently, besides
having a fair knowledge of Spanish and Italian. It must be
remembered, too, that though the later phases of his education
were chiefly scientific (it is true that at the University he studied
philosophy for a short time) at school he had learnt the classics
and never lost his affection for them. We happen to have a letter
written by him at the age of seventeen to a school friend[1]. In it
he describes his varying success in the different papers of his
school-leaving examination: in Latin a passage from Virgil, and
in Greek thirty-three lines from, of all things, *Oedipus Rex*.

In short, we might regard Freud as what in England we
should consider the best kind of product of a Victorian upbringing. His tastes in literature and art would obviously differ
from ours, his views on ethics, though decidedly liberal, would
not belong to the post-Freudian age. But we should see in him
a man who lived a life full of emotion and of much suffering
without embitterment. Complete honesty and directness were
qualities that stood out in him, and so too did his intellectual
readiness to take in and consider any fact, however new or
extraordinary, that was presented to him. It was perhaps an
inevitable corollary and extension of these qualities, combined
with a general benevolence which a surface misanthropy failed
to disguise, that led to some features of a surprising kind. In
spite of his subtlety of mind he was essentially unsophisticated,
and there were sometimes unexpected lapses in his critical
faculty – a failure, for instance, to perceive an untrustworthy
authority in some subject that was off his own beat such as
Egyptology or philology, and, strangest of all in someone
whose powers of perception had to be experienced to be believed, an occasional blindness to defects in his acquaintances.
But though it may flatter our vanity to declare that Freud was a

1. [Emil Fluss. The letter is included in the volume of Freud's correspondence (1960a).]

human being of a kind like our own, that satisfaction can easily be carried too far. There must in fact have been something very extraordinary in the man who was first able to recognize a whole field of mental facts which had hitherto been excluded from normal consciousness, the man who first interpreted dreams, who first accepted the facts of infantile sexuality, who first made the distinction between the primary and secondary processes of thinking – the man who first made the unconscious mind real to us.

JAMES STRACHEY

[Those in search of further information will find it in the three-volume biography of Freud by Ernest Jones, an abridged version of which was published in Pelican in 1964 (reissued 1974), in the important volume of Freud's letters edited by his son and daughter-in-law, Ernst and Lucie Freud (1960a), in several further volumes of his correspondence, with Wilhelm Fliess (1950a), Karl Abraham (1965a), C. G. Jung (1974a), Oskar Pfister (1963a), Lou Andreas-Salomé (1966a), Edoardo Weiss (1970a) and Arnold Zweig (1968a), and above all in the many volumes of Freud's own works.]

CHRONOLOGICAL TABLE

This table traces very roughly some of the main turning-points in Freud's intellectual development and opinions. A few of the chief events in his external life are also included in it.

1856. 6 May. Birth at Freiberg in Moravia.

1860. Family settles in Vienna.

1865. Enters Gymnasium (secondary school).

1873. Enters Vienna University as medical student.

1876–82. Works under Brücke at the Institute of Physiology in Vienna.

1877. First publications: papers on anatomy and physiology.

1881. Graduates as Doctor of Medicine.

1882. Engagement to Martha Bernays.

1882–5. Works in Vienna General Hospital, concentrating on cerebral anatomy: numerous publications.

1884–7. Researches into the clinical uses of cocaine.

1885. Appointed *Privatdozent* (University Lecturer) in Neuropathology.

1885 (October)–1886 (February). Studies under Charcot at the Salpêtrière (hospital for nervous diseases) in Paris. Interest first turns to hysteria and hypnosis.

1886. Marriage to Martha Bernays. Sets up private practice in nervous diseases in Vienna.

1886–93. Continues work on neurology, especially on the cerebral palsies of children at the Kassowitz Institute in Vienna, with numerous publications. Gradual shift of interest from neurology to psychopathology.

1887. Birth of eldest child (Mathilde).

1887–1902. Friendship and correspondence with Wilhelm Fliess in Berlin. Freud's letters to him during this period, published posthumously in 1950, throw much light on the development of his views.

1887. Begins the use of hypnotic suggestion in his practice.

c. 1888. Begins to follow Breuer in using hypnosis for cathartic treatment of hysteria. Gradually drops hypnosis and substitutes free association.

1889. Visits Bernheim at Nancy to study his suggestion technique.

1889. Birth of eldest son (Martin).

1891. Monograph on Aphasia.

Birth of second son (Oliver).

1892. Birth of youngest son (Ernst).

1893. Publication of Breuer and Freud 'Preliminary Communication': exposition of trauma theory of hysteria and of cathartic treatment.

Birth of second daughter (Sophie).

1893–8. Researches and short papers on hysteria, obsessions, and anxiety.

1895. Jointly with Breuer, *Studies on Hysteria*: case histories and description by Freud of his technique, including first account of transference.

1893–6. Gradual divergence of views between Freud and Breue . Freud introduces concepts of defence and repression and of neurosis being a result of a conflict between the ego and the libido.

1895. *Project for a Scientific Psychology*: included in Freud's letters to Fliess and first published in 1950. An abortive attempt to state psychology in neurological terms; but foreshadows much of Freud's later theories.

Birth of youngest child (Anna).

1896. Introduces the term 'psychoanalysis'.

Death of father (aged 80).

1897. Freud's self-analysis, leading to the abandonment of the trauma theory and the recognition of infantile sexuality and the Oedipus complex.

1900. *The Interpretation of Dreams*, with final chapter giving first full account of Freud's dynamic view of mental processes, of the unconscious, and of the dominance of the 'pleasure principle'.

1901. *The Psychopathology of Everyday Life*. This, together with the book on dreams, made it plain that Freud's theories applied not only to pathological states but also to normal mental life.

1902. Appointed Professor Extraordinarius.

1905. *Three Essays on the Theory of Sexuality*: tracing for the first time the course of development of the sexual instinct in human beings from infancy to maturity.

c. 1906. Jung becomes an adherent of psychoanalysis.

1908. First international meeting of psychoanalysts (at Salzburg).

1909. Freud and Jung invited to the USA to lecture.

Case history of the first analysis of a child (Little Hans, aged five): confirming inferences previously made from adult analyses, especially as to infantile sexuality and the Oedipus and castration complexes.

c. 1910. First emergence of the theory of 'narcissism'.

1911–15. Papers on the technique of psychoanalysis.

1911. Secession of Adler.

Application of psychoanalytic theories to a psychotic case: the autobiography of Dr Schreber.

1913–14. *Totem and Taboo*: application of psychoanalysis to anthropological material.

1914. Secession of Jung.

'On the History of the Psycho-Analytic Movement'. Includes a polemical section on Adler and Jung.

Writes his last major case history, of the 'Wolf Man' (not published till 1918).

1915. Writes a series of twelve 'metapsychological' papers on basic theoretical questions, of which only five have survived.

1915–17. *Introductory Lectures*: giving an extensive general account of the state of Freud's views up to the time of the First World War.

1919. Application of the theory of narcissism to the war neuroses.

1920. Death of second daughter.

Beyond the Pleasure Principle: the first explicit introduction of the concept of the 'compulsion to repeat' and of the theory of the 'death instinct'.

1921. *Group Psychology*. Beginnings of a systematic analytic study of the ego.

1923. *The Ego and the Id*. Largely revised account of the structure and functioning of the mind with the division into an id, an ego, and a super-ego.

1923. First onset of cancer.

1925. Revised views on the sexual development of women.

1926. *Inhibitions, Symptoms, and Anxiety*. Revised views on the problem of anxiety.

1927. *The Future of an Illusion*. A discussion of religion: the first of a number of sociological works to which Freud devoted most of his remaining years.

1930. *Civilization and its Discontents*. This includes Freud's first extensive study of the destructive instinct (regarded as a manifestation of the 'death instinct').

Freud awarded the Goethe Prize by the City of Frankfurt.

Death of mother (aged 95).

1933. Hitler seizes power in Germany: Freud's books publicly burned in Berlin.

1934–8. *Moses and Monotheism*: the last of Freud's works to appear during his lifetime.

1936. Eightieth birthday. Election as Corresponding Member of Royal Society.

1938. Hitler's invasion of Austria. Freud leaves Vienna for London. *An Outline of Psycho-Analysis*. A final, unfinished, but profound exposition of psychoanalysis.

1939. 23 September. Death in London.

JAMES STRACHEY

ON THE GROUNDS FOR DETACHING A PARTICULAR SYNDROME FROM NEURASTHENIA UNDER THE DESCRIPTION ' ANXIETY NEUROSIS '

(1895 [1894])

EDITOR'S NOTE

ÜBER DIE BERECHTIGUNG, VON DER NEURASTHENIE EINEN BESTIMMTEN SYMPTOMENKOMPLEX ALS 'ANGSTNEUROSE' ABZUTRENNEN

(A) GERMAN EDITIONS:

1895   *Neurol. Zentbl.*, **14** (2), 50–66. (January 15.)
1925   *Gesammelte Schriften*, **1**, 306–33.
1952   *Gesammelte Werke*, **1**, 315–42.

(B) ENGLISH TRANSLATIONS:

'On the Right to Separate from Neurasthenia a
Definite Symptom-Complex as "Anxiety Neurosis" '

1909   *Selected Papers on Hysteria*, 133–54. (Tr. A. A. Brill.)
       (1912, 2nd ed.; 1920, 3rd ed.)

'The Justification for Detaching from Neurasthenia
a Particular Syndrome: the Anxiety-Neurosis'

1924   *Collected Papers*, **1**, 76–106. (Tr. J. Rickman.)
1962   *Standard Edition*, **3**, 85–115. (Appendix, ibid., 116–17.)
       (Based on the version of 1924, with a new title.)

The present edition is a corrected reprint of the *Standard Edition* version, with some editorial changes.

This paper may be regarded as the first stretch of a trail that led, with more than one bifurcation and more than one sharp turning, through the whole of Freud's writings.[1] But this is not, strictly speaking, the beginning of the trail. It was preceded by several exploratory starts in the form of drafts submitted by Freud to Wilhelm Fliess, which were only posthumously published (Freud, 1950a). It is advisable to bear in mind in reading Freud's early papers that he was at the time deeply involved in an attempt to state the data of psychology in neurological terms – an attempt which culminated in his abortive 'Project for a Scientific Psychology' (written in the autumn of 1895, a few months after these drafts, but, like them, only posthumously published, in Freud 1950a) and which thereafter foundered completely. He had not yet wholly adopted the hypothesis of there being unconscious mental processes. Thus in the present paper he distinguishes between 'somatic sexual excitation' on the one hand and 'sexual libido, or psychical desire' on the other (p. 54). 'Libido' is regarded as something exclusively 'psychical' though, again, no clear distinction seems yet to have been made between 'psychical' and 'conscious'. It is interesting to notice that in an abstract of this paper which Freud himself wrote only a couple of years later (1897b), he evidently already accepts the view of libido as something potentially unconscious and writes: 'Neurotic anxiety is transformed sexual libido.'

But in whatever terms he expressed this theory, it was one which he held till very late in life, though with a number of qualifying complications. For a long series of changing opinions lay ahead, some account of which will be found in the Editor's Introduction to the last of his major works on the subject, *Inhibitions, Symptoms and Anxiety* (1926d), p. 230 ff. below.

1. Some notes on the English translation of the German word '*Angst*' are given in an Editor's Appendix below (p. 64f.).

ON THE GROUNDS FOR DETACHING A PARTICULAR SYNDROME FROM NEURASTHENIA UNDER THE DESCRIPTION 'ANXIETY NEUROSIS'

[INTRODUCTION]

IT is difficult to make any statement of general validity about neurasthenia, so long as we use that name to cover all the things which Beard[1] has included under it. In my opinion, it can be nothing but a gain to neuropathology if we make an attempt to separate from neurasthenia proper all those neurotic disturbances in which, on the one hand, the symptoms are more firmly linked to one another than to the typical symptoms of neurasthenia (such as intracranial pressure, spinal irritation, and dyspepsia with flatulence and constipation); and which, on the other hand, exhibit essential differences in their aetiology and mechanism from the typical neurasthenic neurosis. If we accept this plan, we shall soon obtain a fairly uniform picture of neurasthenia. We shall then be in a position to differentiate from genuine neurasthenia more sharply than has hitherto been possible various pseudo-neurasthenias (such as the clinical picture of the organically determined nasal reflex neurosis,[2] the nervous disorders of the cachexias and arterio-sclerosis, the preliminary stages of general paralysis of the insane, and of some psychoses). Further, it will be possible – as Möbius has

1. [G. M. Beard (1839–83), the American neurologist, was regarded as the principal authority on neurasthenia. Cf. Beard, 1881 and 1884.]

2. [This was a clinical entity proposed by Fliess (1892 and 1893) and impressed by him upon Freud.]

proposed – to eliminate some of the *status nervosi* [nervous conditions] of hereditarily degenerate individuals; and we shall also discover reasons why a number of neuroses which are today described as neurasthenia – in particular, neuroses of an intermittent or periodical nature – ought rather to be included under melancholia. But the most marked change of all will be introduced if we decide to detach from neurasthenia the syndrome which I propose to describe in the following pages and which satisfies especially fully the conditions set out above. The symptoms of this syndrome are clinically much more closely related to one another than to those of genuine neurasthenia (that is, they frequently appear together and they replace one another in the course of the illness); and both the aetiology and the mechanism of this neurosis are fundamentally different from the aetiology and mechanism of genuine neurasthenia as it will be left after this separation has been effected.

I call this syndrome 'anxiety neurosis',[1] because all its components can be grouped round the chief symptom of anxiety, because each one of them has a definite relationship to anxiety. I thought that this view of the symptoms of anxiety neurosis had originated with me, until an interesting paper by E. Hecker (1893) came into my hands, in which I found the same interpretation expounded with all the clarity and completeness that could be desired.[2] Nevertheless, although Hecker recognizes certain symptoms as equivalents or rudiments of an anxiety attack, he does not separate them from the domain of neurasthenia, as I propose to do. But this is evidently due to his not

1. ['*Angstneurose.*' This was the first time Freud used the word in German in a published work. He had already used the French equivalent 'névrose d'angoisse', in 'Obsessions et Phobies' (1895c). According to Löwenfeld, 1904, 479, both the concept and the term are due to Freud. An attempt had been made a little time earlier by Wernicke (1894) to distinguish an anxiety *psychosis*.]

2. Anxiety is actually brought forward as one of the principal symptoms of neurasthenia in a work by Kaan (1893).

having taken into account the difference between the aetiological determinants in the two cases. When this latter difference is recognized there is no longer any necessity for
designating anxiety symptoms by the same name as genuine
neurasthenic ones; for the principal purpose of giving what is
otherwise an arbitrary name is to make it easier to lay down
general statements.

I

THE CLINICAL SYMPTOMATOLOGY OF
ANXIETY NEUROSIS

What I call 'anxiety neurosis' may be observed in a completely
developed form or in a rudimentary one, in isolation or combined with other neuroses. It is of course the cases which are in
some degree complete and at the same time isolated which give
particular support to the impression that anxiety neurosis is a
clinical entity. In other cases, where the syndrome corresponds
to a 'mixed neurosis', we are faced with the task of picking out
and separating those symptoms which belong, not to neurasthenia or hysteria, and so on, but to anxiety neurosis.

The clinical picture of anxiety neurosis comprises the following symptoms:

(1) General irritability. This is a common nervous symptom
and as such belongs to many status nervosi. I mention it here
because it invariably appears in anxiety neurosis and is important theoretically. Increased irritability always points to an
accumulation of excitation or an inability to tolerate such an
accumulation – that is, to an absolute or a relative accumulation
of excitation. One manifestation of this increased irritability
seems to me to deserve special mention; I refer to auditory hyper-
aesthesia, to an oversensitiveness to noise – a symptom which is
undoubtedly to be explained by the innate intimate relationship
between auditory impressions and fright. Auditory hyper-

aesthesia frequently turns out to be a cause of *sleeplessness*, of which more than one form belongs to anxiety neurosis.

(2) *Anxious expectation*. I cannot better describe the condition I have in mind than by this name and by adding a few examples. A woman, for instance, who suffers from anxious expectation will think of influenzal pneumonia every time her husband coughs when he has a cold, and, in her mind's eye, will see his funeral go past; if, when she is coming towards the house, she sees two people standing by her front door, she cannot avoid thinking that one of her children has fallen out of the window; when she hears the bell ring, it is someone bringing news of a death, and so on – while on all these occasions there has been no particular ground for exaggerating a mere possibility.

Anxious expectation, of course, shades off imperceptibly into normal anxiety, comprising all that is ordinarily spoken of as anxiousness – or a tendency to take a pessimistic view of things; but at every opportunity it goes beyond a plausible anxiousness of this kind, and it is frequently recognized by the patient himself as a kind of compulsion. For one form of anxious expectation – that relating to the subject's own health – we may reserve the old term *hypochondria*. The height reached by the hypochondria is not always parallel with the general anxious expectation; it requires as a precondition the existence of paraesthesias and distressing bodily sensations. Thus hypochondria is the form favoured by genuine neurasthenics when, as often happens, they fall victims to anxiety neurosis.[1]

A further expression of anxious expectation is no doubt to be found in the inclination to *moral anxiety*,[2] to scrupulousness and

1. [Freud made some further remarks on the relation of hypochondria to the other neuroses in his theoretical contribution to *Studies on Hysteria* (1895d), *P.F.L.*, **3**, 340–41. He returned to the subject much later, particularly in Section II of his paper on narcissism (1914c).

2. ['*Gewissensangst*', literally 'conscience anxiety'. This was to be a principal topic in some of Freud's latest writings – for instance in the latter part of *Inhibitions, Symptoms and Anxiety* (1926d). Cf. in particular p. 284 and *n*. as well as pp. 296f. and 304 below.]

pedantry – an inclination which is so often present in people with more than the usual amount of moral sensitiveness and which likewise varies from the normal to an exaggerated form in *doubting mania*.

Anxious expectation is the nuclear symptom of the neurosis. It openly reveals, too, a portion of the theory of the neurosis. We may perhaps say that here a *quantum of anxiety in a freely floating state* is present, which, where there is expectation, controls the choice of ideas and is always ready to link itself with any suitable ideational content.

(3) But anxiousness – which, though mostly latent as regards consciousness, is constantly lurking in the background – has other means of finding expression besides this. It can suddenly break through into consciousness without being aroused by a train of ideas, and thus provoke an *anxiety attack*. An anxiety attack of this sort may consist of the feeling of anxiety, alone, without any associated idea, or accompanied by the interpretation that is nearest to hand, such as ideas of the extinction of life, or of a stroke, or of a threat of madness; or else some kind of paraesthesia (similar to the hysterical aura[1]) may be combined with the feeling of anxiety, or, finally, the feeling of anxiety may have linked to it a disturbance of one or more of the bodily functions – such as respiration, heart action, vaso-motor innervation or glandular activity. From this combination the patient picks out in particular now one, now another, factor. He complains of 'spasms of the heart', 'difficulty in breathing', 'outbreaks of sweating', 'ravenous hunger', and such like; and, in his description, the feeling of anxiety often recedes into the background or is referred to quite unrecognizably as 'being unwell', 'feeling uncomfortable', and so on.

(4) Now it is an interesting fact, and an important one from a diagnostic point of view, that the proportion in which these elements are mixed in an anxiety attack varies to a remarkable

1. [The premonitory sensations which precede an epileptic or hysterical attack.

degree, and that almost every accompanying symptom alone
can constitute the attack just as well as can the anxiety itself.
There are consequently *rudimentary anxiety attacks* and *equivalents of anxiety attacks*, all probably having the same significance,
which exhibit a great wealth of forms that has as yet been little
appreciated. A closer study of these larval anxiety-states (as
Hecker [1893] calls them) and their diagnostic differentiation
from other attacks should soon become a necessary task for
neuropathologists.

I append here a list which includes only those forms of
anxiety attack which are known to me:—

(*a*) Anxiety attacks accompanied by disturbances of the *heart
action*, such as palpitation, either with transitory arrhythmia or
with tachycardia of longer duration which may end in serious
weakness of the heart and which is not always easily differentiated from organic heart affection; and, again, pseudo-angina
pectoris – diagnostically a delicate subject!

(*b*) Anxiety attacks accompanied by *disturbances of respiration*,
several forms of nervous dyspnoea, attacks resembling asthma,
and the like. I would emphasize that even these attacks are not
always accompanied by recognizable anxiety.

(*c*) Attacks of *sweating*, often at night.

(*d*) Attacks of *tremor* and *shivering* which are only too easily
confused with hysterical attacks.

(*e*) Attacks of *ravenous hunger*, often accompanied by vertigo.

(*f*) *Diarrhoea* coming on in attacks.

(*g*) Attacks of locomotor *vertigo*.

(*h*) Attacks of what are known as *congestions*, including prac-
tically everything that has been termed vasomotor neurasthenia.

(*i*) Attacks of *paraesthesias*. (But these seldom occur without
anxiety or a similar feeling of discomfort.)

(5) *Waking up at night in a fright* (the *pavor nocturnus* of adults),
which is usually combined with anxiety, dyspnoea, sweating

and so on, is very often nothing else than a variant of the anxiety attack. This disturbance is the determinant of a second form of sleeplessness within the field of anxiety neurosis. [Cf. p. 37f.] I have become convinced, moreover, that the *pavor nocturnus* of children, too, exhibits a form which belongs to anxiety neurosis. The streak of hysteria about it, the linking of the anxiety with the reproduction of an appropriate experience or a dream, causes the *pavor nocturnus* of children to appear as something special. But the *pavor* can also emerge in a pure form, without any dream or recurring hallucination.

(6) '*Vertigo*' occupies a prominent place in the group of symptoms of anxiety neurosis. In its mildest form it is best described as 'giddiness'; in its severer manifestations, as 'attacks of vertigo' (with or without anxiety), it must be classed among the gravest symptoms of the neurosis. The vertigo of anxiety neurosis is not rotatory nor does it especially affect certain planes or directions, like Ménière's vertigo. It belongs to the class of locomotor or co-ordinatory vertigo, as does the vertigo in oculomotor paralysis. It consists in a specific state of discomfort, accompanied by sensations of the ground rocking, of the legs giving way and of its being impossible to stand up any more; while the legs feel as heavy as lead and tremble or the knees bend. This vertigo never leads to a fall. On the other hand, I should like to state that an attack of vertigo of this kind may have its place taken by a profound *fainting fit*. Other conditions in the nature of fainting occurring in anxiety neurosis appear to depend upon *cardiac collapse*.

Attacks of vertigo are not seldom accompanied by the worst sort of anxiety, often combined with cardiac and respiratory disturbances. According to my observations, vertigo produced by heights, mountains and precipices is also often present in anxiety neurosis. Furthermore, I am not sure whether it is not also right to recognize alongside of this a *vertigo a stomacho laeso* [of gastric origin].

(7) On the basis of chronic anxiousness (anxious expectation)

on the one hand, and a tendency to anxiety attacks accompanied by vertigo on the other, two groups of typical phobias develop, the first relating to general physiological dangers, the second relating to locomotion. To the first group belong fear of snakes, thunderstorms, darkness, vermin, and so on, as well as the typical moral over-scrupulousness and forms of doubting mania. Here the available anxiety is simply employed to re-inforce aversions which are instinctively implanted in everyone. But as a rule a phobia which acts in an obsessional manner is only formed if there is added to this the recollection of an experience in which the anxiety was able to find expression – as, for instance, after the patient has experienced a thunderstorm in the open. It is a mistake to try to explain such cases as being simply a *persistence of strong impressions*; what makes these experiences significant and the memory of them lasting is, after all, only the anxiety which was able to emerge at the time [of the experience] and which can similarly emerge now. In other words, such impressions remain powerful only in people with 'anxious expectation'.

The other group includes *agoraphobia* with all its accessory forms, the whole of them characterized by their relation to locomotion. We frequently find that this phobia is based on an attack of vertigo that has preceded it; but I do not think that one can postulate such an attack in every case. Occasionally we see that after a first attack of vertigo without anxiety, loco-motion, although henceforward constantly accompanied by a sensation of vertigo, still continues to be possible without re-striction; but that, under certain conditions – such as being alone or in a narrow street – when once anxiety is added to the attack of vertigo, locomotion breaks down.

The relation of these phobias to the phobias of obsessional neurosis, whose mechanism I made clear in an earlier paper[1] in this periodical, is of the following kind. What they have in

1. 'The Neuro-Psychoses of Defence' (1894*a*). – [The term 'obses-sional neurosis (*Zwangsneurose*)' makes its first published appearance in

common is that in both an idea becomes obsessional as a result of being attached to an available affect. The mechanism of *transposition of affect* thus holds good for both kinds of phobia. But in the phobias of anxiety neurosis (1) this affect always has the same colour, which is that of anxiety; and (2) the affect does not originate in a repressed idea, but turns out to be *not further reducible by psychological analysis, nor amenable to psychotherapy*. The mechanism of *substitution*, therefore, does not hold good for the phobias of anxiety neurosis.

Both kinds of phobias (and also obsessions) often appear side by side; although the *atypical* phobias, which are based on obsessions, need not necessarily spring from the soil of anxiety neurosis. A very frequent and apparently complicated mechanism makes its appearance if, in what was originally a simple phobia belonging to an anxiety neurosis, the content of the phobia is replaced by another idea, so that the substitute is *subsequent* to the phobia. What are most often employed as substitutes are the '*protective measures*' that were originally used to combat the phobia. Thus, for instance, 'brooding mania' arises from the subject's endeavours to disprove that he is mad, as his hypochondriacal phobia maintains; the hesitations and doubt, and still more the repetitions, of *folie du doute* [doubting mania] arise from a justifiable doubt about the certainty of one's own train of thought, since one is conscious of its persistent disturbance by ideas of an obsessional sort, and so on. We can therefore assert that many syndromes, too, of obsessional neurosis, such as *folie du doute* and the like, are also to be reckoned, clinically if not conceptually, as belonging to anxiety neurosis.[1]

(8) The digestive activities undergo only a few disturbances in anxiety neurosis; but these are characteristic ones. Sensations such as an inclination to vomit and nausea are not rare, and the

---

this sentence. Löwenfeld (1904, 296 and 487) attributed the origin of both the term and the concept to Freud.]

1. See 'Obsessions and Phobias' (1895c).

symptom of ravenous hunger may, by itself or in conjunction with other symptoms (such as congestions), give rise to a rudimentary anxiety attack. As a chronic change, analogous to anxious expectation, we find an inclination to diarrhoea, and this has been the occasion of the strangest diagnostic errors. Unless I am mistaken, it is this diarrhoea to which Möbius (1894) has drawn attention recently in a short paper. I suspect, further, that Peyer's reflex diarrhoea, which he derives from disorders of the prostate (Peyer, 1893), is nothing else than this diarrhoea of anxiety neurosis. The illusion of a reflex relationship is created because the same factors come into play in the aetiology of anxiety neurosis as are at work in the setting up of such affections of the prostate and similar disorders.

The behaviour of the gastro-intestinal tract in anxiety neurosis presents a sharp contrast to the influence of neurasthenia on those functions. Mixed cases often show the familiar 'alternation between diarrhoea and constipation'. Analogous to this diarrhoea is the need to urinate that occurs in anxiety neurosis.

(9) The *paraesthesias* which may accompany attacks of vertigo or anxiety are interesting because they, like the sensations of the hysterical aura, become associated in a definite sequence; although I find that these associations, in contrast to the hysterical ones, are atypical and changing. A further similarity to hysteria is provided by the fact that in anxiety neurosis a kind of *conversion*[1] takes place on to bodily sensations, which may easily be overlooked – for instance, on to rheumatic muscles. A whole number of what are known as rheumatic individuals – who, moreover, can be shown to *be* rheumatic – are in reality suffering from anxiety neurosis. Along with this increase of sensitivity to pain, I have also observed in a number of cases of anxiety neurosis a tendency to *hallucinations*; and these could not be interpreted as hysterical.

(10) Several of the symptoms I have mentioned, which

1. See 'The Neuro-Psychoses of Defence' (1894a) [cf. also the paper on 'Hysterical Phantasies' (1908a), pp. 89–90 below.]

accompany or take the place of an anxiety attack, also appear in a chronic form. In that case they are still less easy to recognize, since the anxious sensation which goes with them is less clear than in an anxiety attack. This is especially true of diarrhoea, vertigo and paraesthesias. Just as an attack of vertigo can be replaced by a fainting fit, so chronic vertigo can be replaced by a constant feeling of great feebleness, lassitude and so on.

II

INCIDENCE AND AETIOLOGY OF ANXIETY NEUROSIS

In some cases of anxiety neurosis no aetiology at all is to be discovered. It is worth noting that in such cases there is seldom any difficulty in establishing evidence of a grave hereditary taint.

But where there are grounds for regarding the neurosis as an *acquired* one, careful enquiry directed to that end reveals that a set of noxae and influences from *sexual life* are the operative aetiological factors. These appear at first sight to be of a varied nature, but they soon disclose the common character which explains why they have a similar effect on the nervous system. Further, they are present either alone or together with other noxae of a 'stock'[1] kind, to which we may ascribe a contributory effect. This sexual aetiology of anxiety neurosis can be demonstrated with such overwhelming frequency that I venture, *for the purpose of this short paper*, to disregard those cases where the aetiology is doubtful or different.

In order that the aetiological conditions under which anxiety neurosis makes its appearance may be presented with greater accuracy, it will be advisable to consider males and females separately. In females – disregarding for the moment their

1. [This word was adopted in the *Standard Edition* translations of Freud's early papers as a rendering of the German-French adjective '*banal*'.]

innate disposition – anxiety neurosis occurs in the following cases:

(a) As *virginal anxiety* or *anxiety in adolescents*. A number of unambiguous observations have shown me that anxiety neurosis can be produced in girls who are approaching maturity by their first encounter with the problem of sex, by any more or less sudden revelation of what had till then been hidden – for instance, by witnessing the sexual act, or being told or reading about these things. Such an anxiety neurosis is combined with hysteria in an almost typical fashion.[1]

(b) As *anxiety in the newly-married*. Young married women who have remained anaesthetic during their first cohabitations not seldom fall ill of an anxiety neurosis, which disappears once more as soon as the anaesthesia gives place to normal sensitivity. Since most young wives remain healthy where there is initial anaesthesia of this kind, it follows that, in order that this kind of anxiety shall emerge, other determinants are required; and these I will mention later.

(c) As anxiety in women whose husbands suffer from ejaculatio praecox or from markedly impaired potency; and (d) whose husbands practise coitus interruptus or reservatus. These cases [(c) and (d)] belong together, for on analysing a great number of instances it is easy to convince oneself that they depend simply on whether the woman obtains satisfaction in coitus or not. If not, the condition for the genesis of an anxiety neurosis is given. On the other hand, she is saved from the

1. [Freud quoted the gist of this paragraph in a footnote to his second paper on the neuro-psychoses of defence (1896*b*), and added: 'I know now that the occasion on which this "virginal anxiety" breaks out in young girls does not actually represent their *first* encounter with sexuality, but that an experience of sexual passivity had previously occurred in their childhood, the memory of which is aroused by this "first encounter".' The case of 'Katharina' in *Studies on Hysteria* was described by Freud as an example of 'virginal anxiety'. See *P.F.L.*, 3, 192, 201 and 342–3.]

neurosis if the husband who is afflicted with ejaculatio praecox is able immediately to repeat coitus with better success. Coitus reservatus *by means of condoms* is not injurious to the woman, provided she is very quickly excitable and the husband very potent; otherwise, this kind of preventive intercourse is no less injurious than the others. Coitus interruptus is nearly always a noxa. But for the wife it is only so if the husband practises it regardlessly – that is to say, if he breaks off intercourse as soon as *he* is near emission, without troubling himself about the course of the excitation in *her*. If, on the other hand, the husband waits for his wife's satisfaction, the coitus amounts to a normal one for *her*; but *he* will fall ill of an anxiety neurosis. I have collected and analysed a large number of observations, on which these assertions are based.

(*e*) Anxiety neurosis also occurs as anxiety in *widows* and intentionally *abstinent women*, not seldom in a typical combination with obsessional ideas; and

(*f*) As anxiety in the *climacteric* during the last major increase of sexual need.

Cases (*c*) (*d*) and (*e*) comprise the conditions under which anxiety neurosis in the female sex arises most frequently and most readily, independently of hereditary disposition. It is in reference to these cases of anxiety neurosis – these curable acquired cases – that I shall try to show that the sexual noxae discovered in them are really the aetiological factor of the neurosis.

Before doing so, however, I will discuss the sexual determinants of anxiety neurosis in *men*. I propose to distinguish the following groups, all of which have their analogies in women:

(*a*) Anxiety of intentionally *abstinent* men, which is frequently combined with symptoms of *defence* (obsessional ideas, hysteria). The motives which are responsible for intentional abstinence imply that a number of people with a hereditary disposition, eccentrics, etc., enter into this category.

(*b*) Anxiety in men in a state of *unconsummated excitation* (e.g. during the period of engagement before marriage), or in those

who (from fear of the consequences of sexual intercourse) content themselves with touching or looking at women. This
group of determinants – which, incidentally, can be applied
unaltered to the other sex (during engagements or relations in
which sexual intercourse is avoided) – provides the purest cases
of the neurosis.

(c) Anxiety in men who practise coitus interruptus. As has
been said, coitus interruptus is injurious to the *woman* if it is
practised without regard to her satisfaction; but it is injurious
to the *man* if, in order to obtain satisfaction for her, he directs
coitus voluntarily and postpones emission. In this way it becomes intelligible that when a married couple practise coitus
interruptus, it is, as a rule, only *one* partner who falls ill. Moreover, in men coitus interruptus only rarely produces a pure
anxiety neurosis; it usually produces a mixture of anxiety
neurosis and neurasthenia.

(d) Anxiety in *senescent* men. There are men who have a
climacteric like women, and who produce an anxiety neurosis
at the time of their decreasing potency and increasing libido.[1]

Finally, I must add two other cases which apply to both
sexes:

(α) People who, as a result of practising masturbation, have
become neurasthenics,[2] fall victims to anxiety neurosis as soon
as they give up their form of sexual satisfaction. Such people
have made themselves particularly incapable of tolerating
abstinence.

I may note here, as being important for an understanding of
anxiety neurosis, that any pronounced development of that
affection only occurs among men who have remained potent
and women who are not anaesthetic. Among neurotics whose
potency has already been severely damaged by masturbation,

1. [This seems to be Freud's first published use of the term 'libido'
and is probably its original introduction in this technical sense, preceding Moll's use of it in 1898.]

2. [See below, p. 56, footnote 1.]

the anxiety neurosis resulting from abstinence is very slight and is mostly restricted to hypochondria and mild chronic vertigo. The majority of women, indeed, are to be regarded as 'potent'; a really impotent – i.e. a really anaesthetic – woman is in a similar way little susceptible to anxiety neurosis, and she tolerates the noxae I have described remarkably well.

How far, in addition to this, we are justified in postulating any constant relation between particular aetiological factors and particular symptoms in the complex of anxiety neurosis, I should not like to discuss as yet in this paper.

(β) The last of the aetiological conditions I have to bring forward appears at first sight not to be of a sexual nature at all. Anxiety neurosis also arises – and in both sexes – as a result of the factor of overwork or exhausting exertion – as, for instance, after night-watching, sick-nursing, or even after severe illness.

The main objection to my postulate of a sexual aetiology for anxiety neurosis will probably be to the following effect. Abnormal conditions in sexual life of the kind I have described are found so extremely frequently that they are bound to be forthcoming wherever one looks for them. Their presence in the cases of anxiety neurosis which I have enumerated does not, therefore, prove that we have unearthed in them the aetiology of the neurosis. Moreover, the number of people who practise coitus interruptus and the like is incomparably larger than the number who are afflicted with anxiety neurosis, and the great majority of the former tolerate this noxa very well.

To this I must reply in the first place that, considering the admittedly enormous frequency of the neuroses and especially of anxiety neurosis, it would certainly not be right to expect to find an aetiological factor for them that is of *rare* occurrence; in the second place, that a postulate of pathology is in fact satisfied, if in an aetiological investigation it can be shown that the *presence* of an aetiological factor is more frequent than its effects, since, in order for these latter to occur, other conditions may have to exist in addition (such as disposition, summation of specific aetiological elements, or reinforcement by other, stock noxae); and further, that a detailed dissection of suitable cases of anxiety neurosis proves beyond question the importance of the sexual factor. I will confine myself here, however, to the single aetiological factor of coitus interruptus and to bringing out certain observations which confirm it.

(1) So long as an anxiety neurosis in young married women is not yet established, but only appears in bouts and disappears again spontaneously, it is possible to demonstrate that each such bout of the neurosis is traceable to a coitus which was deficient in satisfaction. Two days after this experience – or, in the case of people with little resistance, the day after – the attack of anxiety or vertigo regularly appears, bringing in its train other symptoms of the neurosis. All this vanishes once more, provided that marital intercourse is comparatively rare. A chance absence of the husband from home, or a holiday in the mountains which necessitates a separation of the couple, has a good effect. The gynaecological treatment which is usually resorted to in the first instance is beneficial because, while it lasts, marital intercourse is stopped. Curiously enough the success of local treatment is only transitory: the neurosis sets in again in the mountains, as soon as the husband begins his holiday too; and so on. If, as a physician who understands this aetiology, one arranges, in a case in which the neurosis has not yet been established, for coitus interruptus to be replaced by normal intercourse, one obtains a *therapeutic* proof of the assertion I have made. The anxiety is removed, and – unless there is fresh cause for it of the same sort – it does not return.

(2) In the anamneses of many cases of anxiety neurosis we find, both in men and women, a striking oscillation in the intensity of its manifestations, and, indeed, in the coming and going of the whole condition. One year, they will tell you, was almost entirely good, but the next one was dreadful; on one occasion the improvement seemed to be due to a particular

treatment, which, however, turned out to be quite useless at the next attack; and so on. If we enquire into the number and sequence of the children and compare this record of the marriage with the peculiar history of the neurosis, we arrive at the simple solution that the periods of improvement or good health coincided with the wife's pregnancies, during which, of course, the need for preventive intercourse was no longer present. The husband benefited by the treatment after which he found his wife pregnant – whether he received it from Pastor Kneipp[1] or at a hydropathic establishment.

(3) The anamnesis of patients often discloses that the symptoms of anxiety neurosis have at some definite time succeeded the symptoms of some other neurosis – neurasthenia, perhaps – and have taken their place. In these instances it can quite regularly be shown that, shortly before this change of the picture, a corresponding change has occurred in the form of the sexual noxa.

Observations of this sort, which can be multiplied at will, positively thrust a sexual aetiology on the doctor for a certain category of cases. And other cases, which would otherwise remain unintelligible, can at least be understood and classified without inconsistency by employing that aetiology as a key. I have in mind those very numerous cases in which, it is true, everything is present that has been found in the previous category – on the one hand the manifestations of anxiety neurosis, and on the other the specific factor of coitus interruptus – but in which something else as well intrudes itself: namely, a long interval between the presumed aetiology and its effects, and also perhaps aetiological factors that are not of a sexual nature. Take, for instance, a man who, on receiving news of his father's death, had a heart attack and from that moment fell a victim to an anxiety neurosis. The case is not comprehensible, for, till

1. [Sebastian Kneipp (1821–97), of Bad Wörishofen in Swabia, was famous for his cold-water and 'nature' cure. Part of his treatment consisted in walking barefoot through wet grass.]

then, the man was not neurotic. The death of his father, who was well advanced in years, did not take place under in any way special circumstances, and it will be admitted that the normal and expected decease of an aged father is not one of those experiences which usually cause a healthy adult to fall ill. Perhaps the aetiological analysis will become clearer if I add that this man had been practising coitus interruptus for eleven years, with due consideration for his wife's satisfaction. The clinical symptoms are, at least, exactly the same as those which appear in other people after only a short sexual noxa of the same kind, and without the interpolation of any other trauma. A similar assessment must be made of the case of a woman whose anxiety neurosis broke out after the loss of her child, or of the student whose preparatory studies for his final examination were interfered with by an anxiety neurosis. I think that in these instances, too, the effect is not explained by the ostensible aetiology. One is not necessarily 'overworked' by study,[1] and a healthy mother as a rule reacts only with normal grief to the loss of a child. Above all, however, I should have expected the student, as a result of his overwork, to acquire cephalasthenia,[2] and the mother, as a result of her bereavement, hysteria. That both should have been overtaken by anxiety neurosis leads me to attach importance to the fact that the mother had been living for eight years in conditions of marital coitus interruptus, and that the student had for three years had an ardent love-affair with a 'respectable' girl whom he had to avoid making pregnant.

These considerations lead us to the conclusion that the specific sexual noxa of coitus interruptus, even when it is not able on its own account to provoke an anxiety neurosis in the subject, does at least *dispose* him to acquire it. The anxiety

1. [Cf. some discussion of 'overwork' in the *Three Essays* (1905*d*), *P.F.L.*, 7, 124.]

2. [Freud referred to this case again in a later paper on anxiety neurosis (1895*f*.), using the term 'cerebral neurasthenia'.]

neurosis breaks out as soon as there is added to the latent effect of the specific factor the effect of another, stock noxa. The latter can act in the sense of the specific factor quantitatively but cannot replace it qualitatively. The specific factor always remains decisive for the *form* taken by the neurōsis. I hope to be able to prove this assertion concerning the aetiology of the neuroses more comprehensively too.

In addition, these latter remarks contain an assumption which is not in itself improbable, to the effect that a sexual noxa like coitus interruptus comes into force through summation. A shorter or longer time is needed – depending on the individual's disposition and any other inherited weaknesses of his nervous system – before the effect of this summation becomes visible. Those individuals who apparently tolerate coitus interruptus without harm, in fact become disposed by it to the disorders of anxiety neurosis, and these may break out at some time or other, either spontaneously or after a stock trauma which would not ordinarily suffice for this; just as, by the path of summation, a chronic alcoholic will in the end develop a cirrhosis or some other illness, or will, under the influence of a fever, fall a victim to delirium.[1]

III

FIRST STEPS TOWARDS A THEORY OF ANXIETY NEUROSIS

The following theoretical discussion can only claim to have the value of a first, groping attempt; criticism of it ought not to affect an acceptance of the *facts* which have been brought forward above. Moreover, an assessment of this 'theory of anxiety neurosis' is made the more difficult from being only a fragment of a more comprehensive account of the neuroses.

1. [The 'summation' of traumas in cases of hysteria had been discussed by Freud in *Studies on Hysteria* (1895*d*), P.F.L., **3**, 245–6.]

What we have so far said about anxiety neurosis already provides a few starting points for gaining an insight into the mechanism of this neurosis. In the first place there was our suspicion that we had to do with an accumulation of excitation [p. 37]; and then there was the extremely important fact that the anxiety which underlies the clinical symptoms of the neurosis can be traced to *no psychical origin*. Such an origin would exist, for instance, if it was found that the anxiety neurosis was based on a single or repeated justifiable fright, and that that fright had since provided the source for the subject's readiness for anxiety. But this is not so. Hysteria or a traumatic neurosis can be acquired from a single fright, but never anxiety neurosis. Since coitus interruptus takes such a prominent place among the causes of anxiety neurosis, I thought at first that the source of the continuous anxiety might lie in the fear, recurring every time the sexual act was performed, that the technique might go wrong and conception consequently take place. But I have found that this state of feeling, either in the man or the woman, during coitus interruptus has no influence on the generation of anxiety neurosis, that women who are basically indifferent about the consequence of a possible conception are just as liable to the neurosis as those who shudder at the possibility, and that everything depends simply on which partner has forfeited satisfaction in this sexual technique.

A further point of departure is furnished by the observation, not so far mentioned, that in whole sets of cases anxiety neurosis is accompanied by a most noticeable decrease of sexual libido or *psychical desire*,[1] so that on being told that their complaint results from 'insufficient satisfaction', patients regularly reply that that is impossible, for precisely now all sexual need has become extinguished in them. From all these indications – that we have to do with an accumulation of excitation; that the anxiety which probably corresponds to this accumulated excitation is of somatic origin, so that what is being accumulated

1. [See Editor's Note, p. 34 above.]

is a *somatic* excitation; and, further, that this somatic excitation is of a sexual nature and that a decrease of *psychical* participation in the sexual processes goes along with it – all these indications, I say, incline us to expect that *the mechanism of anxiety neurosis is to be looked for in a deflection of somatic sexual excitation from the psychical sphere, and in a consequent abnormal employment of that excitation.*

This concept of the mechanism of anxiety neurosis can be made clearer if one accepts the following view of the sexual process, which applies, in the first instance, to men. In the sexually mature male organism somatic sexual excitation is produced – probably continuously – and periodically becomes a stimulus to the psyche. In order to make our ideas on this point firmer, I will add by way of interpolation that this somatic excitation is manifested as a pressure on the walls of the seminal vesicles, which are lined with nerve endings; thus this visceral excitation will develop continuously, but it will have to reach a certain height before it is able to overcome the resistance of the intervening path of conduction to the cerebral cortex and express itself as a psychical stimulus.[1] When this has happened, however, the group of sexual ideas which is present in the psyche becomes supplied with energy and there comes into being the psychical state of libidinal tension which brings with it an urge to remove that tension. A psychical unloading of this kind is only possible by means of what I shall call *specific* or *adequate* action. This adequate action consists, for the male sexual instinct, in a complicated spinal reflex act which brings about the unloading of the nerve-endings, and in all the psychical preparations which have to be made in order to set off that reflex. Anything other than the adequate action would be fruitless, for once the somatic sexual excitation has reached threshold value it is turned continuously into psychical exci-

1. [This theory of the process of sexual excitation was stated again by Freud in Section 2 of the third of his *Three Essays* (1905*d*), P.F.L., **7,** 133 ff.; but he there also stated certain objections to it.]

tation, and something must positively take place which will free the nerve-endings from the load of pressure on them – which will, accordingly, remove the whole of the existing somatic excitation and allow the subcortical path of conduction to re-establish its resistance.

I shall refrain from describing more complicated instances of the sexual process in a similar way. I will only state that in essentials this formula is applicable to women as well, in spite of the confusion introduced into the problem by all the artificial retarding and stunting of the female sexual instinct. In women too we must postulate a somatic sexual excitation and a state in which this excitation becomes a psychical stimulus – libido – and provokes the urge to the specific action to which voluptuous feeling is attached. Where women are concerned, however, we are not in a position to say what the process analogous to the relaxation of tension of the seminal vesicles may be.

We can include within the framework of this description of the sexual process not only the aetiology of anxiety neurosis but that of genuine neurasthenia. Neurasthenia develops whenever the adequate unloading (the adequate action) is replaced by a less adequate one – thus, when normal coition, carried out in the most favourable conditions, is replaced by masturbation or spontaneous emission.[1] Anxiety neurosis, on the other hand, is the product of all those factors which prevent the somatic sexual excitation from being worked over psychically.[2] The

1. [References to masturbation as the source of neurasthenia occur many times in the Fliess letters (Freud, 1950a), as well as in other papers written within two or three years of the present one. Freud's views on the significance of masturbation at different stages in human life were expressed later, in *Three Essays* (1905d), P.F.L., **7**, 102 ff. and in the 'Rat Man' case history (1909d), P.F.L., **9**, 82–3. The connection of masturbation with phantasies is described in the paper on hysterical phantasies (1908a), pp. 89 ff. below, [and the question of why a sense of guilt attaches to it is discussed in the paper on beating-phantasies (1919e), p. 174–7 and 180–83 below.]

2. [Freud was still able to repeat these words with approval in Chapter VIII of *Inhibitions, Symptoms and Anxiety* (1926d), p. 298 below.]

manifestations of anxiety neurosis appear when the somatic excitation which has been deflected from the psyche is expended subcortically in totally inadequate reactions.

I will now attempt to discover whether the aetiological conditions for anxiety neurosis which I set out above [p. 45 ff.] exhibit the common character that I have just attributed to them. The first aetiological factor I postulated for men was intentional abstinence [p. 47]. Abstinence consists in the withholding of the specific action which ordinarily follows upon libido. Such withholding may have two consequences. In the first place, the somatic excitation accumulates; it is then deflected into other paths, which hold out greater promise of discharge than does the path through the psyche. Thus the libido will in the end sink, and the excitation will manifest itself subcortically as anxiety. In the second place, if the libido is *not* diminished, or if the somatic excitation is expended, by a short cut, in emissions, or if, in consequence of being forced back, the excitation really ceases, then all kinds of things other than an anxiety neurosis will ensue. Abstinence, then, leads to anxiety neurosis in the manner described above. But it is also the operative agent in my second aetiological group, that of unconsummated excitation [p. 47 f.]. My third group, that of coitus reservatus with consideration for the woman [p. 48], operates by disturbing the man's psychical preparedness for the sexual process, in that it introduces alongside of the task of mastering the sexual affect another psychical task, one of a deflecting sort. In consequence of this psychical deflection, once more, libido gradually disappears, and the further course of things is then the same as in the case of abstinence. Anxiety in senescence (the male climacteric) [p. 48] requires another explanation. Here there is no diminution of libido; but, as in the female climacteric, so great an increase occurs in the production of somatic excitation that the psyche proves relatively insufficient to master it.

The aetiological conditions applying to women can be

brought into the framework of my scheme with no greater difficulties than in the case of men. Virginal anxiety [p. 46] is a particularly clear example. For here the groups of ideas to which the somatic sexual excitation should become attached are not yet enough developed. In the newly-married woman who is anaesthetic [ibid], anxiety only appears if the first cohabitations arouse a sufficient amount of somatic excitation. When the local indications of such excitement (spontaneous sensations of stimulation, desire to micturate and so on) are lacking, anxiety is also absent. The case of ejaculatio praecox and of coitus interruptus [pp. 46–7] can be explained on the same lines as in men, namely that the libidinal desire for the psychically unsatisfying act gradually disappears, while the excitation which has been aroused during the act is expended subcortically. The *alienation* between the somatic and the psychical sphere, in the course taken by sexual excitation, is established more readily and is more difficult to remove in women than in men. The cases of widowhood and of voluntary abstinence, and also that of the climacteric [p. 47], are dealt with in the same way in both sexes; but where abstinence is concerned there is in the case of women no doubt the further matter of intentional repression of the sexual circle of ideas, to which an abstinent woman, in her struggle against temptation, must often make up her mind. The horror which, at the time of the menopause, an ageing woman feels at her unduly increased libido may act in a similar sense.

The two last aetiological conditions on our list seem to fall into place without difficulty. The tendency to anxiety in masturbators who have become neurasthenic [p. 48] is explained by the fact that it is very easy for them to pass into a state of 'abstinence' after they have been accustomed for so long to discharging even the smallest quantity of somatic excitation, faulty though that discharge is. Finally, the last case, – the generation of anxiety neurosis through severe illness, overwork, exhausting sick-nursing, etc. [p. 49], – finds an easy interpretation

when brought into relation with the effects of coitus interruptus. Here the psyche, on account of its deflection, would
seem to be no longer capable of mastering the somatic excitation, a task on which, as we know, it is continuously engaged.
We are aware to what a low level libido can sink under these
conditions; and we have here a good example of a neurosis
which, although it exhibits *no sexual aetiology, nevertheless
exhibits a sexual mechanism.*

The view here developed depicts the symptoms of anxiety
neurosis as being in a sense *surrogates* of the omitted specific
action following on sexual excitation. In further support of
this view, I may point out that in normal copulation too the
excitation expends itself, among other things, in accelerated
breathing, palpitation, sweating, congestion, and so on. In the
corresponding anxiety attacks of our neurosis we have before us
the dyspnoea, palpitations, etc. of copulation in an isolated and
exaggerated form.[1]

A further question may be asked. Why, under such conditions of psychical insufficiency in mastering sexual excitation,
does the nervous system find itself in the peculiar affective state
of *anxiety*? An answer may be suggested as follows. The psyche
finds itself in the *affect* of anxiety if it feels unable to deal by
appropriate reaction with a task (a danger) *approaching from
outside*; it finds itself in the *neurosis* of anxiety if it notices that it
is unable to even out the (sexual) excitation originating *endo-
genously*—that is to say, *it behaves as though it were projecting that
excitation outwards*. The affect and its corresponding neurosis are
firmly related to each other. The first is a reaction to an exogenous excitation, the second a reaction to the analogous endogenous one. The affect is a state which passes rapidly, the neurosis

1. [This theory was brought up again by Freud in Chapter II of the
'Dora' case history (1905*e*), *P.F.L.*, **8**, 116–17. Later on, in Chapter VIII
of *Inhibitions, Symptoms and Anxiety* (1926*d*), pp. 288–9 below, he
related these same symptoms of anxiety to the accompaniments of
birth.]

is a chronic one; because, while exogenous excitation operates with a single impact, the endogenous excitation operates as a constant force.[1] *In the neurosis, the nervous system is reacting against a source of excitation which is internal, whereas in the corresponding affect it is reacting against an analogous source of excitation which is external.*

IV
RELATION TO OTHER NEUROSES

There are still a few words to be said about the relations of anxiety neurosis to the other neuroses as regards their onset and their internal connections.

The purest cases of anxiety neurosis are usually the most marked. They are found in sexually potent youthful individuals with an undivided aetiology, and an illness that is not of too long standing.

More often, however, symptoms of anxiety occur at the same time as, and in combination with, symptoms of neurasthenia, hysteria, obsessions or melancholia. If we were to allow ourselves to be restrained by a clinical intermixture like this from acknowledging anxiety neurosis as an independent entity, we ought, logically, also to abandon once more the separation which has been so laboriously achieved between hysteria and neurasthenia.

For the purposes of analysing 'mixed neuroses' I can state this important truth: *Wherever a mixed neurosis is present, it will be possible to discover an intermixture of several specific aetiologies.*

A multiplicity of aetiological factors such as this, which

1. [Freud stated this again twenty years later in almost identical words, except that instead of 'exogenous excitation' and 'endogenous excitation' he spoke of 'stimulus' and 'instinct'. See a passage fairly near the beginning of the metapsychological paper on 'Instincts and their Vicissitudes' (1915*c*).]

determine a mixed neurosis, may occur purely fortuitously. For instance, a fresh noxa may add its effects to those of an already existing one. Thus, a woman who has always been hysterical may begin at a certain point in her marriage to experience coitus reservatus; she will then acquire an anxiety neurosis in addition to her hysteria. Or again, a man who has hitherto masturbated and has become neurasthenic, may get engaged and become sexually excited by his fiancée; his neurasthenia will now be joined by a new anxiety neurosis.

In other cases the multiplicity of aetiological factors is by no means fortuitous: one of the factors has brought the other into operation. For example, a woman with whom her husband practises coitus reservatus without regard to her satisfaction may find herself compelled to masturbate in order to put an end to the distressing excitation that follows such an act; as a result, she will produce, not an anxiety neurosis pure and simple, but an anxiety neurosis accompanied by symptoms of neurasthenia. Another woman suffering from the same noxa may have to fight against lascivious images against which she tries to defend herself; and in this way she will, through the coitus interruptus, acquire obsessions as well as an anxiety neurosis. Finally, as a result of coitus interruptus, a third woman may lose her affection for her husband and feel an attraction for another man, which she carefully keeps secret; in consequence, she will exhibit a mixture of anxiety neurosis and hysteria.

In a third category of mixed neuroses the interconnection between the symptoms is still more intimate, in that the same aetiological determinant regularly and simultaneously provokes both neuroses. Thus, for instance, the sudden sexual enlightenment, which we have found present in virginal anxiety, always gives rise to hysteria as well [as anxiety neurosis]; by far the majority of cases of intentional abstinence become linked from the beginning with true obsessional ideas; coitus interruptus in men never seems to me to be able to provoke a pure anxiety neurosis, but always a mixture of it with neurasthenia.

From these considerations it appears that we must further distinguish the aetiological conditions for the *onset* of the neuroses from their specific aetiological factors. The former – for example, coitus interruptus, masturbation or abstinence – are still ambiguous, and each of them can produce different neuroses. Only the aetiological factors which can be picked out in them, such as *inadequate disburdening, psychical insufficiency or defence accompanied by substitution*, have an unambiguous and specific relation to the aetiology of the individual major neuroses.

As regards its intimate nature, anxiety neurosis presents the most interesting agreements with, and differences from, the other major neuroses, in particular neurasthenia and hysteria. It shares with neurasthenia one main characteristic – namely that the source of excitation, the precipitating cause of the disturbance, lies in the somatic field instead of the psychical one, as is the case in hysteria and obsessional neurosis. In other respects we rather find a kind of antithesis between the symptoms of anxiety neurosis and of neurasthenia, which might be brought out by such labels as 'accumulation of excitation' and 'impoverishment of excitation'. This antithesis does not prevent the two neuroses from being intermixed with each other; but it nevertheless shows itself in the fact that the most extreme forms of each are in both cases also the purest.

The symptomatology of hysteria and anxiety neurosis show many points in common, which have not yet been sufficiently considered. The appearance of symptoms either in a chronic form or in attacks, the paraesthesias, grouped like aurae, the hyperaesthesias and pressure-points which are found in certain surrogates of an anxiety attack (in dyspnoea and heart-attacks), the intensification, through conversion, of pains which perhaps have an organic justification – these and other features which the two illnesses have in common even allow of a suspicion that not a little of what is attributed to hysteria might with more justice be put to the account of anxiety neurosis. If one goes into the mechanism of the two neuroses, so far as it has been possible to discover it hitherto, aspects come to light which suggest that anxiety neurosis is actually the somatic counterpart to hysteria. In the latter just as in the former there is an accumulation of excitation (which is perhaps the basis for the similarity between their symptoms we have mentioned). In the latter just as in the former we find a *psychical insufficiency, as a consequence of which abnormal somatic processes arise*. In the latter just as in the former, too, instead of a psychical working-over of the excitation, a deflection of it occurs into the somatic field; the difference is merely that in anxiety neurosis the excitation, in whose displacement the neurosis expresses itself, is purely somatic (somatic sexual excitation), whereas in hysteria it is psychical (provoked by conflict). Thus it is not to be wondered at that hysteria and anxiety neurosis regularly combine with each other, as is seen in 'virginal anxiety' or in 'sexual hysteria', and that hysteria simply borrows a number of its symptoms from anxiety neurosis, and so on. These intimate relations which anxiety neurosis has with hysteria provide a fresh argument, moreover, for insisting on the detachment of anxiety neurosis from neurasthenia; for if this detachment is not granted, we shall also be unable any longer to maintain the distinction which has been acquired with so much labour and which is so indispensable for the theory of the neuroses, between neurasthenia and hysteria.

VIENNA, *December* 1894.

EDITOR'S APPENDIX

THE TERM 'ANGST' AND ITS ENGLISH TRANSLATION

There are at least three passages in which Freud discusses the various shades of meaning expressed by the German word 'Angst' and the cognate 'Furcht' and 'Schreck'.[1] Though he stresses the anticipatory element and absence of an object in 'Angst', the distinctions he draws are not entirely convincing, and his actual usage is far from invariably obeying them. And this is scarcely surprising, since 'Angst' is a word in common use in ordinary German speech and by no means exclusively a technical psychiatric term. It may on occasion be translated by any one of half a dozen similarly common English words – 'fear', 'fright', 'alarm' and so on – and it is therefore quite unpractical to fix on some single English term as its sole translation. Nevertheless 'Angst' does often appear as a psychiatric term (particularly in such combinations as 'Angstneurose' or 'Angstanfall') and for such occasions an English technical equivalent seems to be called for. The word universally, and perhaps unfortunately, adopted for the purpose has been 'anxiety' – unfortunately, since 'anxiety' too has a current everyday meaning, and one which has only a rather remote connection with any of the uses of the German 'Angst'. There is, however, a well-established psychiatric, or at least medical, use of the English 'anxiety', going back (so the Oxford Dictionary tells us) to the middle of the seventeenth century. Indeed,

---

1. See the beginning of Chapter II of Beyond the Pleasure Principle (1920g), Inhibitions, Symptoms and Anxiety (1926d), pp. 324–5 below and a paragraph near the beginning of Lecture 25 of the Introductory Lectures (1916–17), P.F.L., 1, 440–43.

the psychiatric use of the two words brings to light their parallel origins. '*Angst*' is akin to '*eng*', the German word for 'narrow', 'restricted'; 'anxiety' is derived from the Latin '*angere*', 'to throttle' or 'squeeze'; in both cases the reference is to the choking feelings which characterize severe forms of the psychological state in question. A still more acute condition is described in English by the word 'anguish', which has the same derivation; and it is to be remarked that Freud in his French papers used the kindred word '*angoisse*' (as well as the synonymous '*anxiété*') to render the German '*Angst*'.

The English translator is thus driven to compromise: he must use 'anxiety' in technical or semi-technical connections, and must elsewhere choose whatever everyday English word seems most appropriate. Incidentally, the solution adopted in many of the earlier Freud translations of rendering '*Angst*' by 'morbid anxiety' seems especially ill-judged. One of the main theoretical problems discussed by Freud is precisely whether, and if so why, '*Angst*' is sometimes pathological and sometimes normal. (See, for instance, Addendum B to *Inhibitions, Symptoms and Anxiety*, p. 324ff. below.)

MY VIEWS ON THE PART PLAYED
BY SEXUALITY IN THE
AETIOLOGY OF THE NEUROSES

(1906 [1905])

EDITOR'S NOTE

MEINE ANSICHTEN ÜBER DIE ROLLE DER SEXUALITÄT IN DER ÄTIOLOGIE DER NEUROSEN

(A) GERMAN EDITIONS:

(1905   June. Date of MS.)

1906   In Löwenfeld's *Sexualleben und Nervenleiden*, 4th. ed., Wiesbaden: Bergmann. (1914, 5th. ed., 313–22).

1924   *Gesammelte Schriften*, **5**, 123–33.

1942   *Gesammelte Werke*, **5**, 149–59.

(B) ENGLISH TRANSLATIONS:

'My Views on the Role of Sexuality in the Etiology of the Neuroses'

1909   *Selected Papers on Hysteria*, 186–93. (Tr. A. A. Brill) (1912, 2nd. ed.; 1920, 3rd. ed.)

'My Views on the Part Played by Sexuality in the Aetiology of the Neuroses'

1924   *Collected Papers*, **1**, 272–83. (Tr. J. Bernays.)

1953   *Standard Edition*, **7**, 269–79. (A new translation.)

The present edition is a corrected reprint of the *Standard Edition* version, with some editorial additions.

Earlier editions of this book of Löwenfeld's had included discussions of Freud's views; but for the 4th edition Löwenfeld persuaded Freud to write this paper. He agreed to revise it for the 5th edition, but in fact only made a single trivial alteration.

The most notable feature of this paper is that it contains Freud's first fully expressed withdrawal from his belief in the traumatic aetiology of hysteria and his first insistence on the importance of phantasies (views which he had communicated privately to Fliess many years before). See below, pp. 74 ff. 5 and 75 n. It also gives a very good summary of the development of Freud's views up to this time.

MY VIEWS ON THE PART PLAYED
BY SEXUALITY IN THE
AETIOLOGY OF THE NEUROSES

My theory of the aetiological importance of the sexual factor in the neuroses can best be appreciated, in my opinion, by following the history of its development. For I have no desire whatever to deny that it has gone through a process of evolution and been modified in the course of it. My professional colleagues may find a guarantee in this admission that the theory is nothing other than the product of continuous and ever deeper-going experience. What is born of speculation, on the contrary, may easily spring into existence complete and thereafter remain unchangeable.

Originally my theory related only to the clinical pictures comprised under the term 'neurasthenia', among which I was particularly struck by two, which occasionally appear as pure types and which I described as 'neurasthenia proper' and 'anxiety neurosis'. It had, to be sure, always been a matter of common knowledge that sexual factors *may* play a part in the causation of these forms of illness; but those factors were not regarded as invariably operative, nor was there any idea of giving them precedence over other aetiological influences. I was surprised to begin with at the frequency of gross disturbances in the *vita sexualis* of nervous patients; the more I set about looking for such disturbances – bearing in mind the fact that everyone hides the truth in matters of sex – and the more skilful I became at pursuing my enquiries in the face of a preliminary denial, the more regularly was I able to discover pathogenic factors in sexual life, till little seemed to stand in the way of my assuming their universal occurrence. It was necessary, however, to presuppose from the start that sexual irregularities occurred with similar frequency in our ordinary society under the pressure of social conditions; and a doubt might remain as to the degree of deviation from normal sexual functioning which should be regarded as pathogenic. I was therefore obliged to attach less importance to the invariable evidence of sexual noxae than to a second discovery which seemed to me less ambiguous. It emerged that the form taken by the illness – neurasthenia or anxiety neurosis – bore a constant relation to the nature of the sexual noxa involved. In typical cases of neurasthenia a history of regular masturbation or persistent emissions was found; in anxiety neurosis factors appeared such as *coitus interruptus*, 'unconsummated excitation', and other conditions – in all of which there seemed to be the common element of an insufficient discharge of the libido that had been produced. It was only after this discovery, which was easy to make and could be confirmed as often as one liked, that I had the courage to claim a preferential position for sexual influences in the aetiology of the neuroses. Furthermore, in the mixed forms of neurasthenia and anxiety neurosis which are so common it was possible to trace a combination of the aetiologies which I had assumed for the two pure forms. Moreover, this twofold form assumed by the neurosis seemed to tally with the polar (i.e. the masculine and feminine) character of sexuality.

At the time at which I was attributing to sexuality this important part in the production of the *simple* neuroses,[1] I was still faithful to a purely psychological theory in regard to the *psychoneuroses* (hysteria and obsessions) – a theory in which the sexual factor was regarded as no more significant than any other emotional source of feeling. On the basis of some observations made by Josef Breuer on a hysterical patient more than ten years earlier, I collaborated with him in a study of the mechanism of the generation of hysterical symptoms, using the method of awakening the patient's memories in a state of

1. In my [first] paper on anxiety neurosis (1895*b*) [p. 35 ff. above].

hypnosis; and we reached conclusions which enabled us to bridge the gap between Charcot's traumatic hysteria and common non-traumatic hysteria (Breuer and Freud, 1895). We were led to the assumption that hysterical symptoms are the permanent results of psychical traumas, the sum of affect attaching to which has, for particular reasons, been prevented from being worked over consciously and has therefore found an abnormal path into somatic innervation. The terms 'strangulated affect', 'conversion' and 'abreaction' cover the distinctive features of this hypothesis.

But in view of the close connections between the psychoneuroses and the simple neuroses, which go so far, indeed, that a differential diagnosis is not always easy for inexperienced observers, it could not be long before the knowledge arrived at in the one field was extended to the other. Moreover, apart from this consideration, a deeper investigation of the psychical mechanism of hysterical symptoms led to the same result. For if the psychical traumas from which the hysterical symptoms were derived were pursued further and further by means of the 'cathartic' procedure initiated by Breuer and me, experiences were eventually reached which belonged to the patient's childhood and related to his sexual life. And this was so, even in cases in which the onset of the illness had been brought about by some commonplace emotion of a non-sexual kind. Unless these sexual traumas of childhood were taken into account it was impossible either to elucidate the symptoms (to understand the way in which they were determined) or to prevent their recurrence. In this way the unique significance of sexual experiences in the aetiology of the psychoneuroses seemed to be established beyond a doubt; and this fact remains to this day one of the corner-stones of my theory.

This theory might be expressed by saying that the cause of life-long hysterical neuroses lies in what are in themselves for the most part the trivial sexual experiences of early childhood; and, put in this way, it might no doubt sound strange. But if we take the historical development of the theory into account, and see as its essence the proposition that hysteria is the expression of a particular behaviour of the individual's sexual function and that this behaviour is decisively determined by the first influences and experiences brought to bear in childhood, we shall be a paradox the poorer but the richer by a motive for turning our attention to something of the highest importance (though it has hitherto been grossly neglected) – the after-effects of the impressions of childhood.

I will postpone until later in this paper a more thorough-going discussion of the question whether we are to regard the sexual experiences of childhood as the causes of hysteria (and obsessional neurosis), and I will now return to the form taken by the theory in some of my shorter preliminary publications during the years 1895 and 1896 (Freud, 1896b and 1896c). By laying stress on the supposed aetiological factors it was possible at that time to draw a contrast between the common neuroses as disorders with a *contemporary* aetiology and psychoneuroses whose aetiology was chiefly to be looked for in the sexual experiences of the remote past. The theory culminated in this thesis: if the *vita sexualis* is normal, there can be no neurosis.

Though even today I do not consider these assertions incorrect, it is not to be wondered at that, in the course of ten years of continuous effort at reaching an understanding of these phenomena, I have made a considerable step forward from the views I then held, and now believe that I am in a position, on the basis of deeper experience, to correct the insufficiencies, the displacements and the misunderstandings under which my theory then laboured. At that time my material was still scanty, and it happened by chance to include a disproportionately large number of cases in which sexual seduction by an adult or by older children played the chief part in the history of the patient's childhood. I thus over-estimated the frequency of such events (though in other respects they were not open to doubt). Moreover, I was at that period unable to distinguish with certainty between falsifications made by hysterics in their memories of childhood and traces of real events. Since then I have learned to explain a number of phantasies of seduction as attempts at fending off memories of the subject's *own* sexual activity (infantile masturbation). When this point had been clarified, the 'traumatic' element in the sexual experiences of childhood lost its importance and what was left was the realization that infantile sexual activity (whether spontaneous or provoked) prescribes the direction that will be taken by later sexual life after maturity. The same clarification (which corrected the most important of my early mistakes) also made it necessary to modify my view of the mechanism of hysterical symptoms. They were now no longer to be regarded as direct derivatives of the repressed memories of childhood experiences; but between the symptoms and the childish impressions there were inserted the patient's *phantasies* (or imaginary memories), mostly produced during the years of puberty, which on the one side were built up out of and over the childhood memories and on the other side were transformed directly into the symptoms. It was only after the introduction of this element of hysterical phantasies that the texture of the neurosis and its relation to the patient's life became intelligible; a surprising analogy came to light, too, between these unconscious phantasies of hysterics and the imaginary creations of paranoics which become conscious as delusions.[1]

1. [This passage was Freud's first explicit published intimation of his change of views on the relative importance of traumatic experiences and unconscious phantasies in childhood, apart from a brief allusion in his *Three Essays* (1905*d*), P.F.L., **7**, 108 f. In fact, however, he had become aware of his error many years earlier, for he revealed it in a letter to Fliess on September 21, 1897 (Freud, 1950*a*, Letter 69). The effects on Freud's own mind of the discovery of his mistake are vividly related by him in the first section of his 'History of the Psycho-Analytic Movement' (1914*d*) and in the third section of his 'Autobiographical Study' (1925*d*). For later developments in Freud's views on these phantasies, see the paper on 'Female Sexuality' (1931*b*), P.F.L., **7**, 386, and the *New Introductory Lectures* (1933*a*), P.F.L., **2**, 154.]

After I had made this correction, 'infantile sexual traumas' were in a sense replaced by the 'infantilism of sexuality'. A second modification of the original theory lay not far off. Along with the supposed frequency of seduction in childhood, I ceased also to lay exaggerated stress on the *accidental* influencing of sexuality on to which I had sought to thrust the main responsibility for the causation of the illness, though I had not on that account denied the constitutional and hereditary factors. I had even hoped to solve the problem of choice of neurosis (the decision to which form of psychoneurosis the patient is to fall a victim) by reference to the details of the sexual experiences of childhood. I believed at that time – though with reservations – that a passive attitude in these scenes produced a predisposition to hysteria and, on the other hand, an active one a predisposition to obsessional neurosis. Later on I was obliged to abandon this view entirely, even though some facts demand that in some way or other the supposed correlation between passivity and hysteria and between activity and obsessional neurosis shall be maintained.[1] Accidental influences derived from experience having thus receded into the background, the factors of constitution and heredity necessarily gained the upper hand once more; but there was this difference between my views and those prevailing in other quarters, that on my theory the 'sexual constitution' took the place of a 'general neuropathic disposition'. In my recently published *Three Essays on the Theory of Sexuality* (1905*d*) I have tried to give a picture of the variegated nature of this sexual constitution as well as of the composite character of the sexual instinct in general and its derivation from contributory sources from different parts of the organism.

1. [Freud's interest in the general question of 'choice of neurosis' goes back at least to the beginning of 1896. He was to return to the subject a few years later in special reference to obsessional neurosis (1913*i*), and indeed the problem never ceased to occupy his mind. The subject is discussed in some detail in the Editor's Note to this latter paper, pp. 130–31 below.]

As a further corollary to my modified view of 'sexual traumas in childhood', my theory now developed further in a direction which had already been indicated in my publications between 1894 and 1896. At that time, and even before sexuality had been given its rightful place as an aetiological factor, I had maintained that no experience could have a pathogenic effect unless it appeared intolerable to the subject's ego and gave rise to efforts at defence.[1] It was to this defence that I traced back the split in the psyche (or, as we said in those days, in consciousness) which occurs in hysteria. If the defence was successful, the intolerable experience with its affective consequences was expelled from consciousness and from the ego's memory. In certain circumstances, however, what had been expelled pursued its activities in what was now an unconscious state, and found its way back into consciousness by means of symptoms and the affects attaching to them, so that the illness corresponded to a failure in defence. This view had the merit of entering into the interplay of the psychical forces and of thus bringing the mental processes in hysteria nearer to normal ones, instead of characterizing the neurosis as nothing more than a mysterious disorder insusceptible to further analysis.

Further information now became available relating to people who had remained normal; and this led to the unexpected finding that the sexual history of *their* childhood did not necessarily differ in essentials from that of neurotics, and, in particular, that the part played by seduction was the same in both cases. As a consequence, accidental influences receded still further into the background as compared with 'repression' (as I now began to say instead of 'defence').[2] Thus it was no longer a

1. 'The Neuro-Psychoses of Defence (An Attempt at a Psychological Theory of Acquired Hysteria, of many Phobias and Obsessions and of Certain Hallucinatory Psychoses)' (1894a).

2. [Actually the term 'repression' had made its first published appearance as early as in the Breuer and Freud 'Preliminary Communication' (1893), *P.F.L.*, **3**, 61, and both terms occur quite often in the *Studies on*

question of what sexual experiences a particular individual had had in his childhood, but rather of his reaction to those experiences – of whether he had reacted to them by 'repression' or not. It could be shown how in the course of development a spontaneous infantile sexual activity was often broken off by an act of repression. Thus a mature neurotic individual was invariably pursued by a certain amount of 'sexual repression' from his childhood; this found expression when he was faced by the demands of real life, and the psychoanalyses of hysterics showed that they fell ill as a result of the conflict between their libido and their sexual repression and that their symptoms were in the nature of compromises between the two mental currents.

I could not further elucidate this part of my theory without a detailed discussion of my views on repression. It will be enough here to refer to my *Three Essays* (1905*d*), in which I have attempted to throw some light – if only a feeble one – on the somatic processes in which the essential nature of sexuality is to be looked for. I have there shown that the constitutional sexual disposition of children is incomparably more variegated than might have been expected, that it deserves to be described as 'polymorphously perverse' and that what is spoken of as the normal behaviour of the sexual function emerges from this disposition after certain of its components have been repressed. By pointing out the infantile elements in sexuality I was able to establish a simple correlation between health, perversion and neurosis. I showed that *normality* is a result of the repression of certain component instincts and constituents of the infantile disposition and of the subordination of the remaining constituents under the primacy of the genital zones in the service of the

---

Hysteria (1895*d*). At that stage the authors seem to have equated the two concepts: cf. their joint preface to the first edition of the *Studies*, P.F.L., **3,** 47. Many years later, in *Inhibitions, Symptoms and Anxiety* (1926*d*) see particularly Chapter XI A(*c*), Freud once more returned to the term 'defence' as denoting a comprehensive concept, of which 'repression' represented only a single form. See p. 322ff. below.]

reproductive function. I showed that *perversions* correspond to disturbances of this coalescence owing to the overpowering and compulsive development of certain of the component instincts, while *neuroses* can be traced back to an excessive repression of the libidinal trends. Since almost all the perverse instincts of the infantile disposition can be recognized as the forces concerned in the formation of symptoms in neuroses, though in a state of repression, I was able to describe neurosis as being the 'negative' of perversion.[1]

I think it is worth emphasizing the fact that, whatever modifications my views on the aetiology of the psychoneuroses have passed through, there are two positions which I have never repudiated or abandoned – the importance of sexuality and of infantilism. Apart from this, accidental influences have been replaced by constitutional factors and 'defence' in the purely psychological sense has been replaced by organic 'sexual repression'. The question may, however, be raised of where convincing evidence is to be found in favour of the alleged aetiological importance of sexual factors in the psychoneuroses, in view of the fact that the onset of these illnesses may be observed in response to the most commonplace emotions or even to somatic precipitating causes, and since I have had to abandon a specific aetiology depending on the particular form of the childhood experiences concerned. To such a question I would reply that the psychoanalytic examination of neurotics is the source from which this disputed conviction of mine is derived. If we make use of that irreplaceable method of research, we discover that *the patient's symptoms constitute his sexual activity*[2] (whether wholly or in part), which arises from the sources of the normal or perverse component instincts of sexuality. Not only is a large part of the symptomatology of hysteria derived directly from expressions of sexual excitement, not only do a

1. [Cf. *Three Essays on the Theory of Sexuality* (1905*d*), P.F.L., **7**, 79–80.]

2. [Cf. *Three Essays*, P.F.L., **7**, 77 and *n.* 2.]

number of erotogenic zones attain the significance of genitals during neuroses owing to an intensification of infantile characteristics, but the most complicated symptoms are themselves revealed as representing, by means of 'conversion', phantasies which have a sexual situation as their subject-matter. Anyone who knows how to interpret the language of hysteria will recognize that the neurosis is concerned only with the patient's repressed sexuality. The sexual function must, however, be understood in its true extent, as it is laid down by disposition in infancy. Wherever some commonplace emotion must be included among the determinants of the onset of the illness, analysis invariably shows that it is the sexual component of the traumatic experience – a component that is never lacking – which has produced the pathogenic result.

We have been led on imperceptibly from the question of the causation of the psychoneuroses to the problem of their essential nature. If we are prepared to take into account what has been learnt from psychoanalysis, we can only say that the essence of these illnesses lies in disturbances of the sexual processes, the processes which determine in the organism the formation and utilization of sexual libido. It is scarcely possible to avoid picturing these processes as being in the last resort of a chemical nature; so that in what are termed the 'actual' neuroses[1] we may recognize the *somatic* effects of disturbances of the sexual metabolism, and in the psychoneuroses the *psychical* effects of those disturbances as well. The similarity of the neuroses to the phenomena of intoxication and abstinence after the use of certain alkaloids, as well as to Graves' disease and Addison's disease, is forced upon our notice clinically. And just as these last two illnesses should no longer be described as 'nervous

1. [i.e. those with a purely contemporary and physical aetiology (neurasthenia and anxiety neurosis). They are discussed again in the paper on visual disturbances (1910*i*), p. 114 below. Very much later Freud returned to a consideration of the subject in *Inhibitions, Symptoms and Anxiety* (1926*d*); cf. below, pp. 264 and 298–9.

diseases', so also the 'neuroses' proper, in spite of their name, may soon have to be excluded from that category as well.[1]

Accordingly, the aetiology of the neuroses comprises everything which can act in a detrimental manner upon the processes serving the sexual function. In the forefront, then, are to be ranked the noxae which affect the sexual function itself – in so far as these are regarded as injurious by the sexual constitution, varying as it does with different degrees of culture and education. In the next place comes every other kind of noxa and trauma which, by causing general damage to the organism, may lead secondarily to injury to its sexual processes. It should not, however, be forgotten that the aetiological problem in the case of the neuroses is at least as complicated as the causative factors of any other illness. A single pathogenic influence is scarcely ever sufficient; in the large majority of cases a *number* of aetiological factors are required, which support one another and must therefore not be regarded as being in mutual opposition. For this reason a state of neurotic illness cannot be sharply differentiated from health. The onset of the illness is the product of a summation and the necessary total of aetiological determinants can be completed from any direction. To look for the aetiology of the neuroses exclusively in heredity or in the constitution would be just as one-sided as to attribute that aetiology solely to the accidental influences brought to bear upon sexuality in the course of the subject's life – whereas better insight shows that the essence of these illnesses lies solely in a disturbance of the organism's sexual processes.

VIENNA, *June* 1905.

1. [Cf. *Three Essays, P.F.L.,* **7,** 137–8 and footnote.]

HYSTERICAL PHANTASIES AND THEIR RELATION TO BISEXUALITY
(1908)

EDITOR'S NOTE

HYSTERISCHE PHANTASIEN UND IHRE BEZIEHUNG ZUR BISEXUALITÄT

(A) German Editions:

1908   *Z. Sexualwissenschaft*, **1** (1) [January], 27–34.
1924   *Gesammelte Schriften*, **5**, 246–254.
1941   *Gesammelte Werke*, **7**, 191–199.

(B) English Translations:

'Hysterical Fancies and their Relation to Bisexuality'

1909   *Selected Papers on Hysteria*, 194–200. (Tr. A. A. Brill.)
          (1912, 2nd ed.; 1920, 3rd ed.)

'Hysterical Phantasies and their Relation to Bisexuality'

1924   *Collected Papers*, 2, 51–8. (Tr. D. Bryan.)
1959   *Standard Edition*, 9, 155–66. (A considerably revised version of the translation published in 1924.)

The present edition is a reprint of the *Standard Edition* version, with some editorial changes.

This paper was published in a new periodical which the editor Magnus Hirschfeld had just started. The importance of phantasies as the basis of hysterical symptoms had been first recognized by Freud in about the year 1897, in connection with his self-analysis. But though he communicated his findings privately to Fliess at the time (see Freud, 1950a), he had only published them fully a couple of years before the present paper was written in the article on sexuality in the neurosis (1906a), pp. 74–5 above. The main part of this paper is a further discussion of the relation between phantasies and symptoms; and, in spite of its title, the subject of bisexuality emerges almost as an afterthought. It may be remarked, incidentally, that the subject of phantasies seems to have been very much in Freud's mind at about the date of this paper. They are further discussed in the papers on 'The Sexual Theories of Children' (1908c), on 'Creative Writers and Day-Dreaming' (1908e), on 'Family Romances' (1909c), and on 'Hysterical Attacks' (1909a, p. 97 ff. below), as well as at many points in the study of *Gradiva* (1907a). Much of the material of the present paper had, of course, been anticipated. See, for instance, the 'Dora' analysis (1905e [1901]), *P.F.L.*, **8**, 80–86, and the *Three Essays* (1905d), *P.F.L.*, **7**, 79–81.

HYSTERICAL PHANTASIES AND
THEIR RELATION TO BISEXUALITY

WE are all familiar with the delusional imaginings of the paranoic, which are concerned with the greatness and the sufferings of his own self and which appear in forms that are quite typical and almost monotonous. We have also become acquainted, through numerous accounts, with the strange performances with which certain perverts stage their sexual satisfaction, whether in idea or reality. Nevertheless, it may be new to some readers to hear that quite analogous psychical structures are regularly present in all the psychoneuroses, particularly in hysteria, and that these latter – which are known as hysterical phantasies – can be seen to have important connections with the causation of the neurotic symptoms.

A common source and normal prototype of all these creations of phantasy is to be found in what are called the day-dreams of youth. These have already received some, though as yet insufficient, notice in the literature of the subject.[1] They occur with perhaps equal frequency in both sexes, though it seems that while in girls and women they are invariably of an erotic nature, in men they may be either erotic or ambitious. Nevertheless the importance of the erotic factor in men, too, should not be given a secondary rating; a closer investigation of a man's day-dreams generally shows that all his heroic exploits are carried out and all his successes achieved only in order to please a woman and to be preferred by her to other men.[2] These phantasies are satisfactions of wishes proceeding from deprivation and longing. They are justly called 'day-

1. Cf. Breuer and Freud (1895), Pierre Janet (1898, 1), Havelock Ellis (1899), Freud (1900a), Pick (1896).

2. Havelock Ellis (1899, [3rd ed., 1910, 185 ff.]) is of the same opinion.

dreams', for they give us the key to an understanding of night-dreams – in which the nucleus of the dream-formation consists of nothing else than complicated day-time phantasies of this kind that have been distorted and are misunderstood by the conscious psychical agency.[1]

These day-dreams are cathected with a large amount of interest; they are carefully cherished by the subject and usually concealed with a great deal of sensitivity, as though they were among the most intimate possessions of his personality. It is easy to recognize a person who is absorbed in day-dreaming in the street, however, by his sudden, as it were absent-minded, smile, his way of talking to himself, or by the hastening of his steps which marks the climax of the imagined situation. Every hysterical attack which I have been able to investigate up to the present has proved to be an involuntary irruption of day-dreams of this kind. For our observations no longer leave any room for doubt that such phantasies may be unconscious just as well as conscious; and as soon as the latter have become unconscious they may also become pathogenic – that is, they may express themselves in symptoms and attacks. In favourable circumstances, the subject can still capture an unconscious phantasy of this sort in consciousness. After I had drawn the attention of one of my patients to her phantasies, she told me that on one occasion she had suddenly found herself in tears in the street and that, rapidly considering what it was she was actually crying about, she had got hold of a phantasy to the following effect. In her imagination she had formed a tender attachment to a pianist who was well known in the town (though she was not personally acquainted with him); she had had a child by him (she was in fact childless); and he had then deserted her and her child and left them in poverty. It was at this point in her romance that she had burst into tears.

1. Cf. *The Interpretation of Dreams* (1900a), *P.F.L.*, 4, 631 ff. – [The contents of this paragraph had been stated more fully by Freud in his almost contemporary paper 'Creative Writers and Day-Dreaming' (1908e).]

Unconscious phantasies have either been unconscious all along and have been formed in the unconscious; or – as is more often the case – they were once conscious phantasies, daydreams, and have since been purposely forgotten and have become unconscious through 'repression'. Their content may afterwards either have remained the same or have undergone alterations, so that the present unconscious phantasies are derivatives of the once conscious ones. Now an unconscious phantasy has a very important connection with the subject's sexual life; for it is identical with the phantasy which served to give him sexual satisfaction during a period of masturbation. At that time the masturbatory act (in the widest sense of the term[1]) was compounded of two parts. One was the evocation of a phantasy and the other some active behaviour for obtaining self-gratification at the height of the phantasy. This compound, as we know, was itself merely soldered together.[2] Originally the action was a purely auto-erotic procedure for the purpose of obtaining pleasure from some particular part of the body, which could be described as erotogenic. Later, this action became merged with a wishful idea from the sphere of object-love and served as a partial realization of the situation in which the phantasy culminated. When, subsequently, the subject renounces this type of satisfaction, composed of masturbation and phantasy, the action is given up, while the phantasy, from being conscious, becomes unconscious. If no other mode of sexual satisfaction supervenes, the subject remains abstinent; and if he does not succeed in sublimating his libido – that is, in deflecting his sexual excitation to higher aims – , the condition is now fulfilled for his unconscious phantasy to be revived and to proliferate, and, at least as regards some part of its content, to put itself into effect, with the whole force of his need for love, in the form of a pathological symptom.

In this way, unconscious phantasies are the immediate

1. [i.e. not in its restricted literal sense of manual friction.]
2. Cf. Freud, *Three Essays* (1905*d*) [*P.F.L.*, **7**, 59 f.].

psychical precursors of a whole number of hysterical symptoms. Hysterical symptoms are nothing other than unconscious phantasies brought into view through 'conversion'; and in so far as the symptoms are somatic ones, they are often enough taken from the circle of the same sexual sensations and motor innervations as those which had originally accompanied the phantasy when it was still conscious. In this way the giving up of the habit of masturbation is in fact undone, and the purpose of the whole pathological process, which is a restoration of the original, primary sexual satisfaction, is achieved – though never completely, it is true, but always in a sort of approximation.

Anyone who studies hysteria, therefore, soon finds his interest turned away from its symptoms to the phantasies from which they proceed. The technique of psychoanalysis enables us in the first place to infer from the symptoms what those unconscious phantasies are and then to make them conscious to the patient. By this means it has been found that the content of the hysteric's unconscious phantasies corresponds completely to the situations in which satisfaction is consciously obtained by perverts; and if anyone is at a loss for examples of such situations he has only to recall the world-famous performances of the Roman Emperors, the wild excesses of which were, of course, determined only by the enormous and unrestrained power possessed by the authors of the phantasies. The delusions of paranoics are phantasies of the same nature, though they are phantasies which have become directly conscious. They rest on the sado-masochistic components of the sexual instinct, and they, too, may find their complete counterpart in certain unconscious phantasies of hysterical subjects. We also know of cases – cases which have their practical importance as well – in which hysterics do not give expression to their phantasies in the form of symptoms but as conscious realizations, and in that way devise and stage assaults, attacks or acts of sexual aggression.

This method of psychoanalytic investigation, which leads from the conspicuous symptoms to the hidden unconscious phantasies, tells us everything that can be known about the sexuality of psychoneurotics, including the fact which is to be the main subject-matter of this short preliminary publication.

Owing, probably, to the difficulties which the unconscious phantasies meet with in their endeavour to find expression, the relationship of the phantasies to the symptoms is not simple, but on the contrary, complicated in many ways.[1] As a rule – when, that is, the neurosis is fully developed and has persisted for some time – a particular symptom corresponds, not to a single unconscious phantasy, but to several such phantasies; and it does so not in an arbitrary manner but in accordance with a regular pattern. At the beginning of the illness these complications are, no doubt, not all fully developed.

For the sake of general interest I will at this point go outside the framework of this paper and interpolate a series of formulas which attempt to give a progressively fuller description of the nature of hysterical symptoms. These formulas do not contradict one another, but some represent an increasingly complete and precise approach to the facts, while others represent the application of different points of view:

(1) Hysterical symptoms are mnemic symbols[2] of certain operative (traumatic) impressions and experiences.

(2) Hysterical symptoms are substitutes, produced by 'conversion', for the associative return of these traumatic experiences.

1. The same is true of the relation between the 'latent' dream-thoughts and the elements of the 'manifest' content of a dream. See the section of my *Interpretation of Dreams* [Chapter VI] which deals with the 'dream-work'.

2. [The term was used by Freud extensively in the *Studies on Hysteria* (1895*d*). In the first of his *Five Lectures* (1910*a*), Freud compared these to the monuments and memorials of large cities, which are 'mnemic symbols' of a material kind and which no longer evoke strong emotions in the onlooker. A hysterical patient, on the contrary, continues to react to painful experiences of the past as though they were still fresh.]

(3) Hysterical symptoms are – like other psychical structures – an expression of the fulfilment of a wish.

(4) Hysterical symptoms are the realization of an unconscious phantasy which serves the fulfilment of a wish.

(5) Hysterical symptoms serve the purpose of sexual satisfaction and represent a portion of the subject's sexual life (a portion which corresponds to one of the constituents of his sexual instinct).

(6) Hysterical symptoms correspond to a return of a mode of sexual satisfaction which was a real one in infantile life and has since been repressed.

(7) Hysterical symptoms arise as a compromise between two opposite affective and instinctual impulses, of which one is attempting to bring to expression a component instinct or a constituent of the sexual constitution, and the other is attempting to suppress it.

(8) Hysterical symptoms may take over the representation of various unconscious impulses which are not sexual, but they can never be without a sexual significance.

Among these various definitions the seventh brings out the nature of hysterical symptoms most completely as the realization of an unconscious phantasy; and the eighth recognizes the proper significance of the sexual factor. Some of the preceding formulas lead up to these two and are contained in them.

This connection between symptoms and phantasies makes it easy to arrive from a psychoanalysis of the former at a knowledge of the components of the sexual instincts which dominate the individual, as I have demonstrated in my *Three Essays on the Theory of Sexuality* [1905d]. In some cases, however, investigation by this means yields an unexpected result. It shows that there are many symptoms where the uncovering of a sexual phantasy (or of a number of phantasies, one of which, the most significant and the earliest, is of a sexual nature) is not enough to bring about a resolution of the symptoms. To resolve it one has to have *two* sexual phantasies, of which one has a masculine and the other a feminine character. Thus one of these phantasies springs from a homosexual impulse. This new finding does not alter our seventh formula. It remains true that a hysterical symptom must necessarily represent a compromise between a libidinal and a repressing impulse; but it may also represent a union of two libidinal phantasies of an opposite sexual character.

I shall refrain from giving examples in support of this thesis. I have found from experience that short analyses, condensed into extracts, can never have the convincing effect which they are designed to produce. And on the other hand, accounts of fully analysed cases must be left for another occasion.

I will therefore content myself with stating the following formula and explaining its significance:

(9) Hysterical symptoms are the expression on the one hand of a masculine unconscious sexual phantasy, and on the other hand of a feminine one.

I must expressly state that I cannot claim the same general validity for this formula as I have done for the others. As far as I can see, it applies neither to all the symptoms of a given case nor to all cases. On the contrary, it is not hard to adduce cases in which the impulses belonging to the opposite sexes have found separate symptomatic expression, so that the symptoms of heterosexuality and those of homosexuality can be as clearly distinguished from each other as the phantasies concealed behind them. Nevertheless, the condition of things stated in the ninth formula is common enough, and, when it occurs, important enough to deserve special emphasis. It seems to me to mark the highest degree of complexity to which the determination of a hysterical symptom can attain, and one may therefore only expect to find it in a neurosis which has persisted for a long time and within which a great deal of organization has taken place.[1]

1. Sadger (1907) has recently discovered this formula independently in his own psychoanalyses. He, however, maintains that it has general validity.

The bisexual nature of hysterical symptoms, which can in any event be demonstrated in numerous cases, is an interesting confirmation of my view that the postulated existence of an innate bisexual disposition in man is especially clearly visible in the analysis of psychoneurotics.[1] An exactly analogous state of affairs occurs in the same field when a person who is masturbating tries in his conscious phantasies to have the feelings both of the man and of the woman in the situation which he is picturing. Further counterparts are to be found in certain hysterical attacks in which the patient simultaneously plays both parts in the underlying sexual phantasy. In one case which I observed, for instance, the patient pressed her dress up against her body with one hand (as the woman), while she tried to tear it off with the other (as the man).[2] This simultaneity of contradictory actions serves to a large extent to obscure the situation, which is otherwise so plastically portrayed in the attack, and it is thus well suited to conceal the unconscious phantasy that is at work.

In psychoanalytic treatment it is very important to be prepared for a symptom's having a bisexual meaning. We need not then be surprised or misled if a symptom seems to persist undiminished although we have already resolved one of its sexual meanings; for it is still being maintained by the – perhaps unsuspected – one belonging to the opposite sex. In the treatment of such cases, moreover, one may observe how the patient avails himself, during the analysis of the one sexual meaning, of the convenient possibility of constantly switching his associations, as though on to an adjoining track, into the field of the contrary meaning.

1. Cf. my *Three Essays* [e.g. *P.F.L.*, **7**, 80 and 142].
2. [This case is mentioned again in the next paper (p. 98 below).]

SOME GENERAL REMARKS ON HYSTERICAL ATTACKS
(1909 [1908])

EDITOR'S NOTE

ALLGEMEINES ÜBER DEN HYSTERISCHEN ANFALL

(A) GERMAN EDITIONS:

(1908   Probable date of composition.)
1909   *Z. Psychother. med. Psychol.*, **1** (1) [January], 10–14.
1924   *Gesammelte Schriften*, **5**, 255–60.
1941   *Gesammelte Werke*, **7**, 235–40.

(B) ENGLISH TRANSLATIONS:

'General Remarks on Hysterical Attacks'

1924   *Collected Papers*, **2**, 100–104. (Tr. D. Bryan.)
1959   *Standard Edition*, **9**, 227–34. (A modified version of the one published in 1924, with a slightly changed title.)

The present edition is a reprint of the *Standard Edition* version, with a few editorial modifications.

This paper was contributed by Freud at the invitation of Albert Moll to the first number of a new periodical which he was founding. He had last discussed the subject in Section 4 of the Breuer and Freud 'Preliminary Communication' (1893*a*) on the *Studies on Hysteria* (*P.F.L.*, **3**, 64–8). The present paper is one of those highly condensed, almost schematic, works in which we can detect the seeds of later developments. (See especially Section B.) But Freud did not return again to the actual theme of hysterical attacks till twenty years later, in his discussion of Dostoevsky's 'epileptic' attacks (1928*b*).

SOME GENERAL REMARKS ON HYSTERICAL ATTACKS

A

WHEN one carries out the psychoanalysis of a hysterical woman patient whose complaint is manifested in attacks, one soon becomes convinced that these attacks are nothing else but phantasies translated into the motor sphere, projected on to motility and portrayed in pantomime. It is true that the phantasies are unconscious; but apart from this they are of the same nature as the phantasies which can be observed directly in day-dreams or which can be elicited by interpretation from dreams at night. Often a dream takes the place of an attack, and still more often it explains it, since the same phantasy finds a different expression in a dream and in an attack. We might expect then that by observing an attack we should be able to get to know the phantasy represented in it; but this is seldom possible. As a rule, owing to the influence of the censorship, the pantomimic portrayal of the phantasy has undergone distortions which are completely analogous to the hallucinatory distortions of a dream, so that both of them have, in the first resort, become unintelligible to the subject's own consciousness as well as to the observer's comprehension. A hysterical attack, therefore, needs to be subjected to the same interpretative revision as we employ for night-dreams. But not only are the forces from which the distortion proceeds and the purpose of the distortion the same as those we have come to know through the interpretation of dreams; the technique employed in the distortion is the same too.

(1) The attack becomes unintelligible through the fact that it represents several phantasies in the same material simultaneously

– that is to say through *condensation*. The elements common to the two (or more) phantasies constitute the nucleus of the representation, as they do in dreams. The phantasies which are thus made to coincide are often of quite a different nature. They may, for instance, be a recent wish and the re-activation of an infantile impression. The same innervations are in that case made to serve both purposes, often in a most ingenious way. Hysterical patients who make a very extensive use of condensation may find a single form of attack sufficient; others express their numerous pathogenic phantasies by a multiplication of the forms of attack.

(2) The attack becomes obscured through the fact that the patient attempts to carry out the activities of both the figures who appear in the phantasy, that is to say, through *multiple identification*. Compare, for instance, the example I mentioned in my paper on 'Hysterical Phantasies and their Relation to Bisexuality' (1908*a*), in which the patient tore off her dress with one hand (as the man) while she pressed it to her body with the other (as the woman).[1]

(3) A particularly extensive distortion is effected by an *antagonistic inversion of the innervations*. This is analogous to the transformation of an element into its opposite, which commonly happens in the dream-work.[2] For instance, an embrace may be represented in the attack by drawing back the arms convulsively till the hands meet over the spinal column. It is possible that the well-known *arc de cercle* which occurs during attacks in major hysteria is nothing else than an energetic repudiation like this, through antagonistic innervation, of a posture of the body that is suitable for sexual intercourse.

(4) Scarcely less confusing and misleading is a *reversal of the chronological order* within the phantasy that is portrayed, which once more has its complete counterpart in a number of dreams

1. [See above, p. 94.]
2. [Cf. a passage added to *The Interpretation of Dreams* (1900*a*) in 1909, *P.F.L.*, **4**, 440 f.]

which begin with the end of the action and end with its beginning. Supposing, for instance, that a hysterical woman has a phantasy of seduction in which she is sitting reading in a park with her skirt slightly lifted so that her foot is visible; a gentleman approaches and speaks to her; they then go somewhere and make love to one another. This phantasy is acted out in the attack by her beginning with the convulsive stage, which corresponds to the coitus, by her then getting up, going into another room, sitting down and reading and presently answering an imaginary remark addressed to her.[1]

The two last-mentioned forms of distortion give us some idea of the intensity of the resistances which the repressed material must take into account even when it breaks through in a hysterical attack.

B

The onset of hysterical attacks follows laws that are easily understandable. Since the repressed complex consists of a libidinal cathexis and an ideational content (the phantasy),[2] the attack can be evoked (1) *associatively*, when the content of the complex (if sufficiently cathected) is touched on by something connected with it in conscious life; (2) *organically*, when, for internal somatic reasons and as a result of psychical influences from outside, the libidinal cathexis rises above a certain degree; (3) in the service of the *primary purpose* – as an expression of a 'flight into illness', when reality becomes distressing or frightening – that is, as a *consolation*; (4) in the service of the *secondary purposes*, with which the illness allies itself, as soon as, by producing an attack, the patient can achieve an aim that is

1. [A fuller and slightly different account of this example was added as a footnote to *The Interpretation of Dreams* in 1909, *P.F.L.*, 4, 441 *n*. 1.]

2. [The distinction indicated here between ideational content and affective energy was to play an important part in Freud's metapsychological account of repression. Cf. 'Repression' (1915*d*) and Section IV of 'The Unconscious' (1915*e*).]

useful to him.[1] In the last case the attack is directed at particular individuals; it can be put off till they are present, and it gives an impression of being consciously simulated.

C

Investigation of the childhood history of hysterical patients shows that the hysterical attack is designed to take the place of an *auto-erotic* satisfaction previously practised and since given up. In a great number of cases this satisfaction (masturbation by contact or by pressure of the thighs, or, again, by movements of the tongue, and so on) recurs during the attack itself, while the subject's consciousness is deflected. Moreover, the onset of an attack that is due to an increase of libido and is in the service of the primary purpose – as a consolation – exactly repeats the conditions under which, at the earlier time, the patient had intentionally sought this auto-erotic satisfaction.[2] The anamnesis of the patient shows the following stages: (*a*) auto-erotic satisfaction, without ideational content; (*b*) the same satisfaction connected with a phantasy which leads to the act of satisfaction; (*c*) renunciation of the act, with retention of the phantasy; (*d*) repression of the phantasy, which then comes into effect as a hysterical attack, either in an unchanged form, or in a modified one and adapted to new environmental impressions. Further-

1. [This seems to be the first appearance of the actual term 'flight into illness', though the notion was an old one of Freud's. The idea of a 'gain from illness' as an aetiological factor was also an old one, but the distinction between a 'primary' and 'secondary' gain is first made clearly in the present passage. The whole question was fully discussed in Lecture 24 of the *Introductory Lectures* (1916–17), *P.F.L.*, **1**, 429–33, and again in a footnote added in 1923 to the 'Dora' case history (1905*e*), *P.F.L.*, **8**, 75–6 *n.*, in which Freud corrects and clarifies his earlier views on the subject.]

2. [Cf. a discussion of this in the Editor's Introduction to *Inhibitions, Symptoms and Anxiety* (1926*d*), p. 235 below, where further references are given.]

more, (e) the phantasy may even reinstate the act of satisfaction belonging to it which had ostensibly been given up. This is a typical cycle of infantile sexual activity: repression, failure of repression, and return of the repressed.

The involuntary passing of urine is certainly not to be regarded as incompatible with the diagnosis of a hysterical attack; it is merely repeating the infantile form of a violent pollution. Moreover, biting the tongue may also be met with in undoubted cases of hysteria. It is no more inconsistent with hysteria than it is with love-making. It occurs more readily in attacks if the patient's attention had been drawn by the doctor's questions to the difficulties of making a differential diagnosis. Self-injury may occur in hysterical attacks (more frequently in the case of men) where it repeats an accident in childhood – as, for instance, the result of a romp.

The loss of consciousness, the 'absence',[1] in a hysterical attack is derived from the fleeting but unmistakable lapse of consciousness which is observable at the climax of every intense sexual satisfaction, including auto-erotic ones. This course of development can be traced with most certainty where hysterical absences arise from the onset of pollutions in young people of the female sex. The so-called 'hypnoid states'[2] – absences during day-dreaming – , which are so common in hysterical subjects, show the same origin. The mechanism of these absences is comparatively simple. All the subject's attention is concentrated to begin with on the course of the process of satisfaction; with the occurrence of the satisfaction, the whole of this cathexis of attention is suddenly removed, so that there ensues a momentary void in her consciousness. This gap in consciousness, which might be termed a physiological one, is then widened in the service of repression, till it can swallow up everything that the repressing agency rejects.

1. [The French term.]
2. [Breuer's term. See Studies on Hysteria (1895d), in particular the Editor's Introduction, P.F.L., 3, 37 and 42.]

D

What points the way for the motor discharge of the repressed libido in a hysterical attack is the reflex mechanism of the act of coition – a mechanism which is ready to hand in everybody, including women, and which we see coming into manifest operation when an unrestrained surrender is made to sexual activity. Already in ancient times coition was described as a 'minor epilepsy'. We might alter this and say that a convulsive hysterical attack is an equivalent of coition. The analogy with an epileptic fit helps us little, since its genesis is even less understood than that of hysterical attacks.[1]

Speaking as a whole, hysterical attacks, like hysteria in general, revive a piece of sexual activity in women which existed during their childhood and at that time revealed an essentially masculine character. It can often be observed that girls who have shown a boyish nature and inclinations up to the years before puberty are precisely those who become hysterical from puberty onwards. In a whole number of cases the hysterical neurosis merely represents an excessive accentuation of the typical wave of repression which, by doing away with her masculine sexuality, allows the woman to emerge.[2]

1. [Cf. Freud's lengthy discussion of the 'epileptic reaction' and the relation between epilepsy and hysterical attacks in his paper on Dostoevsky (1928b).]

2. Cf. my Three Essays on the Theory of Sexuality (1905d). [P.F.L., 7, 141-4.]

THE PSYCHOANALYTIC VIEW OF PSYCHOGENIC DISTURBANCE OF VISION
(1910)

EDITOR'S NOTE

DIE PSYCHOGENE SEHSTÖRUNG IN PSYCHOANALYTISCHER AUFFASSUNG

(A) German Editions:

1910   *Ärztliche Fortbildung*, supplement to *Ärztliche Standes-zeitung*, **9** (9), 42–4 (May 1).
1913   *S.K.S.N.*, **3**, 314–21. (2nd ed. 1921.)
1924   *Gesammelte Schriften*, **5**, 301–9.
1943   *Gesammelte Werke*, **8**, 94–102.

(B) English Translations:

'Psychogenic Visual Disturbance according to Psycho-Analytical Conceptions'

1924   *Collected Papers*, **2**, 105–12. (Tr. E. Colburn Mayne.)
1957   *Standard Edition*, **11**, 209–18. (A new translation, with a different title.)

The present edition is a corrected reprint of the *Standard Edition* version, with a few editorial changes.

This was written as a contribution to a *Festschrift* in honour of Leopold Königstein, a well-known Viennese ophthalmologist, who was one of Freud's oldest friends. He described it in a letter to Ferenczi, written on April 12, 1910, as being a mere *pièce d'occasion* and of no value (Jones, 1955, 274). It contains one passage at least, however, of very special interest. For it was here that for the first time he made use of the term 'ego-instincts', explicitly identified them with the self-preservative instincts and ascribed to them a vital part in the function of repression. It is also worth remarking that in the later paragraphs of this paper (p. 113 f.) Freud expresses with particular definiteness his belief that mental phenomena are ultimately based on physical ones.

THE PSYCHOANALYTIC VIEW OF
PSYCHOGENIC DISTURBANCE
OF VISION

GENTLEMEN, – I propose to take the example of psychogenic disturbance of vision, in order to show you the modifications which have taken place in our view of the genesis of disorders of this kind under the influence of psychoanalytic methods of investigation. As you know, hysterical blindness is taken as the type of a psychogenic visual disturbance. It is generally believed, as a result of the researches of the French School (including such men as Charcot, Janet and Binet), that the genesis of these cases is understood. For we are in a position to produce blindness of this kind experimentally if we have at our disposal someone who is susceptible to somnambulism. If we put him into deep hypnosis and suggest the idea to him that he sees nothing with one of his eyes, he will in fact behave as though he had become blind in that eye, like a hysteric who has developed a visual disturbance spontaneously. We may thus construct the mechanism of spontaneous hysterical disturbances of vision on the model of suggested hypnotic ones. In a hysteric the idea of being blind arises, not from the prompting of a hypnotist, but spontaneously – by autosuggestion, as people say; and in both cases this idea is so powerful that it turns into reality, exactly like a suggested hallucination, paralysis, etc.

This seems perfectly sound and will satisfy anyone who can ignore the many enigmas that lie concealed behind the concepts of hypnosis, suggestion and autosuggestion. Autosuggestion in particular raises further questions. When and under what conditions does an idea become so powerful that it is able to behave like a suggestion and turn into reality without more ado? Closer investigation has taught us that we cannot answer this question without calling the concept of the 'unconscious' to our assistance. Many philosophers rebel against the assumption of a mental unconscious of this kind, because they have not concerned themselves with the phenomena which compel us to make that assumption. Psychopathologists have found that they cannot avoid working with such things as unconscious mental processes, unconscious ideas, and so on.

Appropriate experiments have shown that people who are hysterically blind do nevertheless see in some sense, though not in the full sense. Excitations of the blind eye may have certain psychical consequences (for instance, they may produce affects) even though they do not become conscious. Thus hysterically blind people are only blind as far as consciousness is concerned; in their unconscious they see. It is precisely observations such as this that compel us to distinguish between conscious and unconscious mental processes.

How does it happen that such people develop the unconscious 'autosuggestion' that they are blind, while nevertheless they see in their unconscious? The reply given by the French researches is to explain that in patients predisposed to hysteria there is an inherent tendency to dissociation – to a falling apart of the connections in their mental field – as a consequence of which some unconscious processes do not continue as far as into the conscious. Let us leave entirely on one side the value that this attempted explanation may have as regards an understanding of the phenomena in question, and let us look at the matter from another angle. As you see, Gentlemen, the identity of hysterical blindness with the blindness provoked by suggestion, on which so much stress was laid to begin with, has now been given up. The hysterical patient is blind, not as the result of an autosuggestive idea that he cannot see, but as the result of a dissociation between unconscious and conscious processes in the act of seeing; his idea that he does not see is the well-founded *expression* of the psychical state of affairs and not its *cause*.

If, Gentlemen, you complain of the obscurity of this exposition I shall not find it easy to defend. I have tried to give you a synthesis of the views of different investigators, and in doing so I have probably coupled them together too closely. I wanted to condense into a single composite whole the concepts that have been brought up to make psychogenic disturbances intelligible – their origin from excessively powerful ideas, the distinction between conscious and unconscious mental processes and the assumption of mental dissociation. And I have been no more successful in this than the French writers, at whose head stands Pierre Janet. I hope, therefore, that you will excuse not only the obscurity but the inaccuracy of my exposition, and will allow me to tell you how psychoanalysis has led us to a view of psychogenic disturbances of vision which is more self-consistent and probably closer to the facts.

Psychoanalysis, too, accepts the assumptions of dissociation and the unconscious, but relates them differently to each other. Its view is a dynamic one, which traces mental life back to an interplay between forces that favour or inhibit one another. If in any instance one group of ideas remains in the unconscious, psychoanalysis does not infer that there is a constitutional incapacity for synthesis which is showing itself in this particular dissociation, but maintains that the isolation and state of unconsciousness of this group of ideas have been caused by an active opposition on the part of other groups. The process owing to which it has met with this fate is known as 'repression' and we regard it as something analogous to a condemnatory judgement in the field of logic. Psychoanalysis points out that repressions of this kind play an extraordinarily important part in our mental life, but that they may also frequently fail and that such failures of repression are the precondition of the formation of symptoms.

If, then, as we have learnt, psychogenic disturbances of vision depend on certain ideas connected with seeing being cut off from consciousness, we must, on the psychoanalytic view, assume that these ideas have come into opposition to other, more powerful ones, for which we use the collective concept of the 'ego' – a compound which is made up variously at different times – and have for that reason come under repression. But what can be the origin of this opposition, which makes for repression, between the ego and various groups of ideas? You will no doubt notice that it was not possible to frame such a question before the advent of psychoanalysis, for nothing was known earlier of psychical conflict and repression. Our researches, however, have put us in a position to give us the desired answer. Our attention has been drawn to the importance of the instincts in ideational life. We have discovered that every instinct tries to make itself effective by activating ideas that are in keeping with its aims. These instincts are not always compatible with one another; their interests often come into conflict. Opposition between ideas is only an expression of struggles between the various instincts. From the point of view of our attempted explanation, a quite specially important part is played by the undeniable opposition between the instincts which subserve sexuality, the attainment of sexual pleasure, and those other instincts, which have as their aim the self-preservation of the individual – the ego-instincts.[1] As the poet has said, all the organic instincts that operate in our mind may be classified as 'hunger' or 'love'.[2] We have traced the 'sexual instinct' from its first manifestations in children to its final form, which is described as 'normal'. We have found that it is put together from numerous 'component instincts' which are attached to excitations of regions of the body; and we have come to see that these separate instincts have to pass through a complicated development before they can be brought effec-

1. [This seems to have been the first occasion on which Freud used this term. (See Editor's Note, p. 106.) For a late summary of Freud's theory of the instincts, see the second half of Lecture 32 of the *New Introductory Lectures* (1933*a*), *P.F.L.*, **2**, 127 ff.]

2. [Schiller, 'Die Weltweisen'.]

tively to serve the aims of reproduction.[1] The light thrown by psychology on the evolution of our civilization has shown us that it originates mainly at the cost of the sexual component instincts, and that these must be suppressed, restricted, transformed and directed to higher aims, in order that the mental constructions of civilization may be established. We have been able to recognize as a valuable outcome of these researches something that our colleagues have not yet been willing to believe, namely that the human ailments known as 'neuroses' are derived from the many different ways in which these processes of transformation in the sexual component instincts may miscarry. The 'ego' feels threatened by the claims of the sexual instincts and fends them off by repressions; these, however, do not always have the desired result, but lead to the formation of dangerous substitutes for the repressed and to burdensome reactions on the part of the ego. From these two classes of phenomena taken together there emerge what we call the symptoms of neuroses.

We have apparently digressed widely from our problem, though in doing so we have touched on the manner in which neurotic pathological conditions are related to our mental life as a whole. But let us now return to the narrower question. The sexual and ego-instincts alike have in general the same organs and systems of organs at their disposal. Sexual pleasure is not attached merely to the function of the genitals. The mouth serves for kissing as well as for eating and communication by speech; the eyes perceive not only alterations in the external world which are important for the preservation of life, but also characteristics of objects which lead to their being chosen as objects of love – their charms.[2] The saying that it is not easy for anyone to serve two masters is thus confirmed. The closer the relation into which an organ with a dual function of

1. [See *Three Essays on the Theory of Sexuality* (1905d).]

2. [In German, '*Reize*', which means both 'charms' and 'stimuli'. Cf. Freud's *Three Essays* (1905d), *P.F.L.*, **7**, 69 *n.* 2 and 130.]

this kind enters with *one* of the major instincts, the more it withholds itself from the other. This principle is bound to lead to pathological consequences if the two fundamental instincts are disunited and if the ego maintains a repression of the sexual component instinct concerned.[1] It is easy to apply this to the eye and to seeing. Let us suppose that the sexual component instinct which makes use of looking – sexual pleasure in looking [scopophilia] – has drawn upon itself defensive action by the ego-instincts in consequence of its excessive demands, so that the ideas in which its desires are expressed succumb to repression and are prevented from becoming conscious; in that case there will be a general disturbance of the relation of the eye and of the act of seeing to the ego and consciousness. The ego will have lost its dominance over the organ, which will now be wholly at the disposal of the repressed sexual instinct. It looks as though the repression had been carried too far by the ego, as though it had emptied the baby out with the bath-water: the ego refuses to see anything at all any more, now that the sexual interest in seeing has made itself so prominent. But the alternative picture seems more to the point. This attributes the active role instead to the repressed pleasure in looking. The repressed instinct takes its revenge for being held back from further psychical expansion, by becoming able to extend its dominance over the organ that is in its service. The loss of conscious dominance over the organ is the detrimental substitute for the repression which had miscarried and was only made possible at that price.

This relation of an organ with a double claim on it – its relation to the conscious ego and to repressed sexuality – is to be seen even more clearly in motor organs than in the eye: as when, for instance, a hand which has tried to carry out an act of sexual aggression, and has become paralysed hysterically, is unable, after that act has been inhibited, to do anything else – as

1. [This point had already been made at the end of the second of the *Three Essays*, ibid., 125–6.]

though it were obstinately insisting on carrying out a repressed innervation; or as when the fingers of people who have given up masturbation refuse to learn the delicate movements required for playing the piano or the violin. As regards the eye, we are in the habit of translating the obscure psychical processes concerned in the repression of sexual scopophilia and in the development of the psychogenic disturbance of vision as though a punishing voice was speaking from within the subject, and saying: 'Because you sought to misuse your organ of sight for evil sensual pleasures, it is fitting that you should not see anything at all any more', and as though it was in this way approving the outcome of the process. The idea of talion punishment is involved in this, and in fact our explanation of psychogenic visual disturbance coincides with what is suggested by myths and legends. The beautiful legend of Lady Godiva tells how all the town's inhabitants hid behind their shuttered windows, so as to make easier the lady's task of riding naked through the streets in broad daylight, and how the only man who peeped through the shutters at her revealed loveliness was punished by going blind. Nor is this the only example which suggests that neurotic illness holds the hidden key to mythology as well.

Psychoanalysis is unjustly reproached, Gentlemen, for leading to purely psychological theories of pathological problems. The emphasis which it lays on the pathogenic role of sexuality, which, after all, is certainly not an exclusively psychical factor, should alone protect it from this reproach. Psychoanalysts never forget that the mental is based on the organic, although their work can only carry them as far as this basis and not beyond it. Thus psychoanalysis is ready to admit, and indeed to postulate, that not all disturbances of vision need be psychogenic, like those that are evoked by the repression of erotic scopophilia. If an organ which serves the two sorts of instinct increases its erotogenic role, it is in general to be expected that this will not occur without the excitability and innervation of the organ undergoing changes which will manifest themselves as disturbances of its function in the service of the ego. Indeed, if we find that an organ normally serving the purpose of sense-perception begins to behave like an actual genital when its erotogenic role is increased, we shall not regard it as improbable that *toxic* changes are also occurring in it. For lack of a better name we must retain the old unsuitable term of 'neurotic' disturbances for both classes of functional disturbances – those of physiological as well as those of toxic origin – which follow from an increase in the erotogenic factor. Generally speaking, the neurotic disturbances of vision stand in the same relation to the psychogenic ones as the 'actual neuroses' do to the psycho-neuroses: psychogenic visual disturbances can no doubt hardly ever appear without neurotic ones, but the latter can appear without the former. These 'neurotic' symptoms are unfortunately little appreciated and understood even today; for they are not directly accessible to psychoanalysis, and other methods of research have left the standpoint of sexuality out of account.[1]

Yet another line of thought extending into organic research branches off from psychoanalysis. We may ask ourselves whether the suppression of sexual component instincts which is brought about by environmental influences is sufficient in itself to call up functional disturbances in organs, or whether special constitutional conditions must be present in order that the organs may be led to an exaggeration of their erotogenic role and consequently provoke repression of the instincts. We should have to see in those conditions the constitutional part of the disposition to fall ill of psychogenic and neurotic disorders. This is the factor to which, as applied to hysteria, I gave the provisional name of 'somatic compliance'.[2]

1. [See some remarks on the 'actual neuroses' in 1906*a* above, p. 80 and *n.*]

2. [Cf. the 'Dora' case history (1905*e*), *P.F.L.*, **8**, 72–4 and 86–8. – In the 1910 edition only, the paper concluded with the following words: 'Alfred Adler's well-known writings seek to give that factor definition in biological terms.']

TYPES OF ONSET OF NEUROSIS
(1912)

EDITOR'S NOTE

ÜBER NEUROTISCHE ERKRANKUNGSTYPEN

(A) GERMAN EDITIONS:

1912   *Zentbl. Psychoanal.*, **2** (6) [March], 297–302.
1924   *Gesammelte Schriften*, **5**, 400–408.
1943   *Gesammelte Werke*, **8**, 322–30.

(B) ENGLISH TRANSLATIONS:

'Types of Neurotic Nosogenesis'

1924   *Collected Papers*, **2**, 113–21. (Tr. E. C. Mayne.)
1958   *Standard Edition*, **12**, 227–38. (A new translation, with a different title.)

The present edition is a corrected reprint of the *Standard Edition* version, with one or two editorial modifications.

The theme of this paper is the classification of the precipitating causes of neurotic illnesses. Freud had, of course, often dealt with it before; but in his earlier writings the position was obscured by the prominence given in them to traumatic events. After he had more or less completely abandoned the trauma theory, his interest was largely focussed (e.g. in the 'Summary' at the end of the *Three Essays* (1905*d*), *P.F.L.*, **7**, 160 ff.) on the various *predisposing* causes of neurosis. The precipitating causes are mentioned in one or two contemporary papers, but only in the most general and somewhat deprecating terms. (See, for instance, the paper on the aetiology of the neuroses (1906*a*), pp.

79–81 above.) It is true, however, that the notion of 'deprivation' makes an occasional appearance, but only in the sense of deprivation due to some external circumstance. The possibility of neurosis resulting from an *internal* obstacle to satisfaction emerges at a somewhat later date – in the paper, for instance, on the effects of 'civilized' morality (1908*d*) – perhaps, as Freud suggests below (p. 121), under the impact of Jung's work. In the last-mentioned paper the term 'frustration' is used to describe the internal obstacle. It reappears, but this time with reference only to *external* obstacles, in the rather earlier Schreber analysis (1911*c*), as well as in a paper contemporary with this one – on the tendency to debasement in love (1912*d*), *P.F.L.*, **7**, 250–55. But in the present paper, Freud used the word for the first time to introduce a more embracing concept, covering *both* kinds of obstacle.

From this time forward 'frustration' as a principal precipitating cause of neurosis became one of the most commonly used weapons in Freud's clinical armoury, and it recurs in many of his later writings. The most elaborate of these later discussions will be found in Lecture 22 of the *Introductory Lectures* (1916–17), *P.F.L.*, **1**, 389–97. The apparently contradictory case of a person falling ill at the moment of attaining success – the very opposite of frustration – was brought up and resolved by Freud in the course of a paper on various types of character (1916*d*), and he returned once more to the same point in his open letter to Romain Rolland describing a visit to the Acropolis (1936*a*). In a passage in the case history of the 'Wolf Man' (1918*b*), Freud pointed out that there was an omission in the present list of types of onset of neurosis – the type resulting from a *narcissistic* frustration (*P.F.L.*, **9**, 361–2).

TYPES OF ONSET OF NEUROSIS

IN the pages which follow, I shall describe, on the basis of impressions arrived at empirically, the changes which conditions must undergo in order to bring about the outbreak of a neurotic illness in a person with a disposition to it. I shall thus be dealing with the question of the precipitating factors of illnesses and shall have little to say about their forms. The present discussion of the precipitating causes will differ from others in that the changes to be enumerated will relate exclusively to the subject's libido. For psychoanalysis has taught us that the vicissitudes of the libido are what decide in favour of nervous health or sickness. Nor are words to be wasted in this connection on the concept of disposition.[1] It is precisely psychoanalytic research which has enabled us to show that neurotic disposition lies in the history of the development of the libido, and to trace back the operative factors in that development to innate varieties of sexual constitution and to influences of the external world experienced in early childhood.

(*a*) The most obvious, the most easily discoverable and the most intelligible precipitating cause of an onset of neurosis is to be seen in the external factor which may be described in general terms as *frustration*. The subject was healthy so long as his need for love was satisfied by a real object in the external world; he becomes neurotic as soon as this object is withdrawn from him without a substitute taking its place. Here happiness coincides with health and unhappiness with neurosis. It is easier for fate to bring about a cure than for the physician;[2] for it can offer the

1. [On this see the Editor's Note to Freud's paper on 'The Disposition to Obsessional Neurosis' (1913*i*) below, p. 130 ff.]

2. [Freud had used almost the same words in the last paragraph of his contribution to the *Studies on Hysteria* (1895*d*), P.F.L., **3**, 393.]

patient a substitute for the possibility of satisfaction which he has lost.

Thus with this type, to which, no doubt, the majority of human beings on the whole belong, the possibility of falling ill arises only when there is abstinence. And it may be judged from this what an important part in the causation of neuroses may be played by the limitation imposed by civilization on the field of accessible satisfactions. Frustration has a pathogenic effect because it dams up libido, and so submits the subject to a test as to how long he can tolerate this increase in psychical tension and as to what methods he will adopt for dealing with it. There are only two possibilities for remaining healthy when there is a persistent frustration of satisfaction in the real world. The first is by transforming the psychical tension into active energy which remains directed towards the external world and eventually extorts a real satisfaction of the libido from it. The second is by renouncing libidinal satisfaction, sublimating the dammed-up libido and turning it to the attainment of aims which are no longer erotic and which escape frustration. That these two possibilities are realized in men's lives proves that unhappiness does not coincide with neurosis and that frustration does not alone decide whether its victim remains healthy or falls ill. The immediate effect of frustration lies in its bringing into play the dispositional factors which have hitherto been inoperative.

Where these are present and sufficiently strongly developed, there is a risk of the libido becoming 'introverted'.[1] It turns away from reality, which, owing to the obstinate frustration, has lost its value for the subject, and turns towards the life of phantasy, in which it creates new wishful structures and revives the traces of earlier, forgotten ones. In consequence of the intimate connection between the activity of phantasy and

1. To use a term introduced by C. G. Jung [1910]. [Some further comments on Jung's use of the term will be found in Lecture 23 of the *Introductory Lectures* (1916–17), *P.F.L.*, 1, 421. Freud used the term extremely seldom in his later writings.]

material present in everyone which is infantile and repressed and has become unconscious, and thanks to the exceptional position enjoyed by the life of phantasy in regard to reality-testing,[1] the libido may thenceforward move on a backward course; it may follow the path of *regression* along infantile lines, and strive after aims that correspond with them. If these strivings, which are incompatible with the subject's present-day individuality, acquire enough intensity, a conflict must result between them and the other portion of his personality, which has maintained its relation to reality. This conflict is resolved by the formation of symptoms, and is followed by the onset of manifest illness. The fact that the whole process originated from frustration in the real world is reflected in the resulting event that the symptoms, in which the ground of reality is reached once more, represent substitutive satisfactions.

(b) The second type of precipitating cause of falling ill is by no means so obvious as the first; and it was in fact only possible to discover it through searching analytic investigations following on the Zurich school's theory of complexes.[2] Here the subject does not fall ill as a result of a change in the external world which has replaced satisfaction by frustration, but as a result of an internal effort to obtain the satisfaction which is accessible to him in reality. He falls ill of his attempt to adapt himself to reality and to fulfil *the demands of reality* – an attempt in the course of which he comes up against insurmountable internal difficulties.

It is advisable to draw a sharp distinction between the two types of onset of illness – a sharper distinction than observation as a rule permits. In the first type what is prominent is a change in the external world; in the second type the accent falls on an internal change. In the first type the subject falls ill from an

1. See my 'Formulations on the Two Principles of Mental Functioning' (1911b). [Cf. also pp. 225–6 below in (1924e).]
2. Cf. Jung (1909).

experience; in the second type it is from a developmental process. In the first case he is faced by the task of renouncing satisfaction, and he falls ill from his incapacity for resistance; in the second case his task is to exchange one kind of satisfaction for another, and he breaks down from his inflexibility. In the second case the conflict, which is between the subject's effort to remain as he is and the effort to change himself in order to meet fresh purposes and fresh demands from reality, is present from the first. In the former case the conflict only arises after the dammed-up libido has chosen other, and incompatible, possibilities of satisfaction. The part played by the conflict and the previous fixation of the libido is incomparably more obvious in the second type than in the first, in which such unserviceable fixations may perhaps only emerge as a result of the external frustration.

A young man who has hitherto satisfied his libido by means of phantasies ending in masturbation, and who now seeks to replace a régime approximating to auto-erotism by the choice of a real object – or a girl who has given her whole affection to her father or brother and who must now, for the sake of a man who is courting her, allow her hitherto unconscious incestuous libidinal wishes to become conscious – or a married woman who would like to renounce her polygamous inclinations and phantasies of prostitution so as to become a faithful consort to her husband and a perfect mother to her child – all of these fall ill from the most laudable efforts, if the earlier fixations of their libido are powerful enough to resist a displacement; and this point will be decided, once again, by the factors of disposition, constitution and infantile experience. All of them, it might be said, meet with the fate of the little tree in the Grimms' fairy tale, which wished it had different leaves.[1] From the hygienic point of view – which, to be sure, is not the only one to be taken into account – one could only wish for them that they had

1. [This episode does not, in fact, appear in the Grimm collection, but in a children's poem by Friedrich Rückert (1788–1866).]

continued to be as undeveloped, as inferior and as useless as they were before they fell ill. The change which the patients strive after, but bring about only imperfectly or not at all, invariably has the value of a step forward from the point of view of real life. It is otherwise if we apply ethical standards: we see people falling ill just as often when they discard an ideal as when they seek to attain it.

In spite of the very clear differences between the two types of onset of illness that we have described, they nevertheless coincide in essentials and can without difficulty be brought together into a unity. Falling ill from frustration may also be regarded as incapacity for adaptation to reality – in the particular case, that is, in which reality frustrates satisfaction of libido. Falling ill under the conditions of the second type leads directly to a special case of frustration. It is true that reality does not here frustrate *every* kind of satisfaction; but it frustrates the one kind which the subject declares is the only possible one. Nor does the frustration come immediately from the external world but primarily from certain trends in the subject's ego. Nevertheless, frustration remains the common factor and the more inclusive one. In consequence of the conflict which immediately sets in in the second type, both kinds of satisfaction – the habitual one as well as the one aimed at – are equally inhibited; a damming-up of libido, with all its consequences, comes about just as it does in the first case. The psychical events leading to the formation of symptoms are if anything easier to follow in the second type than in the first; for in the second type the pathogenic fixations of the libido do not need to be freshly established, but have already been in force while the subject was healthy. A certain amount of introversion of libido is, as a rule, already present; and there is a saving of some part of the subject's regression to the infantile stage, owing to the fact that his forward development has not yet completed its course.

(c) The next type, which I shall describe as falling ill from *an inhibition in development*, looks like an exaggeration of the second one – falling ill from *the demands of reality*. There is no theoretical reason for distinguishing it, but only a practical one; for those we are here concerned with are people who fall ill as soon as they get beyond the irresponsible age of childhood, and who have thus never reached a phase of health – a phase, that is, of capacity for achievement and enjoyment which is on the whole unrestricted. The essential feature of the dispositional process is in these cases quite plain. Their libido has never left its infantile fixations; the demands of reality are not suddenly made upon a wholly or partly mature person, but arise from the very fact of growing older, since it is obvious that they constantly alter with the subject's increasing age. Thus conflict falls into the background in comparison with insufficiency. But here, too, all our other experience leads us to postulate an effort at overcoming the fixations of childhood; for otherwise the outcome of the process could never be neurosis but only a stationary infantilism.

(*d*) Just as the third type has brought the dispositional determinant before us almost in isolation, so the fourth type, which now follows, draws our attention to another factor, which comes into consideration in every single case and might easily for that very reason be overlooked in a theoretical discussion. We see people fall ill who have hitherto been healthy, who have met with no fresh experience and whose relation to the external world has undergone no change, so that the onset of their illness inevitably gives an impression of spontaneity. A closer consideration of such cases, however, shows us that none the less a change *has* taken place in them whose importance we must rate very highly as a cause of illness. As a result of their having reached a particular period of life, and in conformity with regular biological processes, the *quantity* of libido in their mental economy has experienced an increase which is in itself enough to upset the equilibrium of their health and to set up the necessary conditions for a neurosis. It is well known that more or less sudden increases of libido of this kind are habitually associated with puberty and the menopause – with the attainment of a certain age in women; in some people they may in addition be manifested in periodicities that are still unknown. Here the damming-up of libido is the primary factor; it becomes pathogenic as a consequence of a *relative* frustration on the part of the external world, which would still have granted satisfaction to a smaller claim by the libido. The unsatisfied and dammed-up libido can once again open up paths to regression and kindle the same conflicts which we have demonstrated in the case of absolute external frustration. We are reminded in this way that the quantitative factor should not be left out of account in any consideration of the precipitating causes of illness. All the other factors – frustration, fixation, developmental inhibition – remain ineffective unless they affect a certain amount of libido and bring about a damming-up of libido of a certain height. It is true that we are unable to measure this amount of libido which seems to us indispensable for a pathogenic effect; we can only postulate it after the resulting illness has started. There is only one direction in which we can determine it more precisely. We may assume that it is not a question of an *absolute* quantity, but of the relation between the quota of libido in operation and the quantity of libido which the individual ego is able to deal with – that is, to hold under tension, to sublimate or to employ directly. For this reason a *relative* increase in the quantity of libido may have the same effects as an absolute one. An enfeeblement of the ego owing to organic illness or owing to some special demand upon its energy will be able to cause the emergence of neuroses which would otherwise have remained latent in spite of any disposition that might be present.

The importance in the causation of illness which must be ascribed to *quantity* of libido is in satisfactory agreement with two main theses of the theory of the neuroses to which psychoanalysis has led us: first, the thesis that the neuroses are derived from the conflict between the ego and the libido, and secondly, the discovery that there is no *qualitative* distinction between the determinants of health and those of neurosis, and that, on the contrary, healthy people have to contend with the same tasks of mastering their libido – they have simply succeeded better in them.

It remains to say a few words on the relation of these types to the facts of observation. If I survey the set of patients on whose analysis I am at the moment engaged, I must record that not one of them is a pure example of any of the four types of onset. In each of them, rather, I find a portion of frustration operating alongside of a portion of incapacity to adapt to the demands of reality; inhibition in development, which coincides, of course, with inflexibility of fixations, has to be reckoned with in all of them, and, as I have already said, the importance of quantity of libido must never be neglected. I find, indeed, that in several of these patients their illness has appeared in successive waves, between which there have been healthy intervals, and that each of these waves has been traceable to a different type of precipitating cause. Thus the erection of these four types cannot lay claim to any high theoretical value; they are merely different ways of establishing a particular pathogenic constellation in the mental economy – namely the damming-up of libido, which the ego cannot, with the means at its command, ward off without damage. But this situation itself only becomes pathogenic as a result of a quantitative factor; it does not come as a novelty to mental life and is not created by the impact of what is spoken of as a 'cause of illness'.

A certain *practical* importance may readily be allowed to these types of onset. They are to be met with in their pure form, indeed, in individual cases; we should not have noticed the third and fourth types if they had not in some subjects constituted the sole precipitating causes of the illness. The first type keeps before our eyes the extraordinarily powerful influence of the external world, and the second the no less important influence – which opposes the former one – of the subject's peculiar individuality. Pathology could not do justice to the problem of the precipitating factors in the neuroses so long as it was merely concerned with deciding whether those affections were of an 'endogenous' or 'exogenous' nature. It was bound to meet every observation which pointed to the importance of abstinence (in the widest sense of the word) as a precipitating cause with the objection that other people tolerate the same experiences without falling ill. If, however, it sought to lay stress on the peculiar individuality of the subject as being the essential factor decisive between illness and health, it was obliged to put up with the proviso that people possessing such a peculiarity can remain healthy indefinitely, just so long as they are able to retain that peculiarity. Psychoanalysis has warned us that we must give up the unfruitful contrast between external and internal factors, between experience and constitution,[1] and has taught us that we shall invariably find the cause of the onset of neurotic illness in a particular psychical situation which can be brought about in a variety of ways.

1. [Freud, however, continues to pursue this 'unfruitful contrast' to some extent in the next paper in this volume, 'The Disposition to Obsessional Neurosis' (1913*i*).]

THE DISPOSITION TO
OBSESSIONAL NEUROSIS

(A CONTRIBUTION TO THE PROBLEM OF
CHOICE OF NEUROSIS)
(1913)

EDITOR'S NOTE

DIE DISPOSITION ZUR ZWANGSNEUROSE
EIN BEITRAG ZUM PROBLEM DER NEUROSENWAHL

(A) GERMAN EDITIONS:

1913 *Int. Z. ärztl. Psychoanal.*, **1** (6), 525–32.
1918 *S.K.S.N.*, **4**, 113–24. (1922, 2nd ed.)
1924 *Gesammelte Schriften*, **5**, 277–87.
1943 *Gesammelte Werke*, **8**, 442–52.

(B) ENGLISH TRANSLATIONS:

'The Predisposition to Obsessional Neurosis: A Contribution to the Problem of the Option of Neurosis'

1924 *Collected Papers*, **2**, 122–32. (Tr. E. Glover and E. C. Mayne.)
1958 *Standard Edition*, **12**, 311–26. (A new translation with a modified title.)

The present edition is a corrected reprint of the *Standard Edition* version, with some editorial changes.

This paper was read by Freud before the Fourth International Psycho-Analytical Congress, held at Munich on September 7 and 8, 1913, and was published at the end of that year.

Two topics of special importance are discussed in it. First, there is the problem of 'choice of neurosis',[1] which gives the work its sub-heading. It was a problem that had vexed Freud from very early times. References to the subject first appear in

1. In all this, of course, only the *psychoneuroses* are concerned.

his published writings in 1896; it also finds mention in several of his communications to Fliess at that period and during the next two or three years (Freud, 1950a).

In these early discussions of the problem two different solutions may be distinguished, which were alike, however, in postulating a traumatic aetiology for the neuroses. First there was the passive and active theory mentioned in the present paper (below, p. 136), the theory that passive sexual experiences in early childhood predisposed to hysteria and active ones to obsessional neurosis. Ten years later, in a discussion of the part played by sexuality in the neuroses (1906a), Freud repudiated this theory entirely (cf. above, p. 76).

The second of these early theories, not kept completely distinct from the first, attributed the decisive factor to chronological considerations. The form taken by a neurosis was supposed to depend on the period of life at which the traumatic experience occurred, or on the period of life at which defensive action was taken against the revival of the traumatic experience.

A considerable time passed before Freud published anything in the way of an elaboration or modification of these views. And then, in the closing pages of his *Three Essays* (1905d), *P.F.L.*, **7**, 160 ff., the complicated process of sexual development suggested a new version of the chronological theory: the notion of a succession of possible 'fixation points', at which that process is liable to be held up, and to which a regression may take place if difficulties are met with in later life. It was not for several years, however, that any explicit statement was made of the relation between this succession of fixation points and the choice of neurosis. This was in the paper on the two principles of mental functioning (1911b), and (at much greater length) in the almost contemporary Schreber analysis (1911c), *P.F.L.*, **9**, pp. 206 etc. (It seems probable that this last discussion was what Freud had in mind in speaking here (p. 136) of an earlier approach to the problem.) But the whole question is examined in more general terms in the present paper.

This leads us to the second topic of special importance which it discusses – the topic, namely, of pregenital 'organizations' of the libido. The notion is now such a familiar one that we are surprised to learn that it made its first appearance here; but the whole section of the *Three Essays* dealing with it (*P.F.L.*, **7,** 116–18) was in fact only added in 1915, two years after this paper was published. The knowledge of there being non-genital component sexual instincts goes back, of course, very much further, and is prominent in the first edition of the *Three Essays* (1905*d*). What is new is the idea of there being regular stages in sexual development at which one or other of the component instincts dominates the whole picture.

Only one such stage, the anal-sadistic one, is discussed in the present paper. Freud had, however, already distinguished two earlier stages of sexual development; but these were not characterized by the dominance of any one component instinct. The very earliest of all, that of auto-erotism, before any object-choice has been made, appears in the first edition of the *Three Essays* (*P.F.L.*, **7,** 97).[1] The next stage, the first in which object-choice occurs but where the object is the person's own self, had been brought forward by Freud, under the name of narcissism, some three or four years before the present paper (see a footnote added in 1910 to the *Three Essays*, *P.F.L.*, **7,** 56 *n*.). Two other organized stages in the development of the libido remained to be described – one earlier and one later than the anal-sadistic one. The earlier one, the oral stage, once again showed the dominance of a component instinct; it was first mentioned in the section of the 1915 edition of the *Three Essays* already alluded to (*P.F.L.*, **7,** 116 f.). The later stage, no longer pregenital but not yet fully genital in the adult sense, the 'phallic' stage, only appeared on the scene many years later, in Freud's paper on 'The Infantile Genital Organization' (1923*e*, *P.F.L.*, **7,** 308 ff.).

1. Freud borrowed the actual term 'auto-erotism' from Havelock Ellis, who introduced it in a paper published in the previous year, 1898.

THE DISPOSITION TO
OBSESSIONAL NEUROSIS

A CONTRIBUTION TO THE PROBLEM OF
CHOICE OF NEUROSIS

THE problem of why and how a person may fall ill of a neurosis is certainly among those to which psychoanalysis should offer a solution. But it will probably be necessary to find a solution first to another and narrower problem – namely, why it is that this or that person must fall ill of a particular neurosis and of none other. This is the problem of 'choice of neurosis'.

What do we know so far about this problem? Strictly speaking, only one single general proposition can be asserted on the subject with certainty. It will be recalled that we divide the pathogenic determinants concerned in the neuroses into those which a person brings along with him into his life and those which life brings to him – the constitutional and the accidental – by whose combined operation alone the pathogenic determinant is as a rule established. The general proposition, then, which I have alluded to above, lays it down that the grounds for determining the choice of neurosis are entirely of the former kind – that is, that they are in the nature of dispositions[1] and are independent of experiences which operate pathogenically.

Where are we to look for the source of these dispositions? We have become aware that the psychical functions concerned

[1. [In this paper Freud seems always to use the word 'disposition' in the sense of something purely constitutional or hereditary. In later writings he gives the word a wider meaning, and includes it under the effects of experience in infancy. This is made perfectly clear in Lecture 23 of his *Introductory Lectures* (1916–17), *P.F.L.*, **1**, 407–9. – The 'general proposition' quoted in the text had already been asserted by Freud in his paper on sexuality in the neuroses (1906*a*), p. 76 above.]

– above all, the sexual function, but various important ego-functions too – have to undergo a long and complicated development before reaching the state characteristic of the normal adult. We can assume that these developments are not always so smoothly carried out that the total function passes through this regular progressive modification. Wherever a portion of it clings to a previous stage, what is known as a 'point of fixation' results, to which the function may regress if the subject falls ill through some external disturbance.

Thus our dispositions are inhibitions in development. We are confirmed in this view by the analogy of the facts of general pathology of other illnesses. But before the question as to what factors can bring about such disturbances of development the work of psychoanalysis comes to a stop: it leaves that problem to biological research.[1]

Already a few years back we ventured, with the help of these hypotheses, to approach the problem of choice of neurosis.[2] Our method of work, which aims at discovering normal conditions by studying their disturbances, led us to adopt a very singular and unexpected line of attack. The order in which the main forms of psychoneurosis are usually enumerated – Hysteria, Obsessional Neurosis, Paranoia, Dementia Praecox – corresponds (even though not quite exactly) to the order of the ages at which the onset of these disorders occurs. Hysterical forms of illness can be observed even in earliest childhood; obsessional neurosis usually shows its first symptoms in the second period of childhood (between the ages of six and eight); while the two other psychoneuroses, which I have brought together under the heading of 'paraphrenia',[3] do not appear

1. Since Wilhelm Fliess's writings have revealed the biological significance of certain periods of time it has become conceivable that disturbances of development may be traceable to temporal changes in the successive waves of development.

2. [See Editor's Note, p. 132.]

3. [In the first edition only this clause ran 'which are termed by me

until after puberty and during adult life. It is these disorders – the last to emerge – which were the first to show themselves accessible to our enquiry into the dispositions that result in the choice of neurosis. The characteristics peculiar to both of them – megalomania, turning away from the world of objects, increased difficulty in transference – have obliged us to conclude that their dispositional fixation is to be looked for in a stage of libidinal development *before* object-choice has been established – that is, in the phase of auto-erotism and of narcissism. Thus these forms of illness, which make their appearance so late, go back to very early inhibitions and fixations.

This would accordingly lead us to suppose that the disposition to hysteria and obsessional neurosis, the two transference neuroses proper, which produce their symptoms at an early age, lies in later phases of libidinal development. But at what point in them should we find a developmental inhibition? and, above all, what would be the difference in phases that would determine a disposition to obsessional neurosis as contrasted with hysteria? For a long time nothing was to be learned about this; and my earlier attempts at discovering these two dispositions – the notion, for instance, that hysteria might be determined by passivity and obsessional neurosis by activity in infantile experience – had soon to be abandoned as incorrect.[1]

I shall now take my footing once more on the clinical observation of an individual case. Over a long period I studied a woman patient whose neurosis underwent an unusual change. It began, after a traumatic experience, as a straightforward anxiety hysteria and retained that character for a few years. One day, however, it suddenly changed into an obsessional neurosis of the severest type. A case of this kind could not fail to become significant in more than one direction. On the one hand, it might perhaps claim to be looked upon like a bilingual docu-

---

paraphrenia and paranoia'. Some further discussion of the use of these terms occurs in the Schreber analysis (1911c): cf. *P.F.L.*, 9, 215 and *n.* 2.]

1. [See Editor's Note, p. 132.]

ment and to show how an identical content could be expressed by the two neuroses in different languages. On the other hand, it threatened to contradict completely our theory that disposition arises from developmental inhibition, unless we were prepared to accept the supposition that a person could innately possess more than one weak spot in his libidinal development.[1] I told myself that we had no right to dismiss this latter possibility; but I was greatly interested to arrive at an understanding of the case.

When in the course of the analysis this came about, I was forced to see that the situation was quite different from what I had imagined. The obsessional neurosis was not a further reaction to the same trauma which had first provoked the anxiety hysteria; it was a reaction to a second experience, which had completely wiped out the first. (Here, then, we have an exception – though, it is true, a not indisputable one – to our proposition affirming that choice of neurosis is independent of experience [p. 134].)

Unfortunately I am unable, for familiar reasons, to enter into the history of the case as far as I should like, and I must restrict myself to the account which follows. Up to the time of her falling ill the patient had been a happy and almost completely satisfied wife. She wanted to have children, from motives based on an infantile fixation of her wishes, and she fell ill when she learned that it was impossible for her to have any by the husband who was the only object of her love. The anxiety hysteria with which she reacted to this frustration corresponded, as she herself soon learned to understand, to the repudiation of phantasies of seduction in which her firmly implanted wish for a child found expression. She now did all she could to prevent her husband from guessing that she had fallen ill owing to the frustration of which he was the cause. But I have had good reason for asserting that everyone possesses in his own uncon-

1. [Cf. some remarks on this in the Schreber case history (1911c), P.F.L., 9, 217.]

scious an instrument with which he can interpret the utterances of the unconscious in other people.[1] Her husband understood, without any admission or explanation on her part, what his wife's anxiety meant; he felt hurt, without showing it, and in his turn reacted neurotically by – for the first time – failing in sexual intercourse with her. Immediately afterwards he started on a journey. His wife believed that he had become permanently impotent, and produced her first obsessional symptoms on the day before his expected return.

The content of her obsessional neurosis was a compulsion for scrupulous washing and cleanliness and extremely energetic protective measures against severe injuries which she thought other people had reason to fear from her – that is to say, reaction-formations against her own *anal-erotic* and *sadistic* impulses. Her sexual need was obliged to find expression in these shapes after her genital life had lost all its value owing to the impotence of the only man of whom there could be any question for her.

This is the starting-point of the small new fragment of theory which I have formulated. It is of course only in appearance that it is based on this one observation; actually it brings together a large number of earlier impressions, though an understanding of them was only made possible by this last experience. I told myself that my schematic picture of the development of the libidinal function called for an extra insertion in it. To begin with, I had only distinguished, first the phase of auto-erotism, during which the subject's component instincts, each on its own account, seek for the satisfaction of their desires in his own body, and then the combination of all the component instincts for the choice of an object, under the primacy of the genitals acting on behalf of reproduction. The analysis of the para-phrenias has, as we know, necessitated the insertion between them of a stage of narcissism, during which the choice of an object has already taken place but that object coincides with

1. [Cf. 'The Unconscious' (1915e), near the end of Section VI.]

the subject's own ego.[1] And now we see the need for yet another stage to be inserted before the final shape is reached – a stage in which the component instincts have already come together for the choice of an object and that object is already something extraneous in contrast to the subject's own self, but in which *the primacy of the genital zones has not yet been established*. On the contrary, the component instincts which dominate this *pregenital organization*[2] of sexual life are the anal-erotic and sadistic ones.

I am aware that any such hypotheses sound strange at first. It is only by discovering their relations to our former knowledge that they become familiar to us; and in the end it is often their fate to be regarded as minor and long-foreseen innovations. Let us therefore turn with anticipations such as these to a discussion of the 'pregenital sexual ordering'.

(a) The extraordinary part played by impulses of hatred and anal erotism in the symptomatology of obsessional neurosis has already struck many observers and has recently been emphasized with particular clarity by Ernest Jones (1913). This follows directly from our hypothesis if we suppose that in that neurosis the component instincts in question have once more taken over the representation of the genital instincts, whose forerunners they were in the process of development.

At this point a portion of our case history fits in, which I have so far kept back. The patient's sexual life began in her earliest childhood with beating-phantasies. After they were suppressed, an unusually long period of latency set in, during which the girl passed through a period of exalted moral growth, without any awakening of female sexual feelings. Her marriage, which took place at an early age, opened a time of normal sexual

1. [See Freud's later paper on narcissism (1914c); he had already put forward the idea in several places, particularly in the Schreber analysis (1911c), *P.F.L.*, **9**, 197.]

2. [The term is here used for the first time.]

activity. This period, during which she was a happy wife, continued for a number of years, until her first great frustration brought on the hysterical neurosis. When this was followed by her genital life losing all its value, her sexual life, as I have said, returned to the infantile stage of sadism.

It is not difficult to determine the characteristic which distinguishes this case of obsessional neurosis from those more frequent ones which start at an early age and thereafter run a chronic course with exacerbations of a more or less striking kind. In these other cases, once the sexual organization which contains the disposition to obsessional neurosis is established it is never afterwards completely surmounted; in our case it was replaced to begin with by the higher stage of development, and was then re-activated by regression from the latter.

(b) If we wish to bring our hypothesis into contact with biological lines of thought, we must not forget that the antithesis between male and female, which is introduced by the reproductive function, cannot be present as yet at the stage of pregenital object-choice. We find in its place the antithesis between trends with an active and with a passive aim, an antithesis which later becomes firmly attached to that between the sexes. Activity is supplied by the common instinct of mastery, which we call sadism when we find it in the service of the sexual function; and even in fully developed normal sexual life it has important subsidiary services to perform. The passive trend is fed by anal erotism, whose erotogenic zone corresponds to the old, undifferentiated cloaca. A stressing of this anal erotism in the pregenital stage of organization leaves behind a significant predisposition to homosexuality in men when the next stage of the sexual function, the primacy of the genitals, is reached. The way in which this last phase is erected upon the preceding one and the accompanying remoulding of the libidinal cathexes present analytic research with the most interesting problems.

The view may be taken that all the difficulties and complications involved in this can be avoided by denying that there is any pregenital organization of sexual life and by holding that sexual life coincides with the genital and reproductive function and begins with it. It would then be asserted, having regard to the unmistakable findings of analytic research, that the neuroses are compelled by the process of sexual repression to give expression to sexual trends through other, non-sexual instincts, and thus to sexualize the latter by way of compensation. But this line of argument would place us outside psychoanalysis. It would place us where we were before psychoanalysis and would mean abandoning the understanding which psychoanalysis has given us of the relations between health, perversion and neurosis. Psychoanalysis stands or falls with the recognition of the sexual component instincts, of the erotogenic zones and of the extension thus made possible of the concept of a 'sexual function' in contrast to the narrower 'genital function'. Moreover the observation of the normal development of children is in itself enough to make us reject any such temptation.

(c) In the field of the development of *character* we are bound to meet with the same instinctual forces which we have found at work in the neuroses. But a sharp theoretical distinction between the two is necessitated by the single fact that the failure of repression and the return of the repressed – which are peculiar to the mechanism of neurosis – are absent in the formation of character. In the latter, repression either does not come into action or smoothly achieves its aim of replacing the repressed by reaction-formations and sublimations. Hence the processes of the formation of character are more obscure and less accessible to analysis than neurotic ones.[1]

But it is precisely in the field of character-development that

1. [Freud gave few accounts of the nature of 'character' and its formation. A list of the most important will be found in the Editor's introductory note to the earlier paper on the subject, 'Character and Anal Erotism' (1908b), P.F.L., 7, 207–8.]

we come across a good analogy with the case we have been describing – a confirmation, that is, of the occurrence of the pregenital sadistic anal-erotic sexual organization. It is a well-known fact, and one that has given much ground for complaint, that after women have lost their genital function their character often undergoes a peculiar alteration. They become quarrelsome, vexatious and overbearing, petty and stingy; that is to say, they exhibit typically sadistic and anal-erotic traits which they did not possess earlier, during their period of womanliness. Writers of comedy and satirists have in all ages directed their invectives against the 'old dragon' into which the charming girl, the loving wife and the tender mother have been transformed. We can see that this alteration of character corresponds to a regression of sexual life to the pregenital sadistic and anal-erotic stage, in which we have discovered the disposition to obsessional neurosis. It seems, then, to be not only the precursor of the genital phase but often enough its successor as well, its termination after the genitals have fulfilled their function.

A comparison between such a change of character and obsessional neurosis is very impressive. In both cases the work of regression is apparent. But whereas in the former we find complete regression following repression (or suppression) that has occured smoothly, in the neurosis there are conflict, an effort to prevent regression from occurring, reaction-formations against it and symptom-formations produced by compromises between the two opposing sides, and a splitting of the psychical activities into some that are admissible to consciousness and others that are unconscious.

(*d*) Our hypothesis of a pregenital sexual organization is incomplete in two respects. In the first place, it takes no account of the behaviour of other component instincts, in regard to which there is plenty that would repay examination and discussion, and it is content with stressing the striking primacy of sadism and anal erotism.[1] In particular we often gain an impression that the instinct for knowledge can actually take the place of sadism in the mechanism of obsessional neurosis. Indeed it is at bottom a sublimated off-shoot of the instinct of mastery exalted into something intellectual, and its repudiation in the form of doubt plays a large part in the picture of obsessional neurosis.[2]

The second gap in our hypothesis is far more important. As we know, the developmental disposition to a neurosis is only complete if the phase of the development of the ego at which fixation occurs is taken into account as well as that of the libido. But our hypothesis has only related to the latter, and therefore does not include all the knowledge that we should demand. The stages of development of the ego-instincts are at present very little known to us; I know of only one attempt – the highly promising one made by Ferenczi (1913) – to approach these questions. I cannot tell if it may seem too rash if, on the basis of such indications as we possess, I suggest the possibility that a chronological outstripping of libidinal development by ego development should be included in the disposition to obsessional neurosis. A precocity of this kind would necessitate the choice of an object under the influence of the ego-instincts, at a time at which the sexual instincts had not yet assumed their final shape, and a fixation at the stage of the pregenital sexual organization would thus be left. If we consider that obsessional neurotics have to develop a super-morality in order to protect their object-love from the hostility lurking behind it, we shall be inclined to regard some degree of this precocity of ego development as typical of human nature and to derive the capacity for the origin of morality from the fact that in the order of development hate is the precursor of love. This is perhaps the meaning

1. [The existence of an earlier pregenital organization, characterized by the primacy of the oral zone, was not pointed out by Freud until some years later. See Editor's Note, p. 133 above.]

2. [See the 'Rat Man' case history (1909d), P.F.L., 9, 120–23.]

of an assertion by Stekel (1911, 536), which at the time I found incomprehensible, to the effect that hate and not love is the primary emotional relation between men.[1]

(e) It follows from what has been said that there remains for hysteria an intimate relation to the final phase of libidinal development, which is characterized by the primacy of the genitals and the introduction of the reproductive function. In hysterical neurosis this acquisition is subjected to repression, which does not involve regression to the pregenital stage. The gap in determining the disposition owing to our ignorance of ego development is even more obvious here than with obsessional neurosis.

On the other hand, it is not hard to show that another regression to an earlier level occurs in hysteria too. The sexuality of female children, is, as we know, dominated and directed by a masculine organ (the clitoris) and often behaves like the sexuality of boys. This masculine sexuality has to be got rid of by a last wave of development at puberty, and the vagina, an organ derived from the cloaca, has to be raised into the dominant erotogenic zone. Now, it is very common in hysterical neurosis for this repressed masculine sexuality to be reactivated and then for the defensive struggle on the part of the ego-syntonic instincts to be directed against it. But it seems to me too early to enter here into a discussion of the problems of the disposition to hysteria.

1. [This was elaborated by Freud at the end of his metapsychological paper on 'Instincts and their Vicissitudes' (1915c).]

A CASE OF PARANOIA RUNNING
COUNTER TO THE
PSYCHOANALYTIC THEORY
OF THE DISEASE
(1915)

EDITOR'S NOTE

MITTEILUNG EINES DER PSYCHOANALYTISCHEN THEORIE WIDERSPRECHENDEN FALLES VON PARANOIA

(A) GERMAN EDITIONS:

1915   *Int. Z. ärztl. Psychoanal.,* **3** (6), 321–9.
1924   *Gesammelte Schriften,* **5,** 288–300.
1946   *Gesammelte Werke,* **10,** 234–46.

(B) ENGLISH TRANSLATIONS:

'A Case of Paranoia Running Counter to the Psycho-Analytical Theory of the Disease'

1924   *Collected Papers,* **2,** 150–61. (Tr. E. Glover.)
1957   *Standard Edition,* **14,** 261–72 (Based on the version published in 1924, with a slightly modified title.)

The present edition is a corrected reprint of the Standard Edition version with one or two editorial modifications.

The case history presented in this paper serves as a confirmation of the view put forward by Freud in his Schreber analysis (1911c) that there is a close connection between paranoia and homosexuality. It is incidentally an object-lesson to practitioners on the danger of basing a hasty opinion of a case on a superficial knowledge of the facts. The last few pages contain some interesting remarks of a more general kind on the processes at work during a neurotic conflict.

A CASE OF PARANOIA RUNNING COUNTER TO THE PSYCHOANALYTIC THEORY OF THE DISEASE

SOME years ago a well-known lawyer consulted me about a case which had raised some doubts in his mind. A young woman had asked him to protect her from the molestations of a man who had drawn her into a love-affair. She declared that this man had abused her confidence by getting unseen witnesses to photograph them while they were making love, and that by exhibiting these pictures it was now in his power to bring disgrace on her and force her to resign the post she occupied. Her legal adviser was experienced enough to recognize the pathological stamp of this accusation; he remarked, however, that, as what appears to be incredible often actually happens, he would appreciate the opinion of a psychiatrist in the matter. He promised to call on me again, accompanied by the plaintiff.

(Before I continue the account, I must confess that I have altered the *milieu* of the case in order to preserve the incognito of the people concerned, but that I have altered nothing else. I consider it a wrong practice, however excellent the motive may be, to alter any detail in the presentation of a case. One can never tell what aspect of a case may be picked out by a reader of independent judgement, and one runs the risk of leading him astray.)[1]

Shortly afterwards I met the patient in person. She was thirty

1. [Cf. a footnote to the same effect added in 1924 at the end of Freud's case history of 'Katharina' in Breuer and Freud, *Studies on Hysteria* (1895), *P.F.L.*, **3**, 201 *n.* 2, and some remarks in the Introduction to the 'Rat Man' case history (1909*d*), *P.F.L.*, **9**, 36–7.]

years old, a most attractive and handsome girl, who looked much younger than her age and was of a distinctly feminine type. She obviously resented the interference of a doctor and took no trouble to hide her distrust. It was clear that only the influence of her legal adviser, who was present, induced her to tell me the story which follows and which set me a problem that will be mentioned later. Neither in her manner nor by any kind of expression of emotion did she betray the slightest shame or shyness, such as one would have expected her to feel in the presence of a stranger. She was completely under the spell of the apprehension brought on by her experience.

For many years she had been on the staff of a big business concern, in which she held a responsible post. Her work had given her satisfaction and had been appreciated by her superiors. She had never sought any love-affairs with men, but had lived quietly with her old mother, of whom she was the sole support. She had no brothers or sisters; her father had died many years before. Recently an employee in her office, a highly cultivated and attractive man, had paid her attentions and she in turn had been drawn towards him. For external reasons, marriage was out of the question, but the man would not hear of giving up their relationship on that account. He had pleaded that it was senseless to sacrifice to social convention all that they both longed for and had an indisputable right to enjoy, something that could enrich their life as nothing else could. As he had promised not to expose her to any risk, she had at last consented to visit him in his bachelor rooms in the daytime. There they kissed and embraced as they lay side by side, and he began to admire the charms which were now partly revealed. In the midst of this idyllic scene she was suddenly frightened by a noise, a kind of knock or click. It came from the direction of the writing-desk, which was standing across the window; the space between desk and window was partly taken up by a heavy curtain. She had at once asked her friend what this noise meant, and was told, so she said, that it probably came from the small clock on the writing-desk. I shall venture, however, to make a comment presently on this part of her narrative.

As she was leaving the house she had met two men on the staircase, who whispered something to each other when they saw her. One of the strangers was carrying something which was wrapped up and looked like a small box. She was much exercised over this meeting, and on her way home she had already put together the following notions: the box might easily have been a camera, and the man a photographer who had been hidden behind the curtain while she was in the room; the click had been the noise of the shutter; the photograph had been taken as soon as he saw her in a particularly compromising position which he wished to record. From that moment nothing could abate her suspicion of her lover. She pursued him with reproaches and pestered him for explanations and re-assurances, not only when they met but also by letter. But it was in vain that he tried to convince her that his feelings were sincere and that her suspicions were entirely without foundation. At last she called on the lawyer, told him of her experience and handed over the letters which the suspect had written to her about the incident. Later I had an opportunity of seeing some of these letters. They made a very favourable impression on me, and consisted mainly in expression of regret that such a beautiful and tender relationship should have been destroyed by this 'unfortunate morbid idea'.

I need hardly justify my agreement with this judgement. But the case had a special interest for me other than a merely diagnostic one. The view had already been put forward in psychoanalytic literature that patients suffering from paranoia are struggling against an intensification of their homosexual trends – a fact pointing back to a narcissistic object-choice. And a further interpretation had been made: that the persecutor is at bottom someone whom the patient loves or has loved in the past.[1] A synthesis of the two propositions would lead us to the

1. [See Part III of Freud's Schreber analysis (1911c), *P.F.L.*, **9**, 196 ff.]

necessary conclusion that the persecutor must be of the same sex as the person persecuted. We did not maintain, it is true, as universally and without exception valid the thesis that paranoia is determined by homosexuality; but this was only because our observations were not sufficiently numerous; the thesis was one of those which in view of certain considerations become important only when universal application can be claimed for them. In psychiatric literature there is certainly no lack of cases in which the patient imagines himself persecuted by a person of the opposite sex. It is one thing, however, to read of such cases, and quite a different thing to come into personal contact with one of them. My own observations and analyses and those of my friends had so far confirmed the relation between paranoia and homosexuality without any difficulty. But the present case emphatically contradicted it. The girl seemed to be defending herself against love for a man by directly transforming the lover into a persecutor: there was no sign of the influence of a woman, no trace of a struggle against a homosexual attachment.

In these circumstances the simplest thing would have been to abandon the theory that the delusion of persecution invariably depends on homosexuality, and at the same time to abandon everything that followed from that theory. Either the theory must be given up or else, in view of this departure from our expectations, we must side with the lawyer and assume that this was no paranoic combination but an actual experience which had been correctly interpreted. But I saw another way out, by which a final verdict could for the moment be postponed. I recollected how often wrong views have been taken about people who are ill psychically, simply because the physician has not studied them thoroughly enough and has thus not learnt enough about them. I therefore said that I could not form an immediate opinion, and asked the patient to call on me a second time, when she could relate her story again at greater length and add any subsidiary details that might have been omitted. Thanks to the lawyer's influence I secured this promise from the reluctant patient; and he helped me in another way by saying that at our second meeting his presence would be unnecessary.

The story told me by the patient on this second occasion did not conflict with the previous one, but the additional details she supplied resolved all doubts and difficulties. To begin with, she had visited the young man in his rooms not once but twice. It was on the second occasion that she had been disturbed by the suspicious noise: in her original story she had suppressed, or omitted to mention, the first visit because it had no longer seemed of importance to her. Nothing noteworthy had happened during this first visit, but something did happen on the day after it. Her department in the business was under the direction of an elderly lady whom she described as follows: 'She has white hair like my mother.' This elderly superior had a great liking for her and treated her with affection, though sometimes she teased her; the girl regarded herself as her particular favourite. On the day after her first visit to the young man's rooms he appeared in the office to discuss some business matter with this elderly lady. While they were talking in low voices the patient suddenly felt convinced that he was telling her about their adventure of the previous day – indeed, that the two of them had for some time been having a love-affair, which she had hitherto overlooked. The white-haired motherly old lady now knew everything, and her speech and conduct in the course of the day confirmed the patient's suspicion. At the first opportunity she took her lover to task about his betrayal. He naturally protested vigorously against what he called a senseless accusation. For the time being, in fact, he succeeded in freeing her from her delusion, and she regained enough confidence to repeat her visit to his rooms a short time – I believe it was a few weeks – afterwards. The rest we know already from her first narrative.

In the first place, this new information removes any doubts as to the pathological nature of her suspicion. It is easy to see that the white-haired elderly superior was a substitute for her mother, that in spite of his youth her lover had been put in the place of her father, and that it was the strength of her mother-complex which had driven the patient to suspect a love-relationship between these ill-matched partners, however unlikely such a relation might be. Moreover, this disposes of the apparent contradiction to the expectation, based on psychoanalytic theory, that the development of a delusion of persecution will turn out to be determined by an over-powerful homosexual attachment. The *original* persecutor – the agency whose influence the patient wishes to escape – is here again not a man but a woman. The superior knew about the girl's love affairs, disapproved of them, and showed her disapproval by mysterious hints. The patient's attachment to her own sex opposed her attempts to adopt a person of the other sex as a love-object. Her love for her mother had become the spokesman of all those tendencies which, playing the part of a 'conscience', seek to arrest a girl's first step along the new road to normal sexual satisfaction – in many respects a dangerous one; and indeed it succeeded in disturbing her relation with men.

When a mother hinders or arrests a daughter's sexual activity, she is fulfilling a normal function whose lines are laid down by events in childhood, which has powerful, unconscious motives, and has received the sanction of society. It is the daughter's business to emancipate herself from this influence and to decide for herself on broad and rational grounds what her share of enjoyment or denial of sexual pleasure shall be. If in the attempt to emancipate herself she falls a victim to a neurosis it implies the presence of a mother-complex which is as a rule over-powerful, and is certainly unmastered. The conflict between this complex and the new direction taken by the libido is dealt with in the form of one neurosis or another, according to the subject's disposition. The manifestation of the neurotic reaction will always be determined, however, not by her present-day relation to her actual mother but by her infantile relations to her earliest image of her mother.

We know that our patient had been fatherless for many years, we may also assume that she would not have kept away from men up to the age of thirty if she had not been supported by a powerful emotional attachment to her mother. This support became a heavy yoke when her libido began to turn to a man in response to his insistent wooing. She tried to free herself, to throw off her homosexual attachment; and her disposition, which need not be discussed here, enabled this to occur in the form of a paranoic delusion. The mother thus became the hostile and malevolent watcher and persecutor. As such she could have been overcome, had it not been that the mother-complex retained power enough to carry out its purpose of keeping the patient at a distance from men. Thus, at the end of the first phase of the conflict the patient had become estranged from her mother without having definitely gone over to the man. Indeed, both of them were plotting against her. Then the man's vigorous efforts succeeded in drawing her decisively to him. She conquered her mother's opposition in her mind and was willing to grant her lover a second meeting. In the later developments the mother did not reappear, but we may safely insist that in this [first] phase the lover had not become the persecutor directly but *via* the mother and in virtue of his relationship to the mother, who had played the leading part in the first delusion.

One would think that the resistance was now definitely overcome, that the girl who until now had been bound to her mother had succeeded in coming to love a man. But after the second visit a new delusion appeared, which, by making ingenious use of some accidental circumstances, destroyed this love and thus successfully carried through the purpose of the mother-complex. It still seems strange that a woman should protect herself against loving a man by means of a paranoic delusion; but before examining this state of things more closely, let us glance at the accidental circumstances that formed the basis of this second delusion, the one aimed exclusively against the man.

Lying partly undressed on the sofa beside her lover, she heard a noise like a click or beat. She did not know its cause, but she arrived at an interpretation of it after meeting two men on the staircase, one of whom was carrying something that looked like a covered box. She became convinced that someone acting on instructions from her lover had watched and photographed her during their intimate *tête-a-tête*. I do not for a moment imagine, of course, that if the unlucky noise had not occurred the delusion would not have been formed; on the contrary, something inevitable is to be seen behind this accidental circumstance, something which was bound to assert itself compulsively in the patient, just as when she supposed that there was a *liaison* between her lover and the elderly superior, her mother-substitute. Among the store of unconscious phantasies of all neurotics, and probably of all human beings, there is one which is seldom absent and which can be disclosed by analysis: this is the phantasy of watching sexual intercourse between the parents. I call such phantasies – of the observation of sexual intercourse between the parents, of seduction, of castration, and others – 'primal phantasies'; and I shall discuss in detail elsewhere their origin and their relation to individual experience.[1] The accidental noise was thus merely playing the part of a provoking factor which activated the typical phantasy of overhearing which is a component of the parental complex. Indeed, it is doubtful whether we can rightly call the noise 'accidental'. As Otto Rank has remarked to me, such noises are on the contrary an indispensible part of the phantasy of listening, and they reproduce either the sounds which betray parental intercourse or those by which the listening child fears to betray itself. But now we know at once where we stand. The patient's lover was still her father, but she herself had taken her mother's place. The part of the listener had then to be allotted to a third person.

1. [The subject of 'primal phantasies' is discussed at length in Lecture 23 of Freud's *Introductory Lectures* (1916–17), P.F.L., 1, 416–18, and in his case history of the 'Wolf Man' (1918b), P.F.L., 9, 294–5 and 337–8.]

We can see by what means the girl had freed herself from her homosexual dependence on her mother. It was by means of a small piece of regression: instead of choosing her mother as a love-object, she identified herself with her – she herself *became* her mother. The possibility of this regression points to the narcissistic origin of her homosexual object-choice and thus to the paranoic disposition in her. One might sketch a train of thought which would bring about the same result as this identification: 'If my mother does it, I may do it too; I've just as good a right as she has.'

One can go a step further in disproving the accidental nature of the noise. We do not, however, ask our readers to follow us, since the absence of any deeper analytic investigation makes it impossible in this case to go beyond a certain degree of probability. The patient mentioned in her first interview with me that she had immediately demanded an explanation of the noise, and had been told that it was probably the ticking of the small clock on the writing-desk. I venture, however, to explain what she told me as a mistaken memory. It seems to me much more likely that at first she did not react to the noise at all, and that it became significant only after she met the two men on the staircase. Her lover, who had probably not even heard the noise, may have tried, perhaps on some later occasion when she assailed him with her suspicions, to account for it in this way: 'I don't know what noise you can have heard. Perhaps it was the small clock; it sometimes ticks like that.' This deferred use of impressions and this displacement of recollections often occur precisely in paranoia and are characteristic of it. But as I never met the man and could not continue the analysis of the woman, my hypothesis cannot be proved.

I might go still further in the analysis of this ostensibly real 'accident'. I do not believe that the clock ever ticked or that there was any noise to be heard at all. The woman's situation justified a sensation of a knock or beat in her clitoris. And it was this that she subsequently projected as a perception of an external object. Just the same sort of thing can occur in dreams. A hysterical woman patient of mine once related to me a short arousal dream to which she could bring no spontaneous associations. She dreamt simply that someone knocked and then she awoke. Nobody had knocked at the door, but during the previous nights she had been awakened by distressing sensations of pollutions: she thus had a motive for awakening as soon as she felt the first sign of genital excitation. There had been a 'knock' in her clitoris.[1] In the case of our paranoic patient, I should substitute for the accidental noise a similar process of projection. I certainly cannot guarantee that in the course of our short acquaintance the patient, who was reluctantly yielding to compulsion, gave me a truthful account of all that had taken place during the two meetings of the lovers. But an isolated contraction of the clitoris would be in keeping with her statement that no contact of the genitals had taken place. In her subsequent rejection of the man, lack of satisfaction undoubtedly played a part as well as 'conscience'.

Let us consider again the outstanding fact that the patient protected herself against her love for a man by means of a paranoic delusion. The key to the understanding of this is to be found in the history of the development of the delusion. As we might have expected, the latter was at first aimed against the woman. But now, *on this paranoic basis, the advance from a female to a male object was accomplished*. Such an advance is unusual in paranoia; as a rule we find that the victim of persecution remains fixated to the same persons, and therefore to the same sex to which his love-objects belonged before the paranoic transformation took place. But neurotic disorder does not preclude an advance of this kind, and our observation may be typical of many others. There are many similar processes occurring outside paranoia which have not yet been looked at

1. [Cf. a similar instance in the case of an agoraphobic and obsessional girl, described by Freud in Lecture 17 of his *Introductory Lectures* (1916–17), *P.F.L.*, 1, 303 ff.]

from this point of view, amongst them some which are very familiar. For instance, the so-called neurasthenic's unconscious attachment to incestuous love-objects prevents him from choosing a strange woman as his object and restricts his sexual activity to phantasy. But within the limits of phantasy he achieves the progress which is denied him, and he succeeds in replacing mother and sister by extraneous objects. Since the veto of the censorship does not come into action with these objects, he can become conscious in his phantasies of his choice of these substitute-figures.

These then are phenomena of an attempted advance from the new ground which has as a rule been regressively acquired; and we may set alongside them the efforts made in some neuroses to regain a position of the libido which was once held and subsequently lost. Indeed we can hardly draw any conceptual distinction between these two classes of phenomena. We are too apt to think that the conflict underlying a neurosis is brought to an end when the symptom has been formed. In reality the struggle can go on in many ways after this. Fresh instinctual components arise on both sides, and these prolong it. The symptom itself becomes an object of this struggle; certain trends anxious to preserve it conflict with others which strive to remove it and to re-establish the *status quo ante*. Methods are often sought of rendering the symptom nugatory by trying to regain along other lines of approach what has been lost and is now withheld by the symptom. These facts throw much light on a statement made by C. G. Jung to the effect that a peculiar 'psychical inertia', which opposes change and progress, is the fundamental precondition of neurosis. This inertia is indeed most peculiar; it is not a general one, but is highly specialized; it is not even all-powerful within its own field, but fights against tendencies towards progress and recovery which remain active even after the formation of neurotic symptoms. If we search for the starting-point of this special inertia, we discover that it is the manifestation of very early linkages –

linkages which it is hard to resolve – between instincts and impressions and the objects involved in those impressions. These linkages have the effect of bringing the development of the instincts concerned to a standstill. Or in other words, this specialized 'psychical inertia' is only a different term, though hardly a better one, for what in psychoanalysis we are accustomed to call a 'fixation'.[1]

1. [This tendency to fixation, or, as he called it elsewhere, 'adhesiveness of the libido', had been alluded to by Freud in the first edition of his *Three Essays* (1905*d*), *P.F.L.*, **7**, 167–8. It was further discussed by him towards the end of his case history of the 'Wolf Man' (1918*b*), *P.F.L.*, **9**, 358–9, and in Lectures 22 and 28 of his *Introductory Lectures* (1916–17), *P.F.L.*, **1**, 392–3 and 508, both of which works were more or less contemporary with the present paper. The special case of 'inertia of the libido' is referred to at the beginning of Chapter V of *Civilization and its Discontents* (1930*a*). A last allusion to 'psychical inertia' occurs near the end of Chapter VI of his posthumously published *Outline of Psycho-Analysis* (1940*a* [1938]).]

'A CHILD IS BEING BEATEN'

(A CONTRIBUTION TO THE STUDY OF THE ORIGIN OF SEXUAL PERVERSIONS)
(1919)

EDITOR'S NOTE

'EIN KIND WIRD GESCHLAGEN'
BEITRAG ZUR KENNTNIS DER ENTSTEHUNG
SEXUELLER PERVERSIONEN

(A) GERMAN EDITIONS:

1919   *Int. Z. ärztl. Psychoanal.*, **5** (3), 151–72.
1922   *S.K.S.N.*, **5**, 195–228.
1924   *Gesammelte Schriften*, **5**, 344–75.
1947   *Gesammelte Werke*, **12**, 197–226.

(B) ENGLISH TRANSLATIONS:

'"A Child is being Beaten"
A Contribution to the Study of the Origin of Sexual Perversions'

1920   *Int. J. Psycho-Analysis*, **1**, 371–95. (Tr. A. and J. Strachey).
1924   *Collected Papers*, **2**, 172–201. (Same translators.)
1955   *Standard Edition*, **17**, 175–204. (A corrected version of the one published in 1924.)

The present edition is a corrected reprint of the *Standard Edition* version, with some editorial changes.

In a letter to Ferenczi of January 24, 1919, Freud announced that he was writing a paper on masochism. The paper was finished and given its present title by the middle of March, 1919, and it was published in the summer of the same year.

The greater part of the paper consists of a very detailed

clinical enquiry into a particular kind of perversion. Freud's findings throw special light on the problem of masochism; and, as the sub-title implies, the paper was also designed to extend our knowledge of the perversions in general. From this point of view, it may be regarded as a supplement to the first of Freud's *Three Essays on the Theory of Sexuality* (1905*d*).

In addition to this, however, the paper includes a discussion, to which Freud attached considerable importance, of the motives which cause repression to be put into operation, with special reference to two theories on the subject, proposed respectively by Fliess and Adler (cf. pp. 188–93). The *mechanism* of repression is exhaustively discussed in two of Freud's meta-psychological papers – in 'Repression' (1915*d*) and in Section IV of 'The Unconscious' (1915*e*); but the question of the *motives* leading to repression, though it is touched upon in the last section of the analysis of the 'Wolf Man' (1918*b*), *P.F.L.*, **9**, 352–3, is nowhere examined more fully than in the present paper. The problem was, of course, one which had interested and also puzzled Freud from very early days, and there are many references to it in the Fliess correspondence (1950*a*). At the very end of his life Freud returned to it once more, in the last section of his 'Analysis Terminable and Interminable' (1937*c*), where he discussed the theories of Fliess and Adler once again.

'A CHILD IS BEING BEATEN'

A CONTRIBUTION TO THE STUDY OF
THE ORIGIN OF SEXUAL PERVERSIONS

I

IT is surprising how often people who seek analytic treatment for hysteria or an obsessional neurosis confess to having indulged in the phantasy: 'A child is being beaten.' Very probably there are still more frequent instances of it among the far greater number of people who have not been obliged to come to analysis by manifest illness.

The phantasy has feelings of pleasure attached to it, and on their account the patient has reproduced it on innumerable occasions in the past or may even still be doing so. At the climax of the imaginary situation there is almost invariably a masturbatory satisfaction – carried out, that is to say, on the genitals. At first this takes place voluntarily, but later on it does so in spite of the patient's efforts, and with the characteristics of an obsession.

It is only with hesitation that this phantasy is confessed to. Its first appearance is recollected with uncertainty. The analytic treatment of the topic is met by unmistakable resistance. Shame and a sense of guilt are perhaps more strongly excited in this connection than when similar accounts are given of memories of the beginning of sexual life.

Eventually it becomes possible to establish that the first phantasies of the kind were entertained very early in life: certainly before school age, and not later than in the fifth or sixth year. When the child was at school and saw other children being beaten by the teacher, then, if the phantasies had become dormant, this experience called them up again, or, if they were still present, it reinforced them and noticeably modified their content. From that time forward it was 'an indefinite number' of children that were being beaten. The influence of the school was so clear that the patients concerned were at first tempted to trace back their beating-phantasies exclusively to these impressions of school life, which dated from later than their sixth year. But it was never possible for them to maintain that position; the phantasies had already been in existence before.

Though in the higher forms at school the children were no longer beaten, the influence of such occasions was replaced and more than replaced by the effects of reading, of which the importance was soon to be felt. In my patients' *milieu* it was almost always the same books whose contents gave a new stimulus to the beating-phantasies: those accessible to young people, such as what was known as the '*Bibliothèque rose*',[1] *Uncle Tom's Cabin*,[2] etc. The child began to compete with these works of fiction by producing his own phantasies and by constructing a wealth of situations and institutions, in which children were beaten, or were punished and disciplined in some other way, because of their naughtiness and bad behaviour.

This phantasy – 'a child is being beaten' – was invariably cathected with a high degree of pleasure and had its issue in an act of pleasurable auto-erotic satisfaction. It might therefore be expected that the sight of another child being beaten at school would also be a source of similar enjoyment. But as a matter of fact this was never so. The experience of real scenes of beating at school produced in the child who witnessed them a peculiarly excited feeling which was probably of a mixed character and in which repugnance had a large share. In a few cases the real experience of the scenes of beating was felt to be intolerable.

1. [A well-known series of books by Mme de Ségur (1799–1874), of which *Les Malheurs de Sophie* was perhaps the most popular.]

2. [The novel (published in 1852) on Negro slavery in America by Harriet Beecher Stowe (1811–96).]

Moreover, it was always a condition of the more sophisticated phantasies of later years that the punishment should do the children no serious injury.

The question was bound to arise of what relation there might be between the importance of the beating-phantasies and the part that real corporal punishment might have played in the child's bringing up at home. It was impossible, on account of the one-sidedness of the material, to confirm the first suspicion that the relation was an inverse one. The individuals from whom the data for these analyses were derived were very seldom beaten in their childhood, or were at all events not brought up by the help of the rod. Naturally, however, each of these children was bound to have become aware at one time or another of the superior physical strength of its parents or educators; the fact that in every nursery the children themselves at times come to blows requires no special emphasis.

As regards the early and simple phantasies which could not be obviously traced to the influence of school impressions or of scenes taken from books, further information would have been welcome. Who was the child that was being beaten? The one who was himself producing the phantasy or another? Was it always the same child or as often as not a different one? Who was it that was beating the child? A grown-up person? And if so, who? Or did the child imagine that he himself was beating another one? Nothing could be ascertained that threw any light upon all these questions – only the hesitant reply: 'I know nothing more about it: a child is being beaten.'

Enquiries as to the sex of the child that was being beaten met with more success, but none the less brought no enlightenment. Sometimes the answer was: 'Always boys', or 'Only girls'; more often it was: 'I don't know', or 'It doesn't matter which'. But the point to which the questions were directed, the discovery of some constant relation between the sex of the child producing the phantasy and that of the child that was being beaten, was never established. Now and again another characteristic detail of the content of the phantasy came to light: 'A small child is being beaten on its naked bottom.'

In these circumstances it was impossible at first even to decide whether the pleasure attaching to the beating-phantasy was to be described as sadistic or masochistic.

II

A phantasy of this kind, arising, perhaps from accidental causes, in early childhood and retained for the purpose of auto-erotic satisfaction, can, in the light of our present knowledge, only be regarded as a primary trait of perversion. One of the components of the sexual function has, it seems, developed in advance of the rest, has made itself prematurely independent, has undergone fixation and in consequence been withdrawn from the later processes of development, and has in this way given evidence of a peculiar and abnormal constitution in the individual. We know that an infantile perversion of this sort need not persist for a whole lifetime; later on it can be subjected to repression, be replaced by a reaction-formation, or be transformed by sublimation. (It is possible that sublimation arises out of some special process[1] which would be held back by repression.) But if these processes do not take place, then the perversion persists to maturity; and whenever we find a sexual aberration in adults – perversion, fetishism, inversion – we are justified in expecting that anamnestic investigation will reveal an event such as I have suggested, leading to a fixation in childhood. Indeed, long before the days of psychoanalysis, observers like Binet were able to trace the strange sexual aberrations of maturity back to similar impressions and to precisely the same period of childhood, namely, the fifth or sixth year.[2] But at this

1. [This may be related to the theory of sublimation touched upon in Chapter III of *The Ego and the Id* (1923*b*).]

2. [This observation of Binet's (1888) was mentioned by Freud in his *Three Essays* (1905*d*) and commented upon in a footnote added to that work in 1920 (*P.F.L.*, **7**, 67).]

point the enquiry was confronted with the limitations of our knowledge; for the impressions that brought about the fixation were without any traumatic force. They were for the most part commonplace and unexciting to other people. It was impossible to say why the sexual impulse had undergone fixation particularly upon them. It was possible, however, to look for their significance in the fact that they offered an occasion for fixation (even though it was an accidental one) to precisely that component which was prematurely developed and ready to press forward. We had in any case to be prepared to come to a provisional end somewhere or other in tracing back the train of causal connection; and the congenital constitution seemed exactly to correspond with what was required for a stopping-place of that kind.

If the sexual component which has broken loose prematurely is the sadistic one, then we may expect, on the basis of knowledge derived from other sources, that its subsequent repression will result in a disposition to an obsessional neurosis.[1] This expectation cannot be said to be contradicted by the results of enquiry. The present short paper is based on the exhaustive study of six cases (four female and two male). Of these, two were cases of obsessional neurosis; one extremely severe and incapacitating, the other of moderate severity and quite well accessible to influence. There was also a third case which at all events exhibited clearly marked individual traits of obsessional neurosis. The fourth case, it must be admitted, was one of straightforward hysteria, with pains and inhibitions; and the fifth patient, who had come to be analysed merely on account of indecisiveness in life, would not have been classified at all by coarse clinical diagnosis, or would have been dismissed as 'psychasthenic'.[2] There is no need for feeling disappointed over these statistics. In the first place, we know that not every disposition is necessarily developed into a disorder; in the

---

1. [See the paper on this subject (1913i), p. 134 ff. above.]
2. [Nothing is said here of the sixth case.]

second place, we ought to be content to explain the facts before us, and ought as a rule to avoid the additional task of making clear why something has *not* taken place.

The present state of our knowledge would allow us to make our way so far and no further towards the comprehension of beating-phantasies. In the mind of the analytic physician, it is true, there remains an uneasy suspicion that this is not a final solution of the problem. He is obliged to admit to himself that to a great extent these phantasies subsist apart from the rest of the content of a neurosis, and find no proper place in its structure. But impressions of this kind, as I know from my own experience, are only too willingly put on one side.

III

Strictly considered – and why should this question not be considered with all possible strictness? – analytic work deserves to be recognized as genuine psychoanalysis only when it has succeeded in removing the amnesia which conceals from the adult his knowledge of his childhood from its beginning (that is, from about the second to the fifth year). This cannot be said among analysts too emphatically or repeated too often. The motives for disregarding this reminder are, indeed, intelligible. It would be desirable to obtain practical results in a shorter period and with less trouble. But at the present time theoretical knowledge is still far more important to all of us than therapeutic success, and anyone who neglects childhood analysis is bound to fall into the most disastrous errors. The emphasis which is laid here upon the importance of the earliest experiences does not imply any underestimation of the influence of later ones. But the later impressions of life speak loudly enough through the mouth of the patient, while it is the physician who has to raise his voice on behalf of the claims of childhood.

It is in the years of childhood between the ages of two and four or five that the congenital libidinal factors are first awakened by actual experiences and become attached to certain complexes. The beating-phantasies which are now under discussion show themselves only towards the end of this period or after its termination. So it may quite well be that they have an earlier history, that they go through a process of development, that they represent an end-product and not an initial manifestation.

This suspicion is confirmed by analysis. A systematic application of it shows that beating-phantasies have a historical development which is by no means simple, and in the course of which they are changed in most respects more than once – as regards their relation to the author of the phantasy, and as regards their object, their content and their significance.

In order to make it easier to follow these transformations in beating-phantasies I shall now venture to confine my descriptions to the female cases, which, since they are four as against two, in any case constitute the greater part of my material. Moreover, beating-phantasies in men are connected with another subject, which I shall leave on one side in this paper.[1] In my description I shall be careful to avoid being more schematic than is inevitable for the presentation of an average case. If then on further observation a greater complexity of circumstances should come to light, I shall nevertheless be sure of having before us a typical occurrence, and one, moreover, that is not of an uncommon kind.

The first phase of beating-phantasies among girls, then, must belong to a very early period of childhood. Some features remain curiously indefinite, as though they were a matter of indifference. The scanty information given by the patients in their first statement, 'a child is being beaten', seems to be justified in respect to this phase. But another of their features can be established with certainty, and to the same effect in every case.

1. [Freud does in fact discuss beating-phantasies in men below (pp. 175 f. and 183 ff.). Their specifically feminine basis is what he probably has in mind in speaking of 'another subject'.]

The child being beaten is never the one producing the phantasy, but is invariably another child, most often a brother or a sister if there is any. Since this other child may be a boy or a girl, there is no constant relation between the sex of the child producing the phantasy and that of the child being beaten. The phantasy, then, is certainly not masochistic. It would be tempting to call it sadistic, but one cannot neglect the fact that the child producing the phantasy is never doing the beating herself. The actual identity of the person who does the beating remains obscure at first. Only this much can be established: it is not a child but an adult. Later on this indeterminate grown-up person becomes recognizable clearly and unambiguously as the (girl's) *father*.

This first phase of the beating-phantasy is therefore completely represented by the phrase: '*My father is beating the child.*' I am betraying a great deal of what is to be brought forward later when instead of this I say: 'My father is beating the child *whom I hate.*' Moreover, one may hesitate to say whether the characteristics of a 'phantasy' can yet be ascribed to this first step towards the later beating-phantasy. It is perhaps rather a question of recollections of events which have been witnessed, or of desires which have arisen on various occasions. But these doubts are of no importance.

Profound transformations have taken place between this first phase and the next. It is true that the person beating remains the same (that is, the father); but the child who is beaten has been changed into another one and is now invariably the child producing the phantasy. The phantasy is accompanied by a high degree of pleasure, and has now acquired a significant content, with the origin of which we shall be concerned later. Now, therefore, the wording runs: '*I am being beaten by my father.*' It is of an unmistakably masochistic character.

This second phase is the most important and the most momentous of all. But we may say of it in a certain sense that it has never had a real existence. It is never remembered, it has never succeeded in becoming conscious. It is a construction of analysis, but it is no less a necessity on that account.

The third phase once more resembles the first. It has the wording which is familiar to us from the patient's statement. The person beating is never the father, but is either left undetermined just as in the first phase, or turns in a characteristic way into a representative of the father, such as a teacher. The figure of the child who is producing the beating-phantasy no longer itself appears in it. In reply to pressing enquiries the patients only declare: 'I am probably looking on.' Instead of the one child that is being beaten, there are now a number of children present as a rule. Most frequently it is boys who are being beaten (in girls' phantasies), but none of them is personally known to the subject. The situation of being beaten, which was originally simple and monotonous, may go through the most complicated alterations and elaborations; and punishments and humiliations of another kind may be substituted for the beating itself. But the essential characteristic which distinguishes even the simplest phantasies of this phase from those of the first, and which establishes the connection with the intermediate phase, is this: the phantasy now has strong and unambiguous sexual excitement attached to it, and so provides a means for masturbatory satisfaction. But this is precisely what is puzzling. By what path has the phantasy of strange and unknown boys being beaten (a phantasy which has by this time become sadistic) found its way into the permanent possession of the little girl's libidinal trends?

Nor can we conceal from ourselves that the interrelations and sequence of the three phases of the beating-phantasy, as well as all its other peculiarities, have so far remained quite unintelligible.

IV

If the analysis is carried through the early period to which the beating-phantasies are referred and from which they are recollected, it shows us the child involved in the agitations of its parental complex.

The affections of the little girl are fixed on her father, who has probably done all he could to win her love, and in this way has sown the seeds of an attitude of hatred and rivalry towards her mother. This attitude exists side by side with a current of affectionate dependence on her, and as years go on it may be destined to come into consciousness more and more clearly and forcibly, or else to give an impetus to an excessive reaction of devotion to her. But it is not with the girl's relation to her mother that the beating-phantasy is connected. There are other children in the nursery, only a few years older or younger, who are disliked on all sorts of other grounds, but chiefly because the parents' love has to be shared with them, and for this reason they are repelled with all the wild energy characteristic of the emotional life of those years. If the child in question is a younger brother or sister (as in three of my four cases) it is despised as well as hated; yet it attracts to itself the share of affection which the blinded parents are always ready to give the youngest child, and this is a spectacle the sight of which cannot be avoided. One soon learns that being beaten, even if it does not hurt very much, signifies a deprivation of love and a humiliation. And many children who believed themselves securely enthroned in the unshakeable affection of their parents have by a single blow been cast down from all the heavens of their imaginary omnipotence. The idea of the father beating this hateful child is therefore an agreeable one, quite apart from whether he has actually been seen doing so. It means: 'My father does not love this other child, *he loves only me*.'

This then is the content and meaning of the beating-phantasy in its first phase. The phantasy obviously gratifies the child's jealousy and isdependent upon the erotic side of its life, but is also powerfully reinforced by the child's egoistic interests. Doubt remains, therefore, whether the phantasy ought to be described as purely 'sexual', nor can one venture to call it 'sadistic'.

As is well known, all the signs on which we are accustomed to base our distinctions tend to lose their clarity as we come nearer to the source. So perhaps we may say in terms recalling the prophecy made by the Three Witches to Banquo: 'Not clearly sexual, not in itself sadistic, but yet the stuff from which both will later come.'[1] In any case, however, there is no ground for suspecting that in this first phase the phantasy is already at the service of an excitation which involves the genitals and finds its outlet in a masturbatory act.

It is clear that the child's sexual life has reached the stage of genital organization, now that its incestuous love has achieved this premature choice of an object. This can be demonstrated more easily in the case of boys, but is also indisputable in the case of girls. Something like a premonition of what are later to be the final and normal sexual aims governs the child's libidinal trends. We may justly wonder why this should be so, but we may regard it as a proof of the fact that the genitals have already begun playing their part in the process of excitation. With boys the wish to beget a child from their mother is never absent, with girls the wish to have a child by their father is equally constant; and this in spite of their being completely incapable of forming any clear idea of the means for fulfilling these wishes. The child seems to be convinced that the genitals have something to do with the matter, even though in its constant brooding it may look for the essence of the presumed intimacy between its parents in relations of another sort, such as in their sleeping together, micturating in each other's presence, etc.; and material of the latter kind can be more easily apprehended in verbal images than the mystery that is connected with the genitals.

But the time comes when this early blossoming is nipped by

1. ['Lesser than Macbeth, and greater.
Not so happy, yet much happier.
Thou shalt get kings, though thou be none.'
Macbeth, Act I, Scene 3.]

the frost. None of these incestuous loves can avoid the fate of repression. They may succumb to it on the occasion of some discoverable external event which leads to disillusionment – such as unexpected slights, the unwelcome birth of a new brother or sister (which is felt as faithlessness), etc.; or the same thing may happen owing to internal conditions apart from any such events, perhaps simply because their yearning remains unsatisfied too long. It is unquestionably true that such events are not the *effective* causes, but that these love-affairs are bound to come to grief sooner or later, though we cannot say on what particular stumbling block. Most probably they pass away because their time is over, because the children have entered upon a new phase of development in which they are compelled to recapitulate from the history of mankind the repression of an incestuous object-choice, just as at an earlier stage they were obliged to effect an object-choice of that very sort.[1] In the new phase no mental product of the incestuous love-impulses that is present unconsciously is taken over by consciousness; and anything that has already come into consciousness is expelled from it. At the same time as this process of repression takes place, a sense of guilt appears. This is also of unknown origin, but there is no doubt whatever that it is connected with the incestuous wishes, and that it is justified by the persistence of those wishes in the unconscious.[2]

The phantasy of the period of incestuous love had said: 'He (my father) loves only me, and not the other child, for he is beating it.' The sense of guilt can discover no punishment more severe than the reversal of this triumph: 'No, he does not love you, for he is beating you.' In this way the phantasy of the second phase, that of being beaten by her father, is a direct expression of the girl's sense of guilt, to which her love for her father has now succumbed. The phantasy, therefore, has be-

1. Compare the part played by Fate in the myth of Oedipus.
2. [*Footnote added* 1924:] See the continuation of this line of thought in 'The Dissolution of the Oedipus Complex' (1924*d*).

come masochistic. So far as I know, this is always so; a sense of guilt is invariably the factor that transforms sadism into masochism. But this is certainly not the whole content of masochism. The sense of guilt cannot have won the field alone; a share must also fall to the love-impulse. We must remember that we are dealing with children in whom the sadistic component was able for constitutional reasons to develop prematurely and in isolation. We need not abandon this point of view. It is precisely such children who find it particularly easy to hark back to the pregenital, sadistic-anal organization of their sexual life. If the genital organization, when it has scarcely been effected, is met by repression, the result is not only that every psychical representation of the incestuous love becomes unconscious, or remains so, but there is another result as well: a regressive debasement of the genital organization itself to a lower level. 'My father loves me' was meant in a genital sense; owing to the regression it is turned into 'My father is beating me (I am being beaten by my father)'. This being beaten is now a convergence of the sense of guilt and sexual love. *It is not only the punishment for the forbidden genital relation, but also the regressive substitute for that relation,* and from this latter source it derives the libidinal excitation which is from this time forward attached to it, and which finds its outlet in masturbatory acts. Here for the first time we have the essence of masochism.

This second phase – the child's phantasy of being itself beaten by its father – remains unconscious as a rule, probably in consequence of the intensity of the repression. I cannot explain why nevertheless in one of my six cases, that of a male, it was consciously remembered. This man, now grown up, had preserved the fact clearly in his memory that he used to employ the idea of being beaten by his mother for the purpose of masturbation, though to be sure he soon substituted for his own mother the mothers of his school-fellows or other women who in some way resembled her. It must not be forgotten that when a boy's incestuous phantasy is transformed into the corresponding masochistic one, one more reversal has to take place than in the case of a girl, namely the substitution of passivity for activity; and this additional degree of distortion may save the phantasy from having to remain unconscious as a result of repression. In this way the sense of guilt would be satisfied by regression instead of by repression. In the female cases the sense of guilt, in itself perhaps more exacting, could be appeased only by a combination of the two.

In two of my four female cases an elaborate superstructure of day-dreams, which was of great significance for the life of the person concerned, had grown up over the masochistic beating-phantasy. The function of this superstructure was to make possible a feeling of satisfied excitation, even though the masturbatory act was abstained from. In one of these cases the content – being beaten by the father – was allowed to venture again into consciousness, so long as the subject's own ego was made unrecognizable by a thin disguise. The hero of these stories was invariably beaten (or later only punished, humiliated, etc.) by his father.

I repeat, however, that as a rule the phantasy remains unconscious, and can only be reconstructed in the course of the analysis. This fact perhaps vindicates patients who say they remember that with them masturbation made its appearance before the third phase of the beating-phantasy (shortly to be discussed), and that this phase was only a later addition, made perhaps under the impression of scenes at school. Every time I have given credit to these statements I have felt inclined to assume that the masturbation was at first under the dominance of unconscious phantasies and that conscious ones were substituted for them later.

I look upon the beating-phantasy in its familiar third phase, which is its final form, as a substitute of this sort. Here the child who produces the phantasy appears almost as a spectator, while the father persists in the shape of a teacher or some other person in authority. The phantasy, which now resembles that of the first phase, seems to have become sadistic once more. It appears as though in the phrase, 'My father is beating the child, he loves only me', the stress has been shifted back on to the first part after the second part has undergone repression. But only the *form* of this phantasy is sadistic; the satisfaction which is derived from it is masochistic. Its significance lies in the fact that it has taken over the libidinal cathexis of the repressed portion and at the same time the sense of guilt which is attached to the content of that portion. All of the many unspecified children who are being beaten by the teacher are, after all, nothing more than substitutes for the child itself.

We find here for the first time, too, something like a constancy of sex in the persons who play a part in the phantasy. The children who are being beaten are almost invariably boys, in the phantasies of boys just as much as in those of girls. This characteristic is naturally not to be explained by any rivalry between the sexes, as otherwise of course in the phantasies of boys it would be girls who would be being beaten; and it has nothing to do with the sex of the child who was hated in the first phase. But it points to a complication in the case of girls. When they turn away from their incestuous love for their father, with its genital significance, they easily abandon their feminine role. They spur their 'masculinity complex' (Van Ophuijsen [1917]) into activity, and from that time forward only want to be boys. For that reason the whipping-boys who represent them are boys too. In both the cases of day-dreaming – one of which almost rose to the level of a work of art – the heroes were always young men; indeed women used not to come into these creations at all, and only made their first appearance after many years, and then in minor parts.

V

I hope I have brought forward my analytic observations in sufficient detail, and I should only like to add that the six cases

I have mentioned so often do not exhaust my material. Like other analysts, I have at my disposal a far larger number of cases which have been investigated less thoroughly. These observations can be made use of along various lines: for elucidating the genesis of the perversions in general and of masochism in particular, and for estimating the part played by difference of sex in the dynamics of neurosis.

The most obvious result of such a discussion is its application to the origin of the perversions. The view which brought into the foreground in this connection the constitutional reinforcement or premature growth of a single sexual component is not shaken, indeed; but it is seen not to comprise the whole truth. The perversion is no longer an isolated fact in the child's sexual life, but falls into its place among the typical, not to say normal, processes of development which are familiar to us. It is brought into relation with the child's incestuous love-object, with its Oedipus complex. It first comes into prominence in the sphere of this complex, and after the complex has broken down it remains over, often quite by itself, the inheritor of the charge of libido from that complex and weighed down by the sense of guilt that was attached to it. The abnormal sexual constitution, finally, has shown its strength by forcing the Oedipus complex into a particular direction, and by compelling it to leave an unusual residue behind.

A perversion in childhood, as is well known, may become the basis for the construction of a perversion having a similar sense and persisting throughout life, one which consumes the subject's whole sexual life. On the other hand the perversion may be broken off and remain in the background of a normal sexual development, from which, however, it continues to withdraw a certain amount of energy. The first of these alternatives was already known before the days of analysis. Analytic investigation, however, of such fully-developed cases almost bridges the gulf between the two. For we find often enough with these perverts that they too made an attempt at developing normal sexual activity, usually at the age of puberty; but their attempt had not enough force in it and was abandoned in the face of the first obstacles which inevitably arise, whereupon they fell back upon their infantile fixation once and for all.

It would naturally be important to know whether the origin of infantile perversions from the Oedipus complex can be asserted as a general principle. While this cannot be decided without further investigation, it does not seem impossible. When we recall the anamneses which have been obtained in adult cases of perversion we cannot fail to notice that the decisive impression, the 'first experience', of all these perverts, fetishists, etc., is scarcely ever referred back to a time earlier than the sixth year. At this time, however, the dominance of the Oedipus complex is already over; the experience which is recalled, and which has been effective in such a puzzling way, may very well have represented the legacy of that complex. The connections between the experience and the complex which is by this time repressed are bound to remain obscure so long as analysis has not thrown any light on the time before the first 'pathogenic' impression. So it may be imagined how little value is to be attached, for instance, to an assertion that a case of homosexuality is congenital, when the ground given for this belief is that ever since his eighth or sixth year the person in question has felt inclinations only towards his own sex.

If, however, the derivation of perversions from the Oedipus complex can be generally established, our estimate of its importance will have gained added strength. For in our opinion the Oedipus complex is the actual nucleus of neuroses,[1] and the infantile sexuality which culminates in this complex is the true determinant of neuroses. What remains of the complex in the unconscious represents the disposition to the later development of neuroses in the adult. In this way the beating-phantasy and other analogous perverse fixations would also only be precipitates of the Oedipus complex, scars, so to say, left behind after

1. [Cf. p. 192 and n. 4 below.]

the process has ended, just as the notorious 'sense of inferiority' corresponds to a narcissistic scar of the same sort. In taking this view of the matter I must express my unreserved agreement with Marcinowski (1918), who has recently put it forward most happily. As is well known, this neurotic delusion of inferiority is only a partial one, and is completely compatible with the existence of a self-overvaluation derived from other sources. The origin of the Oedipus complex itself, and the destiny which compels man, probably alone among all animals, to begin his sexual life twice over, first like all other creatures in his early childhood, and then after a long interruption once more at the age of puberty – all the problems that are connected with man's 'archaic inheritance' – have been discussed by me elsewhere, and I have no intention of going into them in this place.[1]

Little light is thrown upon the genesis of masochism by our discussion of the beating-phantasy. To begin with, there seems to be a confirmation of the view that masochism is not the manifestation of a primary instinct, but originates from sadism which has been turned round upon the self – that is to say, by means of regression from an object to the ego.[2] Instincts with a passive aim must be taken for granted as existing, especially among women. But passivity is not the whole of masochism. The characteristic of unpleasure belongs to it as well, – a bewildering accompaniment to the satisfaction of an instinct. The transformation of sadism into masochism appears to be due to the influence of the sense of guilt which takes part in the act of repression. Thus repression is operative here in three ways: it renders the consequences of the genital organization unconscious, it compels that organization itself to regress to the

1. [Cf; however, pp. 192–3 below. Freud had discussed these questions at length, not long before, in his *Introductory Lectures* (1916–17), especially in Lectures 21 and 23.]

2. Cf. 'Instincts and their Vicissitudes' (1915c). – [In *Beyond the Pleasure Principle* (1920g), Chapter VI, Freud suggested that there might after all be a primary masochism.]

earlier sadistic-anal stage, and it transforms the sadism of this stage into masochism, which is passive and again in a certain sense narcissistic. The second of these three effects is made possible by the weakness of the genital organization, which must be presupposed in these cases. The third becomes necessary because the sense of guilt takes as much objection to sadism as to incestuous object-choice genitally conceived. Again, the analyses do not tell us the origin of the sense of guilt itself. It seems to be brought along by the new phase upon which the child is entering, and, if it afterwards persists, it seems to correspond to a scar-like formation which is similar to the sense of inferiority. According to our present orientation in the structure of the ego, which is as yet uncertain, we should assign it to the agency in the mind which sets itself up as a critical conscience over against the rest of the ego, which produces Silberer's functional phenomenon in dreams [cf. Silberer 1910], and which cuts itself loose from the ego in delusions of being watched.[1]

We may note too in passing that the analysis of the infantile perversion dealt with here is also of help in solving an old riddle – one which, it is true, has always troubled those who have not accepted psychoanalysis more than analysts themselves. Yet quite recently even Bleuler [1913] regarded it as a remarkable and inexplicable fact that neurotics make masturbation the central point of their sense of guilt. We have long assumed that this sense of guilt relates to the masturbation of early childhood and not to that of puberty, and that in the main it is to be connected not with the act of masturbation but with the phantasy which, although unconscious, lies at its root – that is to say, with the Oedipus complex.[2]

1. [See Part III of Freud's paper on narcissism (1914c). This agency was, of course, later described as the 'super-ego'. Cf. Chapter III of *The Ego and the Id* (1923b).]

2. [Cf. a footnote to the *Three Essays* (1905d), which Freud added in 1915 and extended in 1920 (*P.F.L.*, **7**, 107 *n*.). Cf. also an Editor's footnote to the paper on anxiety neurosis (1895b), p.56 *n*. 1 above, which gives references to other discussions of masturbation.]

As regards the third and apparently sadistic phase of the beating-phantasy, I have already [pp. 176-7] discussed the significance that it gains as the vehicle of the excitation impelling towards masturbation; and I have shown how it arouses activities of the imagination which on the one hand continue the phantasy along the same line, and on the other hand neutralize it through compensation. Nevertheless the second phase, the unconscious and masochistic one, in which the child itself is being beaten by its father, is incomparably the more important. This is not only because it continues to operate through the agency of the phase that takes its place; we can also detect effects upon the character, which are directly derived from its unconscious form. People who harbour phantasies of this kind develop a special sensitiveness and irritability towards anyone whom they can include in the class of fathers. They are easily offended by a person of this kind, and in that way (to their own sorrow and cost) bring about the realization of the imagined situation of being beaten by their father. I should not be surprised if it were one day possible to prove that the same phantasy is the basis of the delusional litigiousness of paranoia.

VI

It would have been quite impossible to give a clear survey of infantile beating-phantasies if I had not limited it, except in one or two connections, to the state of things in females. I will briefly recapitulate my conclusions. The little girl's beating-phantasy passes through three phases, of which the first and third are consciously remembered, the middle one remaining unconscious. The two conscious phases appear to be sadistic, whereas the middle and unconscious one is undoubtedly of a masochistic nature; its content consists in the child's being beaten by her father, and it carries with it the libidinal charge and the sense of guilt. In the first and third phantasies the child who is being beaten is always someone other than the subject;

in the middle phase it is always the child herself; in the third phase it is almost invariably only boys who are being beaten. The person who does the beating is from the first her father, replaced later on by a substitute taken from the class of fathers. The unconscious phantasy of the middle phase had primarily a genital significance and developed by means of repression and regression out of an incestuous wish to be loved by the father. Another fact, though its connection with the rest does not appear to be close, is that between the second and third phases the girls change their sex, for in the phantasies of the latter phase they turn into boys.

I have not been able to get so far in my knowledge of beating-phantasies in boys, perhaps because my material was unfavourable. I naturally expected to find a complete analogy between the state of things in the case of boys and in that of girls, the mother taking the father's place in the phantasy. This expectation seemed to be fulfilled; for the content of the boy's phantasy which was taken to be the corresponding one was actually his being beaten by his mother (or later on by a substitute for her). But this phantasy, in which the boy's own self was retained as the person who was being beaten, differed from the second phase in girls in that it was able to become conscious. If on this account, however, we attempt to draw a parallel between it and the *third* phase of the girl's phantasy, a new difference is found, for the figure of the boy himself is not replaced by a number of unknown, and unspecified children, least of all by a number of girls. Therefore the expectation of there being a complete parallel was mistaken.

My male cases with an infantile beating-phantasy comprised only a few who did not exhibit some other gross injury to their sexual activities; again they included a fairly large number of persons who would have to be described as true masochists in the sense of being sexual perverts. They were either people who obtained their sexual satisfaction exclusively from masturbation accompanied by masochistic phantasies; or they were people who had succeeded in combining masochism with their genital activity in such a way that, along with masochistic performances and under similar conditions, they were able to bring about erection and emission or to carry out normal intercourse. In addition to this there was the rarer case in which a masochist is interfered with in his perverse activities by the appearance of obsessional ideas of unbearable intensity. Now perverts who can obtain satisfaction do not often have occasion to come for analysis. But as regards the three classes of masochists that have been mentioned there may be strong motives to induce them to go to an analyst. The masochist masturbator finds that he is absolutely impotent if after all he does attempt intercourse with a woman; and the man who has hitherto effected intercourse with the help of a masochistic idea or performance may suddenly make the discovery that the alliance which was so convenient for him has broken down, his genital organs no longer reacting to the masochistic stimulus. We are accustomed confidently to promise recovery to psychically impotent patients who come to us for treatment; but we ought to be more guarded in making this prognosis so long as the dynamics of the disturbance are unknown to us. It comes as a disagreeable surprise if the analysis reveals the cause of the 'merely psychical' impotence to be a typically masochistic attitude, perhaps deeply embedded since infancy.

As regards these masochistic men, however, a discovery is made at this point which warns us not to pursue the analogy between their case and that of women any further at present, but to judge each independently. For the fact emerges that in their masochistic phantasies, as well as in the performances they go through for their realization, they invariably transfer themselves into the part of a woman; that is to say, their masochistic attitude coincides with a *feminine* one. This can easily be demonstrated from details of the phantasies; but many patients are even aware of it themselves, and give expression to it as a subjective conviction. It makes no difference if in a fanciful embellishment of the masochistic scene they keep up the fiction that a mischievous boy, or page, or apprentice is going to be punished. On the other hand the persons who administer chastisement are always women, both in the phantasies and the performances. This is confusing enough; and the further question must be asked whether this feminine attitude already forms the basis of the masochistic element in the *infantile* beating-phantasy.[1]

Let us therefore leave aside consideration of the state of things in cases of adult masochism, which it is so hard to clear up, and turn to the infantile beating-phantasy in the male sex. Analysis of the earliest years of childhood once more allows us to make a surprising discovery in this field. The phantasy which has as its content being beaten by the mother, and which is conscious or can become so, is not a primary one. It possesses a preceding stage which is invariably unconscious and has as its content: '*I am being beaten by my father.*' This preliminary stage, then, really corresponds to the second phase of the phantasy in the girl. The familiar and conscious phantasy: 'I am being beaten by my mother', takes the place of the third phase in the girl, in which, as has been mentioned already, unknown boys are the objects that are being beaten. I have not been able to demonstrate among boys a preliminary stage of a sadistic nature that could be set beside the first phase of the phantasy in girls, but I will not now express any final disbelief in its existence, for I can readily see the possibility of meeting with more complicated types.

In the male phantasy – as I shall call it briefly, and, I hope, without any risk of being misunderstood – the being beaten also stands for being loved (in a genital sense), though this has been debased to a lower level owing to regression. So the original form of the unconscious male phantasy was not the provisional one that we have hitherto given: 'I am being beaten by my

1. [*Footnote added* 1924:] Further remarks on this subject will be found in 'The Economic Problem of Masochism' (1924c).

father', but rather: '*I am loved by my father*'. The phantasy has been transformed by the processes with which we are familiar into the conscious phantasy: '*I am being beaten by my mother*'. The boy's beating-phantasy is therefore passive from the very beginning, and is derived from a feminine attitude towards his father. It corresponds with the Oedipus complex just as the female one (that of the girl) does; only the parallel relation which we expected to find between the two must be given up in favour of a common character of another kind. *In both cases the beating-phantasy has its origin in an incestuous attachment to the father.*[1]

It will help to make matters clearer if at this point I enumerate the other similarities and differences between beating-phantasies in the two sexes. In the case of the girl the unconscious masochistic phantasy starts from the normal Oedipus attitude; in that of the boy it starts from the inverted attitude, in which the father is taken as the object of love. In the case of the girl the phantasy has a preliminary stage (the first phase), in which the beating bears no special significance and is performed upon a person who is viewed with jealous hatred. Both of these features are absent in the case of the boy, but this particular difference is one which might be removed by more fortunate observation. In her transition to the conscious phantasy [the third phase] which takes the place of the unconscious one, the girl retains the figure of her father, and in that way keeps unchanged the sex of the person beating; but she changes the figure and sex of the person being beaten, so that eventually a man is beating male children. The boy, on the contrary, changes the figure and sex of the person beating, by putting his mother in the place of his father; but he retains his own figure, with the result that the person beating and the person being beaten are of opposite sexes. In the case of the girl what was originally a masochistic

1. [A beating-phantasy plays some little part in the analysis of the 'Wolf Man' (1918b), *P.F.L.*, **9**, 255 and 279f.]

(passive) situation is transformed into a sadistic one by means of repression, and its sexual quality is almost effaced. In the case of the boy the situation remains masochistic, and shows a greater resemblance to the original phantasy with its genital significance, since there is a difference of sex between the person beating and the person being beaten. The boy evades his homosexuality by repressing and remodelling his unconscious phantasy: and the remarkable thing about his later conscious phantasy is that it has for its content a feminine attitude without a homosexual object-choice. By the same process, on the other hand, the girl escapes from the demands of the erotic side of her life altogether. She turns herself in phantasy into a man, without herself becoming active in a masculine way, and is no longer anything but a spectator of the event which takes the place of a sexual act.

We are justified in assuming that no great change is effected by the *repression* of the original unconscious phantasy. Whatever is repressed from consciousness or replaced in it by something else remains intact and potentially operative in the unconscious. The effect of *regression* to an earlier stage of the sexual organization is quite another matter. As regards this we are led to believe that the state of things changes in the unconscious as well. Thus in both sexes the masochistic phantasy of being beaten by the father, though not the passive phantasy of being loved by him, lives on in the unconscious after repression has taken place. There are, besides, plenty of indications that the repression has only very incompletely attained its object. The boy, who has tried to escape from a homosexual object-choice, and who has not changed his sex, nevertheless feels like a woman in his conscious phantasies, and endows the women who are beating him with masculine attributes and characteristics. The girl, who has even renounced her sex, and who has on the whole accomplished a more thoroughgoing work of repression, nevertheless does not become freed from her father;

she does not venture to do the beating herself; and since she has herself become a boy, it is principally boys whom she causes to be beaten.

I am aware that the differences that I have here described between the two sexes in regard to the nature of the beating-phantasy have not been cleared up sufficiently. But I shall not attempt to unravel these complications by tracing out their dependence on other factors, as I do not consider that the material for observation is exhaustive. So far as it goes, however, I should like to make use of it as a test for two theories. These theories stand in opposition to each other, though both of them deal with the relation between repression and sexual character, and each, according to its own view, represents the relation as a very intimate one. I may say at once that I have always regarded both theories as incorrect and misleading.

The first of these theories is anonymous. It was brought to my notice many years ago by a colleague with whom I was at that time on friendly terms.[1] The theory is so attractive on account of its bold simplicity that the only wonder is that it should not have found its way into the literature of the subject except in a few scattered allusions. It is based on the fact of the bisexual constitution of human beings, and asserts that the motive force of repression in each individual is a struggle between the two sexual characters. The dominant sex of the person, that which is the more strongly developed, has repressed the mental representation of the subordinated sex into the unconscious. Therefore the nucleus of the unconscious (that is to say, the repressed) is in each human being that side of him which belongs to the opposite sex. Such a theory as this can only have an intelligible meaning if we assume that a person's sex is to be determined by the formation of his genitals; for otherwise it would not be certain which is a person's stronger sex and

1. [This was Wilhelm Fliess. Cf. the 'Sketch' of Freud's life and ideas, p.18 above.]

we should run the risk of reaching from the results of our enquiry the very fact which has to serve as its point of departure. To put the theory briefly: with men, what is unconscious and repressed can be brought down to feminine instinctual impulses; and conversely with women.

The second theory is of more recent origin.[1] It is in agreement with the first one in so far as it too represents the struggle between the two sexes as being the decisive cause of repression. In other respects it comes into conflict with the former theory; moreover, it looks for support to sociological rather than biological sources. According to this theory of the 'masculine protest', formulated by Alfred Adler [1910], every individual makes efforts not to remain on the inferior 'feminine line [of development]' and struggles towards the 'masculine line', from which satisfaction can alone be derived. Adler makes the masculine protest responsible for the whole formation both of character and of neuroses. Unfortunately he makes so little distinction between the two processes, which certainly have to be kept separate, and sets altogether so little store in general by the fact of repression, that to attempt to apply the doctrine of the masculine protest to repression brings with it the risk of misunderstanding. In my opinion such an attempt could only lead us to infer that the masculine protest, the desire to break away from the feminine line, was in every case the motive force of repression. The repressing agency, therefore, would always be a masculine instinctual impulse, and the repressed would be a feminine one. But symptoms would also be the result of a feminine impulse, for we cannot discard the characteristic feature of symptoms – that they are substitutes for the repressed, substitutes that have made their way out in spite of repression.

Now let us take these two theories, which may be said to

1. [Adler's theory of repression was discussed briefly in the Schreber analysis (1911c), as well as in the case history of the 'Wolf Man' (1918b), P.F.L., 9, 176 f. and 352–3.]

have in common a sexualization of the process of repression, and test them by applying them to the example of the beating-phantasies which we have been studying. The original phantasy, 'I am being beaten by my father', corresponds, in the case of the boy, to a feminine attitude, and is therefore an expression of that part of his disposition which belongs to the opposite sex. If this part of him undergoes repression, the first theory seems shown to be correct; for this theory set it up as a rule that what belongs to the opposite sex is identical with the repressed. It scarcely answers to our expectations, it is true, when we find that the conscious phantasy, which arises after repression has been accomplished, nevertheless exhibits the feminine attitude once more, though this time directed towards the mother. But we will not go into such doubtful points, when the whole question can be so quickly decided. There can be no doubt that the original phantasy in the case of the girl, 'I am being beaten (i.e. I am loved) by my father', represents a feminine attitude, and corresponds to her dominant and manifest sex; according to the theory, therefore, it ought to escape repression, and there would be no need for its becoming unconscious. But as a matter of fact it does become unconscious, and is replaced by a conscious phantasy which disavows the girl's manifest sexual character. The theory is therefore useless as an explanation of beating-phantasies, and is contradicted by the facts. It might be objected that it is precisely in unmanly boys and unwomanly girls that these beating-phantasies appeared and went through these vicissitudes; or that it was a trait of femininity in the boy and of masculinity in the girl which must be made responsible for the production of a passive phantasy in the boy, and its repression in the girl. We should be inclined to agree with this view, but it would not be any the less impossible to defend the supposed relation between manifest sexual character and the choice of what is destined for repression. In the last resort we can only see that both in male and female individuals masculine as well as feminine instinctual impulses are found, and that each can equally well undergo repression and so become unconscious.

The theory of the masculine protest seems to maintain its ground very much better on being tested in regard to the beating-phantasies. In the case of both boys and girls the beating-phantasy corresponds with a feminine attitude – one, that is, in which the individual is lingering on the 'feminine line' – and both sexes hasten to get free from this attitude by repressing the phantasy. Nevertheless, it seems to be only with the girl that the masculine protest is attended with complete success, and in that instance, indeed, an ideal example is to be found of the operation of the masculine protest. With the boy the result is not entirely satisfactory; the feminine line is not given up, and the boy is certainly not 'on top' in his conscious masochistic phantasy. It would therefore agree with the expectations derived from the theory if we were to recognize that this phantasy was a symptom which had come into existence through the failure of the masculine protest. It is a disturbing fact, to be sure, that the girl's phantasy, which owes its origin to the forces of repression, also has the value and meaning of a symptom. In this instance, where the masculine protest has completely achieved its object, surely the determining condition for the formation of a symptom must be absent.

Before we are led by this difficulty to a suspicion that the whole conception of the masculine protest is inadequate to meet the problem of neuroses and perversions, and that its application to them is unfruitful, we will for a moment leave the passive beating-phantasies and turn our attention to other instinctual manifestations of infantile sexual life – manifestations which have equally undergone repression. No one can doubt that there are also wishes and phantasies which keep to the masculine line from their very nature, and which are the expression of masculine instinctual impulses – sadistic tendencies, for instance, or a boy's lustful feelings towards his mother arising out of the normal Oedipus complex. It is no less certain that these impulses, too, are overtaken by repression. If the masculine protest is to be taken as having satisfactorily explained the repression of passive phantasies (which later become masochistic), then it becomes for that very reason totally inapplicable to the opposite case of active phantasies. That is to say, the doctrine of the masculine protest is altogether incompatible with the fact of repression. Unless we are prepared to throw away all that has been acquired in psychology since Breuer's first cathartic treatment and through its agency,[1] we cannot expect that the principle of the masculine protest will acquire any significance in the elucidation of the neuroses and perversions.

The theory of psychoanalysis (a theory based on observation) holds firmly to the view that the motive forces of repression must not be sexualized. Man's archaic heritage[2] forms the nucleus of the unconscious mind; and whatever part of that heritage has to be left behind in the advance to later phases of development, because it is unserviceable or incompatible with what is new and harmful to it, falls a victim to the process of repression. This selection is made more successfully with one group of instincts than with the other. In virtue of special circumstances which have often been pointed out already,[3] the latter group, that of the sexual instincts, are able to defeat the intentions of repression, and to enforce their representation by substitutive formations of a disturbing kind. For this reason infantile sexuality, which is held under repression, acts as the chief motive force in the formation of symptoms; and the essential part of its content, the Oedipus complex, is the nuclear complex of neuroses.[4] I hope that in this paper I have raised an

1. [The reference is to the case of 'Anna O', published in *Studies on Hysteria* (Breuer and Freud, 1895), *P.F.L.*, **3**, 73 ff.]

2. [Cf. p. 180 and *n.* 1 above.]

3. [See for instance Freud's paper 'Formulations on the Two Principles of Mental Functioning' (1911*b*).]

4. [Freud had first spoken of the 'nuclear complex' in his paper on

expectation that the sexual aberrations of childhood, as well as those of mature life, are ramifications of the same complex.[1]

---

infantile sexual theories (1908c) and had introduced the 'Oedipus complex' in a paper on object-choice in men (1910h); cf. *P.F.L.*, **7**, 192 and *n*. 1 and 238 and *n*. 1. See also a long note added in 1920 (after the present paper) to *Three Essays* (1905d), ibid., 149–50, where, as here, the two terms are brought together.]

1. [Some further remarks on the first phase of the beating-phantasy in girls will be found in a later paper of Freud's on the anatomical distinction between the sexes (1925j), *P.F.L.*, **7**, 338.]

SOME NEUROTIC MECHANISMS IN JEALOUSY, PARANOIA AND HOMOSEXUALITY
(1922 [1921])

EDITOR'S NOTE

ÜBER EINIGE NEUROTISCHE MECHANISMEN BEI EIFERSUCHT, PARANOIA UND HOMOSEXUALITÄT

(A) GERMAN EDITIONS:

(1921   January. Probable date of composition.)

1922   *Int. Z. Psychoanal.*, **8** (3), 249–58.

1924   *Gesammelte Schriften*, **5**, 387–99.

1940   *Gesammelte Werke*, **13**, 195–207.

(B) ENGLISH TRANSLATIONS:

'Certain Neurotic Mechanisms in Jealousy,
Paranoia and Homosexuality'

1923   *Int. J. Psycho-Analysis*, **4**, 1–10. (Tr. Joan Riviere.)

1924   *Collected Papers*, **2**, 232–43. (Same translator.)

1955   *Standard Edition*, **18**, 221–32. (Based on the translation
        published in 1924, with a modified title.)

The present edition is a corrected reprint of the *Standard Edition* version, with some editorial changes.

We learn from Ernest Jones (1957, 85–6) that this paper was in all probability written in January, 1921, and that it was definitely read by Freud to a small group of his closest followers (Abraham, Eitingon, Ferenczi, Rank and Sachs, besides Jones himself), at an informal gathering in the Harz Mountains, in September of that year. Some of the discussion on paranoic delusions (pp. 200–201) goes back to similar remarks in *The Psychopathology of Everyday Life* (1901*b*), Chapter XII, *P.F.L.*, **5**, 317–18 and 321–22.

SOME NEUROTIC MECHANISMS IN JEALOUSY, PARANOIA AND HOMOSEXUALITY

A

JEALOUSY is one of those affective states, like grief, that may be described as normal. If anyone appears to be without it, the inference is justified that it has undergone severe repression and consequently plays all the greater part in his unconscious mental life. The instances of abnormally intense jealousy met with in analytic work reveal themselves as constructed of three layers. The three layers or grades of jealousy may be described as (1) *competitive* or normal, (2) *projected*, and (3) *delusional* jealousy.

There is not much to be said from the analytic point of view about *normal* jealousy. It is easy to see that essentially it is compounded of grief, the pain caused by the thought of losing the loved object, and of the narcissistic wound, in so far as this is distinguishable from the other wound; further, of feelings of enmity against the successful rival, and of a greater or lesser amount of self-criticism which tries to hold the subject's own ego accountable for his loss. Although we may call it normal, this jealousy is by no means completely rational, that is, derived from the actual situation, proportionate to the real circumstances and under the complete control of the conscious ego; for it is rooted deep in the unconscious, it is a continuation of the earliest stirrings of the child's affective life, and it originates in the Oedipus or brother-and-sister complex of the first sexual period. Moreover, it is noteworthy that in some people it is experienced bisexually. That is to say, a man will not only feel pain about the woman he loves and hatred of the man who is

his rival, but also grief about the man, whom he loves unconsciously, and hatred of the woman as his rival; and this latter set
of feelings will add to the intensity of his jealousy. I even know
of a man who suffered exceedingly during his attacks of jealousy
and who, according to his own account, went through un-
endurable torments by consciously imagining himself in the
position of the faithless woman. The sensation of helplessness
which then came over him and the images he used to describe
his condition – exposed to the vulture's beak like Prometheus,
or thrown bound into a nest of serpents – were referred by him
to impressions received during several homosexual acts of
aggression to which he had been subjected as a boy.

The jealousy of the second layer, *projected* jealousy, is derived
in both men and women either from their own actual unfaithfulness in real life or from impulses towards it which have succumbed to repression. It is a matter of everyday experience that
fidelity, especially that degree of it required in marriage, is only
maintained in the face of continual temptations. Anyone who
denies these temptations in himself will nevertheless feel their
pressure so strongly that he will be glad enough to make use of
an unconscious mechanism to alleviate his situation. He can
obtain this alleviation – and, indeed, acquittal by his conscience
– if he projects his own impulses to faithlessness on to the
partner to whom he owes faith. This strong motive can then
make use of the perceptual material which betrays unconscious
impulses of the same kind in the partner, and the subject can
justify himself with the reflection that the other is probably not
much better than he is himself.[1]

Social conventions have wisely taken this universal state of
things into account, by granting a certain amount of latitude to
the married woman's craving to attract and the married man's
thirst to make conquests, in the expectation that this inevitable

1. Cf. Desdemona's song [*Othello*, Act IV, Scene 3]:
   I called my love false love; but what said he then?
   If I court moe women, you'll couch with moe men.

tendency to unfaithfulness will thus find a safety-valve and be rendered innocuous. Convention has laid down that neither partner is to hold the other accountable for these little excursions in the direction of unfaithfulness, and they usually result in the desire that has been awakened by the new object finding satisfaction in some kind of return to faithfulness to the original object. A jealous person, however, does not recognize this convention of tolerance; he does not believe in any such thing as a halt or a turning-back once the path has been trodden, nor that a flirtation may be a safeguard against actual infidelity. In the treatment of a jealous person like this, one must refrain from disputing with him the material on which he bases his suspicions; one can only aim at bringing him to regard the matter in a different light.

The jealousy that arises from such a projection has, it is true, an almost delusional character; it is, however, amenable to the analytic work of exposing the unconscious phantasies of the subject's own infidelity. The position is worse as regards jealousy belonging to the third layer, the true *delusional* type. It too has its origin in repressed impulses towards unfaithfulness; but the object in these cases is of the same sex as the subject. Delusional jealousy is what is left of a homosexuality that has run its course, and it rightly takes its position among the classical forms of paranoia. As an attempt at defence against an unduly strong homosexual impulse it may, in a man, be described in the formula: '*I* do not love him, *she* loves him!'[1] In a delusional case one will be prepared to find jealousy belonging to all three layers, never to the third alone.

B

Paranoia. – Cases of paranoia are for well-known reasons not usually amenable to analytic investigation. I have recently been able, nevertheless, by an intensive study of two paranoics, to discover something new to me.

1. See the Schreber analysis (1911c) [*P.F.L.*, **9**, 196 ff.].

The first case was that of a youngish man with a fully developed paranoia of jealousy, the object of which was his impeccably faithful wife. A stormy period in which the delusion had possessed him uninterruptedly already lay behind him. When I saw him he was only subject to clearly separated attacks, which lasted for several days and which, curiously enough, regularly appeared on the day after he had had sexual intercourse with his wife, which was, incidentally, satisfying to both of them. The inference is justified that after every satiation of the heterosexual libido the homosexual component, likewise stimulated by the act, forced an outlet for itself in the attack of jealousy.

These attacks drew their material from his observation of minute indications, by which his wife's quite unconscious coquetry, unnoticeable to any one else, had betrayed itself to him. She had unintentionally touched the man sitting next to her with her hand; she had turned too much towards him, or she had smiled more pleasantly than when alone with her husband. He was extraordinarily observant of all these manifestations of her unconscious, and always knew how to interpret them correctly, so that he really was always in the right about it, and could furthermore call in analysis to justify his jealousy. His abnormality really reduced itself to this, that he watched his wife's unconscious mind much more closely and then regarded it as far more important than anyone else would have thought of doing.

We are reminded that sufferers from persecutory paranoia act in just the same way. They, too, cannot regard anything in other people as indifferent, and they, too, take up minute indications with which these other, unknown, people present them, and use them in their 'delusions of reference'. The meaning of their delusion of reference is that they expect from all strangers something like love. But these people show them nothing of the kind; they laugh to themselves, flourish their sticks, even spit on the ground as they go by – and one really does not do such things while a person in whom one takes a friendly interest is near. One does them only when one feels quite indifferent to the passer-by, when one can treat him like air; and, considering, too, the fundamental kinship of the concepts of 'stranger' and 'enemy', the paranoic is not so far wrong in regarding this indifference as hate, in contrast to his claim for love.

We begin to see that we describe the behaviour of both jealous and persecutory paranoics very inadequately by saying that they project outwards on to others what they do not wish to recognize in themselves. Certainly they do this; but they do not project it into the blue, so to speak, where there is nothing of the sort already. They let themselves be guided by their knowledge of the unconscious, and displace to the unconscious minds of others the attention which they have withdrawn from their own. Our jealous husband perceived his wife's unfaithfulness instead of his own; by becoming conscious of hers and magnifying it enormously he succeeded in keeping his own unconscious. If we accept his example as typical, we may infer that the enmity which the persecuted paranoic sees in others is the reflection of his own hostile impulses against them. Since we know that with the paranoic it is precisely the most loved person of his own sex that becomes his persecutor, the question arises where this reversal of affect takes its origin; the answer is not far to seek – the ever-present ambivalence of feeling provides its source and the non-fulfilment of his claim for love strengthens it. This ambivalence thus serves the same purpose for the persecuted paranoic as jealousy served for my patient – that of a defence against homosexuality.

The dreams of my jealous patient presented me with a great surprise. They were not simultaneous with the outbreaks of the attacks, it is true, but they occurred within the period which was under the dominance of the delusion; yet they were completely free from delusion and they revealed the underlying homosexual impulses with no more than the usual degree of disguise. Since I had had little experience of the dreams of paranoics, it seemed plausible at the time to suppose that it was true in general that paranoia does not penetrate into dreams.

This patient's homosexual position was easily surveyed. He had made no friendships and developed no social interests; one had the impression that only the delusion had carried forward the development of his relations with men, as if it had taken over some of the arrears that had been neglected. The fact that his father was of no great importance in the family, combined with a humiliating homosexual trauma in early boyhood, had forced his homosexuality into repression and barred the way to its sublimation. The whole of his youth was governed by a strong attachment to his mother. Of all her many sons he was her declared favourite, and he developed marked jealousy of the normal type in regard to her. When later he made his choice of a wife – mainly prompted by an impulse to enrich his mother – his longing for a virgin mother expressed itself in obsessive doubts about his fiancée's virginity. The first years of his marriage were free from jealousy. Then he became unfaithful to his wife and entered upon an intimate relationship with another woman that lasted for a considerable time. Frightened by a certain suspicion, he at length made an end of this love affair, and not until then did jealousy of the second, projected type break out, by means of which he was able to assuage his self-reproaches about his own unfaithfulness. It was soon complicated by an accession of homosexual impulses, of which his father-in-law was the object, and became a fully formed jealous paranoia.

My second case would probably not have been classified as *paranoia persecutoria*, apart from analysis; but I had to recognize the young man as a candidate for a terminal illness of that kind. In his attitude to his father there existed an ambivalence which in its range was quite extraordinary. On the one hand, he was the most pronounced rebel imaginable, and had developed manifestly in every direction in opposition to his father's wishes and ideals; on the other hand, at a deeper level he was still the most submissive of sons, who after his father's death denied himself all enjoyment of women out of a tender sense of guilt. His actual relations with men were clearly dominated by suspiciousness; his keen intellect easily rationalized this attitude; and he knew how to bring it about that both friends and acquaintances deceived and exploited him. The new thing I learned from studying him was that classical persecutory ideas may be present without finding belief or acceptance. They flashed up occasionally during the analysis, but he regarded them as unimportant and invariably scoffed at them. This may occur in many cases of paranoia; it may be that the delusions which we regard as new formations when the disease breaks out have already long been in existence.

It seems to me that we have here an important discovery – namely, that the qualitative factor, the presence of certain neurotic formations, has less practical significance than the quantitative factor, the degree of attention or, more correctly, the amount of cathexis that these structures are able to attract to themselves. Our consideration of the first case, the jealous paranoia, led to a similar estimate of the importance of the quantitative factor, by showing that there also the abnormality essentially consisted in the hypercathexis of the interpretations of someone else's unconscious. We have long known of an analogous fact in the analysis of hysteria. The pathogenic phantasies, derivatives of repressed instinctual impulses, are for a long time tolerated alongside the normal life of the mind, and have no pathogenic effect until by a revolution in the libidinal economy they receive a hypercathexis; not till then does the conflict which leads to the formation of symptoms break out. Thus as our knowledge grows we are increasingly impelled to bring the *economic* point of view into the foreground. I should also like to throw out the question whether this quantitative factor that I am now dwelling on does not suffice to cover the phenomena which Bleuler [1916] and others have lately proposed to name 'switching'. One need only assume that an increase in resistance in the course taken by the psychical current in one direction results in a hypercathexis of another path and thus causes the flow to be switched into that path.

My two cases of paranoia showed an instructive contrast in the behaviour of their dreams. Whereas those of the first case were free from delusion, as has already been said, the other patient produced great numbers of persecutory dreams, which may be regarded as forerunners of or substitutes for the delusional ideas. The pursuer, whom he only managed to escape with great fear, was usually a powerful bull or some other male symbol which even in the dream itself he sometimes recognized as representing his father. One day he produced a very characteristic paranoic transference-dream. He saw me shaving in front of him, and from the scent he realized that I was using the same soap as his father had used. I was doing this in order to oblige him to make a father-transference on to me. The choice of this incident for his dream quite unmistakably betrays the patient's depreciatory attitude to his paranoic phantasies and his disbelief in them; for his own eyes could tell him every day that I was never in a position to make use of shaving-soap and that therefore there was in this respect nothing to which a father-transference could attach itself.

A comparison of the dreams of the two patients shows, however, that the question whether or not paranoia (or any other psychoneurosis) can penetrate into dreams is based on a false conception of dreams. Dreams are distinguished from waking thought by the fact that they can include material (belonging to the region of the repressed) which must not emerge in waking thought. Apart from this, dreams are merely a *form of thinking*, a transformation of preconscious material of thought by the dream-work and its conditions.[1] Our terminology of the neuroses is not applicable to repressed material; this cannot be called hysterical, nor obsessional, nor paranoic. As against this, the other part of the material which is subjected

1. [Cf. *The Interpretation of Dreams* (1900a), P.F.L., **4**, 649–50 n.]

to the process of dream-formation – the preconscious thoughts – may be normal or may bear the character of any neurosis; they may be the products of any of the pathogenic processes in which the essence of a neurosis lies. There seems to be no reason why any such pathological idea should not be transformed into a dream. A dream may therefore quite simply represent a hysterical phantasy, an obsessional idea, or a delusion – that is, may reveal one or other of these upon interpretation. Observation of the two paranoics shows that the dreams of the one were quite normal while he was subject to his delusion, and that those of the other were paranoic in content while he was treating his delusional ideas with contempt. In both cases, therefore, the dream took up the material that was at the time forced into the background in waking life. This too, however, need not necessarily be an invariable rule.

C

Homosexuality. – Recognition of the organic factor in homosexuality does not relieve us of the obligation of studying the psychical processes connected with its origin. The typical process,[1] already established in innumerable cases, is that a few years after the termination of puberty a young man, who until this time has been strongly fixated to his mother, changes his attitude; he identifies himself with his mother, and looks about for love-objects in whom he can re-discover himself, and whom he might then love as his mother loved him. The characteristic mark of this process is that for several years one of the necessary conditions for his love is usually that the male object shall be of the same age as he himself was when the change took place. We have come to know of various factors contributing to this result, probably in different degrees. First there is the fixation on the mother, which makes it difficult to pass on to another

1. [This was described by Freud in Chapter III of his study of Leonardo (1910*c*).]

woman. Identification with the mother is an outcome of this attachment, and at the same time in a certain sense it enables the son to keep true to her, his first object. Then there is the inclination towards a narcissistic object-choice, which in general lies readier to hand and is easier to put into effect than a move towards the other sex. Behind this latter factor there lies concealed another of quite exceptional strength, or perhaps it coincides with it: the high value set upon the male organ and the inability to tolerate its absence in a love-object. Depreciation of women, and aversion to them, even horror of them, are generally derived from the early discovery that women have no penis. We subsequently discovered, as another powerful motive urging towards homosexual object-choice, regard for the father or fear of him; for the renunciation of women means that all rivalry with him (or with all men who may take his place) is avoided. The two last motives – the clinging to the condition of a penis in the object, as well as the retiring in favour of the father – may be ascribed to the castration complex. Attachment to the mother, narcissism, fear of castration – these are the factors (which incidentally have nothing specific about them) that we have hitherto found in the psychical aetiology of homosexuality; and with these must be reckoned the effect of seduction, which is responsible for a premature fixation of the libido, as well as the influence of the organic factor which favours the passive role in love.

We have, however, never regarded this analysis of the origin of homosexuality as complete. I can now point to a new mechanism leading to homosexual object-choice, although I cannot say how large a part it plays in the formation of the extreme, manifest and exclusive type of homosexuality. Observation has directed my attention to several cases in which during early childhood impulses of jealousy, derived from the mother-complex and of very great intensity, arose [in a boy] against rivals, usually older brothers. This jealousy led to an exceedingly hostile and aggressive attitude towards these brothers which might sometimes reach the pitch of actual death-wishes, but which could not maintain themselves in the face of the subject's further development. Under the influences of upbringing – and certainly not uninfluenced also by their own continuing power-lessness – these impulses yielded to repression and underwent a transformation, so that the rivals of the earlier period became the first homosexual love-objects. Such an outcome of the attachment to the mother shows various interesting relations with other processes known to us. First of all it is a complete contrast to the development of *paranoia persecutoria*, in which the person who has before been loved becomes the hated perse-cutor, whereas here the hated rivals are transformed into love-objects. It represents, too, an exaggeration of the process which, according to my view, leads to the birth of social instincts in the individual.[1] In both processes there is first the presence of jealous and hostile impulses which cannot achieve satisfaction; and both the affectionate and the social feelings of identifica-tion arise as reactive formations against the repressed aggressive impulses.

This new mechanism of homosexual object-choice – its origin in rivalry which has been overcome and in aggressive impulses which have become repressed – is sometimes com-bined with the typical conditions already familiar to us. In the history of homosexuals one often hears that the change in them took place after the mother had praised another boy and set him up as a model. The tendency to a narcissistic object-choice was thus stimulated, and after a short phase of keen jealousy the rival became a love-object. As a rule, however, the new mecha-nism is distinguished by the change taking place at a much ear-lier period, and the identification with the mother receding into the background. Moreover, in the cases I have observed, it led only to homosexual attitudes which did not exclude hetero-sexuality and did not involve a *horror feminae*.

1. Cf. my *Group Psychology and the Analysis of the Ego* (1921c). [The second half of Chapter IX].

It is well known that a good number of homosexuals are characterized by a special development of their social instinctual impulses and by their devotion to the interests of the community. It would be tempting, as a theoretical explanation of this, to say that the behaviour towards men in general of a man who sees in other men potential love-objects must be different from that of a man who looks upon other men in the first instance as rivals in regard to women. The only objection to this is that jealousy and rivalry play their part in homosexual love as well, and that the community of men also includes these potential rivals. Apart from this speculative explanation, however, the fact that homosexual object-choice not infrequently proceeds from an early overcoming of rivalry with men cannot be without a bearing on the connection between homosexuality and social feeling.

In the light of psychoanalysis we are accustomed to regard social feeling as a sublimation of homosexual attitudes towards objects. In the homosexuals with marked social interests, it would seem that the detachment of social feeling from object-choice has not been fully carried through.

NEUROSIS AND PSYCHOSIS
(1924 [1923])

EDITOR'S NOTE

NEUROSE UND PSYCHOSE

(A) GERMAN EDITIONS:

1924   *Int. Z. Psychoanal.*, **10** (1), 1–5.
1924   *Gesammelte Schriften*, **5**, 418–22.
1940   *Gesammelte Werke*, **13**, 387–91.

(B) ENGLISH TRANSLATIONS:

'Neurosis and Psychosis'

1924   *Collected Papers*, **2**, 250–54. (Tr. Joan Riviere.)
1961   *Standard Edition*, **19**, 147–53. (Based on the translation of 1924.)

The present edition is a reprint of the *Standard Edition* version, with one or two editorial modifications.

This was written during the late autumn of 1923. It is an application of the new hypotheses put forward in *The Ego and the Id* to the particular question of the genetic difference between neuroses and psychoses. This same discussion was carried further in another paper, written a few months after the present one, 'The Loss of Reality in Neurosis and Psychosis' (1924*e*), p. 221 below. The roots of the matter were already under discussion by Freud in Section III of his first paper on 'The Neuro-Psychoses of Defence' (1894*a*).

In the second paragraph of this paper, Freud speaks of its having been stimulated by 'a train of thought raised in other quarters'. It seems likely that what he was referring to was a work on the psychoanalysis of general paralysis by Hollós and Ferenczi (1922), which had just appeared and to which a theoretical section was contributed by Ferenczi.

NEUROSIS AND PSYCHOSIS

In my recently published work, *The Ego and the Id* (1923b), I have proposed a differentiation of the mental apparatus, on the basis of which a number of relationships can be represented in a simple and perspicuous manner. As regards other points – for instance, in what concerns the origin and role of the super-ego – enough remains obscure and unelucidated. Now one may reasonably expect that a hypothesis of this kind should prove useful and helpful in other directions as well, if only to enable us to see what we already know from another angle, to group it differently and to describe it more convincingly. Such an application of the hypothesis might also bring with it a profitable return from grey theory to the perpetual green of experience.[1]

In the work I have mentioned I described the numerous dependent relationships of the ego, its intermediate position between the external world and the id and its efforts to humour all its masters at once. In connection with a train of thought raised in other quarters, which was concerned with the origin and prevention of the psychoses, a simple formula has now occurred to me which deals with what is perhaps the most important genetic difference between a neurosis and a psychosis: *neurosis is the result of a conflict between the ego and its id, whereas psychosis is the analogous outcome of a similar disturbance in the relations between the ego and the external world.*

There are certainly good grounds for being suspicious of such

1. [Grau, teurer Freund, ist alle Theorie,
   Und grün des Lebens goldner Baum.

   My worthy friend, gray is all theory,
   And green alone Life's golden tree.
   (Trans. Bayard Taylor, emended.)
   Mephistopheles in *Faust*, Part I, Scene 4.]

simple solutions of a problem. Moreover, the most that we may expect is that this formula will turn out to be correct in the roughest outline. But even that would be something. One recalls at once, too, a whole number of discoveries and findings which seem to support our thesis. All our analyses go to show that the transference neuroses originate from the ego's refusing to accept a powerful instinctual impulse in the id or to help it to find a motor outlet, or from the ego's forbidding that impulse the object at which it is aiming. In such a case the ego defends itself against the instinctual impulse by the mechanisms of repression. The repressed material struggles against this fate. It creates for itself, along paths over which the ego has no power, a substitutive representation (which forces itself upon the ego by way of a compromise) – the symptom. The ego finds its unity threatened and impaired by this intruder, and it continues to struggle against the symptom, just as it fended off the original instinctual impulse. All this produces the picture of a neurosis. It is no contradiction to this that, in undertaking the repression, the ego is at bottom following the commands of its super-ego – commands which, in their turn, originate from influences in the external world that have found representation in the super-ego. The fact remains that the ego *has* taken sides with those powers, that in it their demands have more strength than the instinctual demands of the id, and that the ego is the power which sets the repression in motion against the portion of the id concerned and which fortifies the repression by means of the anticathexis of resistance. The ego has come into conflict with the id in the service of the super-ego and of reality; and this is the state of affairs in every transference neurosis.

On the other side, it is equally easy, from the knowledge we have so far gained of the mechanism of the psychosis, to adduce examples which point to a disturbance in the relationship between the ego and the external world. In Meynert's amentia – an acute hallucinatory confusion which is perhaps the most extreme and striking form of psychosis – either the external world is not perceived at all, or the perception of it has no effect whatever.[1] Normally, the external world governs the ego in two ways: firstly, by current, present perceptions which are always renewable, and secondly, by the store of memories of earlier perceptions which, in the shape of an 'internal world', form a possession of the ego and a constituent part of it. In amentia, not only is the acceptance of new perceptions refused, but the internal world, too, which, as a copy of the external world, has up till now represented it, loses its significance (its cathexis). The ego creates, autocratically, a new external and internal world; and there can be no doubt of two facts – that this new world is constructed in accordance with the id's wishful impulses, and that the motive of this dissociation from the external world is some very serious frustration by reality of a wish – a frustration which seems intolerable. The close affinity of this psychosis to normal dreams is unmistakable. A precondition of dreaming, moreover, is a state of sleep, and one of the features of sleep is a complete turning away from perception and the external world.[2]

We know that other forms of psychosis, the schizophrenias, are inclined to end in affective hebetude – that is, in a loss of all participation in the external world. In regard to the genesis of delusions, a fair number of analyses have taught us that the delusion is found applied like a patch over the place where originally a rent had appeared in the ego's relation to the external world. If this precondition of a conflict with the external world is not much more noticeable to us than it now is, that is because, in the clinical picture of the psychosis, the manifestations of the pathogenic process are often overlaid by manifestations of an attempt at a cure or a reconstruction.[3]

1. [A passage in Chapter VIII of Freud's posthumous *Outline of Psycho-Analysis* (1940a [1938]) qualifies this statement. Cf. footnote p. 217 below.]

2. [Cf. the metapsychological paper on dreams (1917d).]

3. [Cf. the Schreber analysis (1911c), *P.F.L.*, **9**, 209–10.]

The aetiology common to the onset of a psychoneurosis and of a psychosis always remains the same. It consists in a frustration, a non-fulfilment, of one of those childhood wishes which are for ever undefeated and which are so deeply rooted in our phylogenetically determined organization. This frustration is in the last resort always an external one;[1] but in the individual case it may proceed from the internal agency (in the super-ego) which has taken over the representation of the demands of reality. The pathogenic effect depends on whether, in a conflictual tension of this kind, the ego remains true to its dependence on the external world and attempts to silence the id, or whether it lets itself be overcome by the id and thus torn away from reality. A complication is introduced into this apparently simple situation, however, by the existence of the super-ego, which, through a link that is not yet clear to us, unites in itself influences coming from the id as well as from the external world, and is to some extent an ideal model of what the whole endeavour of the ego is aiming at – a reconciliation between its various dependent relationships.[2] The attitude of the super-ego should be taken into account – which has not hitherto been done – in every form of psychical illness. We may provisionally assume that there must also be illnesses which are based on a conflict between the ego and the super-ego. Analysis gives us a right to suppose that melancholia is a typical example of this group; and we would set aside the name of 'narcissistic psychoneuroses' for disorders of that kind. Nor will it clash with our impressions if we find reasons for separating states like melancholia from the other psychoses. We now see that we have been able to make our simple genetic formula more complete, without dropping it. Transference neuroses correspond to a conflict between the ego and the id; narcissistic neuroses, to a conflict between the ego and the super-ego; and psychoses, to

1. [See some remarks in the discussion of frustration in 'Types of Onset of Neurosis' (1912c), p. 123 above.]

2. [Cf. 'The Economic Problem of Masochism' (1924c).]

one between the ego and the external world. It is true that we cannot tell at once whether we have really gained any new knowledge by this, or have only enriched our store of formulas; but I think that this possible application of the proposed differentiation of the mental apparatus into an ego, a super-ego and an id cannot fail to give us courage to keep that hypothesis steadily in view.

The thesis that neuroses and psychoses originate in the ego's conflicts with its various ruling agencies – that is, therefore, that they reflect a failure in the functioning of the ego, which is at pains to reconcile all the various demands made on it – this thesis needs to be supplemented in one further point. One would like to know in what circumstances and by what means the ego can succeed in emerging from such conflicts, which are certainly always present, without falling ill. This is a new field of research, in which no doubt the most varied factors will come up for examination. Two of them, however, can be stressed at once. In the first place, the outcome of all such situations will undoubtedly depend on economic considerations – on the relative magnitude of the trends which are struggling with one another. In the second place, it will be possible for the ego to avoid a rupture in any direction by deforming itself, by submitting to encroachments on its own unity and even perhaps by effecting a cleavage or division of itself.[1] In this way the inconsistencies, eccentricities and follies of men would appear in a similar light to their sexual perversions, through the acceptance of which they spare themselves repressions.

In conclusion, there remains to be considered the question of what the mechanism, analogous to repression, can be by

---

1. [This is an early hint at a problem that was to occupy Freud in his later years. It was first discussed at length in the paper on 'Fetishism' (1927e) and afterwards in two unfinished works, in 'Splitting of the Ego in the Process of Defence' (1940e [1938]) and in Chapter VIII of the *Outline* (1940a [1938]).]

means of which the ego detaches itself from the external world. This cannot, I think, be answered without fresh investigations; but such a mechanism, it would seem, must, like repression, comprise a withdrawal of the cathexis sent out by the ego.[1]

1. [This problem, too – the nature of what Freud later called '*Verleugnung*', 'disavowal' – was discussed in the later papers mentioned in the previous footnote. See an Editor's footnote to 'The Infantile Genital Organization' (1923*e*), *P.F.L.*, **7**, 310 *n.* 1, for a fuller discussion of the question.]

THE LOSS OF REALITY IN
NEUROSIS AND PSYCHOSIS
(1924)

EDITOR'S NOTE

DER REALITATSVERLUST BEI NEUROSE UND PSYCHOSE

(A) GERMAN EDITIONS:

1924   *Int. Z. Psychoanal.*, **10** (4), 374–9.
1925   *Gesammelte Schriften*, **6**, 409–14.
1940   *Gesammelte Werke*, **13**, 363–8.

(B) ENGLISH TRANSLATIONS:

'The Loss of Reality in Neurosis and Psychosis'

1924   *Collected Papers*, **2**, 277–82. (Tr. Joan Riviere.)
1961   *Standard Edition*, **19**, 181–7. (Based on the translation of 1924.)

According to a statement in a footnote to the first English translation (*Collected Papers*, **2**, 277), it was actually published before the German original.

The present edition is a corrected reprint of the *Standard Edition* version, with one or two editorial modifications.

This paper was written by the end of May, 1924, for it was read by Abraham during that month. It continues the discussion begun in the earlier paper 'Neurosis and Psychosis' (1924*b*), p. 213 above, which it amplifies and corrects. Some doubts about the validity of the distinction drawn in these two papers were discussed by Freud later, in his paper on 'Fetishism' (1927*e*).

THE LOSS OF REALITY IN
NEUROSIS AND PSYCHOSIS

I HAVE recently[1] indicated as one of the features which differentiate a neurosis from a psychosis the fact that in a neurosis the ego, in its dependence on reality, suppresses a piece of the id (of instinctual life), whereas in a psychosis, this same ego, in the service of the id, withdraws from a piece of reality. Thus for a neurosis the decisive factor would be the predominance of the influence of reality, whereas for a psychosis it would be the predominance of the id. In a psychosis, a loss of reality would necessarily be present, whereas in a neurosis, it would seem, this loss would be avoided.

But this does not at all agree with the observation which all of us can make that every neurosis disturbs the patient's relation to reality in some way, that it serves him as a means of withdrawing from reality, and that, in its severe forms, it actually signifies a flight from real life. This contradiction seems a serious one; but it is easily resolved, and the explanation of it will in fact help us to understand neuroses.

For the contradiction exists only as long as we keep our eyes fixed on the situation at the *beginning* of the neurosis, in which the ego, in the service of reality, sets about the repression of an instinctual impulse. This, however, is not yet the neurosis itself. The neurosis consists rather in the processes which provide a compensation for the portion of the id that has been damaged – that is to say, in the reaction against the repression and in the failure of the repression. The loosening of the relation to reality is a consequence of this second step in the formation of a neurosis, and it ought not to surprise us if a detailed examination shows that the loss of reality affects precisely that piece of

1. 'Neurosis and Psychosis' (1924*b*) [this volume, p. 213 above].

reality as a result of whose demands the instinctual repression ensued.

There is nothing new in our characterization of neurosis as the result of a repression that has failed. We have said this all along,[1] and it is only because of the next context in which we are viewing the subject that it has been necessary to repeat it.

Incidentally, the same objection arises in a specially marked manner when we are dealing with a neurosis in which the exciting cause (the 'traumatic scene') is known, and in which one can see how the person concerned turns away from the experience and consigns it to amnesia. Let me go back by way of example to a case analysed a great many years ago,[2] in which the patient, a young woman, was in love with her brother-in-law. Standing beside her sister's death-bed, she was horrified at having the thought: 'Now he is free and can marry me.' This scene was instantly forgotten, and thus the process of regression, which led to her hysterical pains, was set in motion. It is instructive precisely in this case, moreover, to learn along what path the neurosis attempted to solve the conflict. It took away from the value of the change that had occurred in reality, by repressing the instinctual demand which had emerged – that is, her love for her brother-in-law. The *psychotic* reaction would have been a disavowal[3] of the fact of her sister's death.

We might expect that when a psychosis comes into being, something analogous to the process in a neurosis occurs,

---

1. [The notion that the 'return of the repressed' constitutes 'the illness proper' is already stated in Draft K of the Fliess correspondence, of January 1, 1896 (Freud 1950a). A little later Freud restated this, using the actual words 'failure of defence' as equivalent to 'return of the repressed', in Section II of the second paper on 'The Neuro-Psychoses of Defence' (1896b).]

2. In *Studies on Hysteria* (1895d). [P.F.L., **3**, 226 and 238. The words of the patient, Fräulein Elisabeth von R., are not here quoted verbatim.]

3. [See an Editor's footnote to 'Neurosis and Psychosis' (1924b), p. 218 *n*. above.]

though, of course, between different agencies of the mind; thus we might expect that in a psychosis, too, two steps could be discerned, of which the first would drag the ego away, this time from reality, while the second would try to make good the damage done and re-establish the subject's relations to reality at the expense of the id. And, in fact, some analogy of the sort can be observed in a psychosis. Here, too, there are two steps, the second of which has the character of a reparation. But beyond that the analogy gives way to a far more extensive similarity between the two processes. The second step of the psychosis is indeed intended to make good the loss of reality, not, however, at the expense of a restriction of the id – as happens in neurosis at the expense of the relation to reality – but in another, more autocratic manner, by the creation of a new reality which no longer raises the same objections as the old one that has been given up. The second step, therefore, both in neurosis and psychosis, is supported by the same trends. In both cases it serves the desire for power of the id, which will not allow itself to be dictated to by reality. Both neurosis and psychosis are thus the expression of a rebellion on the part of the id against the external world, of its unwillingness – or, if one prefers, its incapacity – to adapt itself to the exigencies of reality, to ᾿Ανάγκη [Necessity].[1] Neurosis and psychosis differ from each other far more in their first, introductory, reaction than in the attempt at reparation which follows it.

Accordingly, the initial difference is expressed thus in the final outcome: in neurosis a piece of reality is avoided by a sort of flight, whereas in psychosis it is remodelled. Or we might say: in psychosis, the initial flight is succeeded by an active phase of remodelling; in neurosis, the initial obedience is succeeded by a deferred attempt at flight. Or again, expressed in yet another way: neurosis does not disavow the reality, it only ignores it; psychosis disavows it and tries to replace it. We call behaviour normal or 'healthy', if it combines certain features

1. [See 'The Economic Problem of Masochism' (1924c).]

of both reactions – if it disavows the reality as little as does a neurosis, but if it then exerts itself, as does a psychosis, to effect an alteration of that reality. Of course, this expedient, normal, behaviour leads to work being carried out on the external world; it does not stop, as in psychosis, at effecting internal changes. It is no longer *autoplastic* but *alloplastic*.[1]

In a psychosis, the transforming of reality is carried out upon the psychical precipitates of former relations to it – that is, upon the memory-traces, ideas and judgements which have been previously derived from reality and by which reality was represented in the mind. But this relation was never a closed one; it was continually being enriched and altered by fresh perceptions. Thus the psychosis is also faced with the task of procuring for itself perceptions of a kind which shall correspond to the new reality; and this is most radically effected by means of hallucination. The fact that, in so many forms and cases of psychosis, the paramnesias, the delusions and the hallucinations that occur are of a most distressing character and are bound up with a generation of anxiety – this fact is without doubt a sign that the whole process of remodelling is carried through against forces which oppose it violently. We may construct the process on the model of a neurosis, with which we are more familiar. There we see that a reaction of anxiety sets in whenever the repressed instinct makes a thrust forward, and that the outcome of the conflict is only a compromise and does not provide complete satisfaction. Probably in a psychosis the rejected piece of reality constantly forces itself upon the mind, just as the repressed instinct does in a neurosis, and that is why in both cases the consequences too are the same. The elucidation of the various mechanisms which are designed, in the psychoses, to

1. [These terms are possibly due to Ferenczi, who used them in a paper on 'The Phenomena of Hysterical Materialization' (1919, 24; English trans., 1926, 97). But he there appears to attribute them to Freud who, however, does not seem to have used them elsewhere than in this passage.]

turn the subject away from reality and to reconstruct reality – this is a task for specialized psychiatric study which has not yet been taken in hand.[1]

There is, therefore, a further analogy between a neurosis and a psychosis, in that in both of them the task which is undertaken in the second step is partly unsuccessful. For the repressed instinct is unable to procure a full substitute (in neurosis); and the representation of reality cannot be remoulded into satisfying forms (not, at least, in every species of mental illness). But the emphasis is different in the two cases. In a psychosis it falls entirely on the first step, which is pathological in itself and cannot but lead to illness. In a neuroses, on the other hand, it falls on the second step, on the failure of the repression, whereas the first step may succeed, and does succeed in innumerable instances without overstepping the bounds of health – even though it does so at a certain price and not without leaving behind traces of the psychical expenditure it has called for. These distinctions, and perhaps many others as well, are a result of the topographical difference in the initial situation of the pathogenic conflict – namely whether in it the ego yielded to its allegiance to the real world or to its dependence on the id.

A neurosis usually contents itself with avoiding the piece of reality in question and protecting itself against coming into contact with it. The sharp distinction between neurosis and psychosis, however, is weakened by the circumstance that in neurosis, too, there is no lack of attempts to replace a disagreeable reality by one which is more in keeping with the subject's wishes. This is made possible by the existence of a *world of phantasy*, of a domain which became separated from the real external world at the time of the introduction of the reality principle. This domain has since been kept free from the

1. [Cf. however, some beginnings made by Freud himself as regards paranoia, in the Schreber analysis (1911c) (P.F.L., **9**, 208–10), and 'paraphrenia', in his papers on 'Narcissism' (1914c), 'The Unconscious' (1915e) and the metapsychology of dreams (1917d).]

demands of the exigencies of life, like a kind of 'reservation';[1] it is not inaccessible to the ego, but is only loosely attached to it. It is from this world of phantasy that the neurosis draws the material for its new wishful constructions, and it usually finds that material along the path of regression to a more satisfying real past.

It can hardly be doubted that the world of phantasy plays the same part in psychosis and that there, too, it is the storehouse from which the materials or the pattern for building the new reality are derived. But whereas the new, imaginary external world of a psychosis attempts to put itself in the place of external reality, that of a neurosis, on the contrary, is apt, like the play of children, to attach itself to a piece of reality – a different piece from the one against which it has to defend itself – and to lend that piece a special importance and a secret meaning which we (not always quite appropriately) call a *symbolic* one. Thus we see that both in neurosis and psychosis there comes into consideration the question not only of a *loss of reality* but also of a *substitute for reality*.

1. [Cf. the paper on the 'Two Principles of Mental Functioning' (1911*b*). See also the earlier paper on 'Hysterical Phantasies (1908*a*), p. 87 above.]

INHIBITIONS, SYMPTOMS AND
ANXIETY
(1926 [1925])

EDITOR'S INTRODUCTION

HEMMUNG, SYMPTOM UND ANGST

(A) GERMAN EDITIONS:

1926   Leipzig, Vienna and Zurich: Internationaler Psycho-analytischer Verlag. Pp. 136.

1928   *Gesammelte Schriften*, **11**, 23–115.

1931   *Neurosenlehre und Technik*, 205–99.

1948   *Gesammelte Werke*, **14**, 113–205.

(B) ENGLISH TRANSLATIONS:

Inhibition, Symptom and Anxiety

1927   Stamford, Conn.: Psychoanalytical Institute. Pp. vi + 103. (Tr. supervised L. Pierce Clark; Preface S. Ferenczi.)

Inhibitions, Symptoms and Anxiety

1935–6   *Psychoanal. Quart.*, **4** (4), 616–25; **5** (1), 1–28; (2) 261–279; (3) 415–43. (Tr. H. A. Bunker.)

The Problem of Anxiety

1936   New York: Psychoanalytic Quarterly Press and W. W. Norton. Pp. vii + 165. (The above reprinted in volume form.)

Inhibitions, Symptoms and Anxiety

1936   London: Hogarth Press and Institute of Psycho-Analysis. Pp. 179. (Tr. Alix Strachey.)

1959   *Standard Edition*, **20**, 75–175. (Considerably modified version of the above.)

All three of the translations were authorized by Freud, and, as Ernest Jones points out (1957, 139–40), the translators of the last two prepared their work simultaneously, and in complete ignorance of each other's activities.

The present edition is a corrected reprint of the *Standard Edition* version, with several editorial changes.

We learn from Ernest Jones that this book was written in July 1925, and that it was revised in December of the same year and published in the third week of the following February.

The topics with which it deals range over a wide field, and there are signs that Freud found an unusual difficulty in unifying the work. This is shown, for instance, in the way in which the same subject often comes up for discussion at more than one point in very similar terms, in the necessity under which Freud found himself of tidying up a number of separate questions in his 'Addenda', and even in the actual title of the book. It is nevertheless true that – in spite of such important side-issues as the different classes of resistance, the distinction between repression and defence, and the relations between anxiety, pain and mourning – the problem of anxiety is its main theme. This problem was constantly present to Freud's mind from the beginning to the end of his psychological studies, and though on some aspects of the subject his opinions underwent little modification, on others, as he tells us in these pages, they were considerably altered. It will perhaps be of interest to trace, if only roughly, the history of these changes in two or three of the more important issues involved.

(a) ANXIETY AS TRANSFORMED LIBIDO

It was in the course of investigating the 'actual' neuroses that Freud first came upon the problem of anxiety, and his earliest published discussion of it will be found in his first paper on the anxiety neuroses (1895*b*), this volume, p. 35 ff. At that time he was still largely under the influence of his neurological studies and he was deep in his attempt at expressing the data of psychology in physiological terms. In particular, following Fechner, he had taken as a fundamental postulate the 'principle of constancy', according to which there was an inherent tendency in the nervous system to reduce, or at least to keep constant, the amount of excitation present in it. When, therefore, he made the clinical discovery that in cases of anxiety neuroses it was always possible to discover some interference with the discharge of sexual tension, it was natural for him to conclude that the accumulated excitation was finding its way out in the transformed shape of anxiety. He regarded this as a purely physical process without any psychological determinants.

From the first the anxiety occurring in phobias or in obsessional neuroses raised a complication, for here the presence of psychological events could not be excluded. But, as regards the emergence of anxiety, the explanation remained the same. In these cases – in the psychoneuroses – the *reason* for the accumulation of undischarged excitation was a psychological one: repression. But what followed was the same as in the 'actual' neuroses: the accumulated excitation (or libido) was transformed directly into anxiety.

Freud maintained and repeated this view for about thirty years. For example, in 1920 he could still write in a footnote to the fourth edition of the *Three Essays*: 'One of the most important results of psychoanalytic research is this discovery that neurotic anxiety arises out of libido, that it is the product of a transformation of it, and that it is thus related to it in the same kind of way as vinegar is to wine.' (*P.F.L.*, **7**, 147.) It is curious to note, however, that at quite an early stage Freud seems to have been assailed by doubts on the subject. In a letter to Fliess of 14 November 1897 (Freud, 1950*a*, Letters 75), he remarks, without any apparent connection with the rest of what he has been writing about: 'I have decided, then, henceforth to regard

as separate factors what causes libido and what causes anxiety.'
No further evidence is anywhere to be found of this isolated
recantation. In the work before us Freud gave up the theory
he had held for so long. He no longer regarded anxiety as
transformed libido, but as a reaction on a particular model to
situations of danger. But even here he still maintained (p. 298f.)
that it was very possible that in the case of the anxiety neurosis
'what finds discharge in the generating of anxiety is precisely
the surplus of unutilized libido'. This last relic of the old theory
was to be abandoned a few years later. In a passage near the end
of his discussion of anxiety in Lecture 32 of his *New Introductory
Lectures* (1933a) he wrote that in the anxiety neurosis, too, the
appearance of anxiety was a reaction to a traumatic situation:
'we shall no longer maintain that it is the libido itself that is
turned into anxiety in such cases.' (*P.F.L.*, **2**, 127.)

(b) REALISTIC AND NEUROTIC ANXIETY

In spite of his theory that neurotic anxiety was merely transformed libido, Freud was from the first at pains to insist on the
close relation between anxiety due to external and to instinctual dangers. This is clearly stated in his first paper on the
anxiety neuroses (1895b), p. 59 above.

This position, especially in connection with phobias, was
elaborated later in many of Freud's writings – for instance, in
Lecture 25 of the *Introductory Lectures*. But it was difficult to
maintain the sameness of the anxiety in the two classes of case
so long as the direct derivation of anxiety from libido was
insisted upon for the 'actual' neuroses. With the abandonment of this view and with the new distinction between
automatic anxiety and anxiety as a signal, the whole situation
was clarified and there ceased to be any reason for seeing a
generic difference between neurotic and realistic anxiety.

(c) THE TRAUMATIC SITUATION AND
SITUATIONS OF DANGER

It adds to the difficulties of this book that the distinction between anxiety as a direct and automatic reaction to a trauma and anxiety as a signal of the danger of the approach of such a trauma, although touched on at several earlier points, is only clinched in the very last chapter. (A later and shorter account, given in Lecture 32 of the *New Introductory Lectures*, may perhaps be found easier to grasp: *P.F.L.*, **2**, 117–27.)

The fundamental determinant of automatic anxiety is the occurrence of a traumatic situation; and the essence of this is an experience of helplessness on the part of the ego in the face of an accumulation of excitation, whether of external or of internal origin, which cannot be dealt with (pp. 294 and 326). Anxiety 'as a signal' is the response of the ego to the threat of the occurrence of a traumatic situation. Such a threat constitutes a situation of danger. Internal dangers change with the period of life (pp. 305–6), but they have a common characteristic, namely that they involve separation from, or loss of, a loved object, or a loss of its love (p. 309) – a loss or separation which might in various ways lead to an accumulation of unsatisfied desires and so to a situation of helplessness.

The various specific dangers which are liable to precipitate a traumatic situation at different times of life are, put briefly: birth, loss of the mother as an object, loss of the penis, loss of the object's love, loss of the super-ego's love. The question of birth is dealt with in section (*e*) below. The danger of castration with its devastating effects is no doubt the most familiar of all these dangers. But it is worth recalling a footnote added in 1923 to the case history of 'Little Hans' (1909*b*), in which Freud deprecates the application of the name 'castration complex' to the other kinds of separation which the child must inevitably experience (*P.F.L.*, **8**, 172 *n.* 2). We may possibly see in that passage a first hint at the concept of anxiety due to separation which comes into prominence here. The stress laid on the danger of losing the love of the loved object is explicitly related (on p. 300 f.) to the characteristics of female sexuality, which had only recently begun to occupy Freud's mind.[1] Finally, the danger of losing the love of the super-ego carries us back to the long-debated problems of the sense of guilt, which had been re-stated only shortly before in *The Ego and the Id* (1923*b*).

(*d*) ANXIETY AS A SIGNAL

As applied to unpleasure in general, this notion was a very old one of Freud's, dating from the period of his friendship with Fliess, and is closely related to his view that thinking must aim at restricting the development of affect in thought-activity to the minimum needed to act as a signal. In 'The Unconscious' (1915*e*), the idea is already applied to anxiety; similarly in Lecture 25 of the *Introductory Lectures* the state of 'anxious expectancy' is described in one or two places as offering a 'signal' to prevent an outbreak of severe anxiety. From this it was not a long step to the illuminating exposition in these pages, where the concept is, incidentally, also first introduced as a signal of 'unpleasure' (p. 243) and only subsequently as one of 'anxiety'.

(*e*) ANXIETY AND BIRTH

There remains the question of what it is that determines the *form* in which anxiety is manifested. This, too, was discussed by

1. In his papers on 'The Dissolution of the Oedipus Complex' (1924*d*) and on the physiological distinction between the sexes (1925*j*), Freud had begun to emphasize the differences between the sexual development of boys and girls and at the same time to insist on the fact that in both sexes the mother is the first love-object. The history of this shift of emphasis in his views will be found discussed in the Editor's Note to the second of these two papers (*P.F.L.*, **7**, 326 ff.).

Freud in his early writings. To begin with (consistently with his view of anxiety as transformed libido) he regarded the most striking of its symptoms – the breathlessness and palpitations – as elements in the act of copulation, which, in the absence of the normal means of discharging the excitation, made their appearance in an isolated and exaggerated shape. Cf. the first paper on anxiety neurosis (1895b), p. 59 and n. above. It is not clear how all this fitted in with Freud's views on the expression of the emotions in general. These seem certainly to have been ultimately derived from Darwin. In the Studies on Hysteria (1895d) he twice quoted Darwin's volume on the subject (Darwin, 1872), and on the second occasion recalled that Darwin has taught us that the expression of the emotions 'consists of actions which originally had a meaning and served a purpose' (P.F.L., 3, 254). Much later, in Lecture 25 of the Introductory Lectures (1916–17), P.F.L., 1, 444, he took up this point again, and expressed his belief that the 'nucleus' of an affect is 'the repetition of some particular significant experience'. He recalled, too, the explanation he had earlier given of hysterical attacks (1909a, p. 100 above) as revivals of events in infancy, and added his conclusion that 'a hysterical attack may be likened to a freshly constructed individual affect, and a normal affect to the expression of a general hysteria which has become a heritage'. He repeats this theory in almost the same terms in the present work (pp. 244f. and 289f.).

Whatever part this theory of the affects played in Freud's earlier explanation of the form taken by anxiety, it played an essential one in his new explanation, which emerged, apparently without warning, in a footnote added to the second edition (1909) of The Interpretation of Dreams (1900a, P.F.L., 4, 525–6 n.) At the end of some discussion of phantasies about life in the womb, he went on (and printed the sentence in spaced type); 'Moreover, the act of birth is the first experience of anxiety, and thus the source and prototype of the affect of anxiety.' Thereafter that theory was never dropped. Freud gave it special prominence in the first of his papers on the psychology of love (1910*h*). The connection between anxiety and birth also re-appears in Lecture 25 of the *Introductory Lectures* (loc. cit) and near the end of *The Ego and the Id* (1923*b*), where Freud spoke of birth as 'the first great anxiety-state'. This carries us up to the time of the publication of Rank's book *The Trauma of Birth* (1924).

Rank's book was far more than an adoption of Freud's ex-planation of the *form* taken by anxiety. He argued that all later attacks of anxiety were attempts at 'abreacting' the trauma of birth. He accounted for all neuroses on similar lines, in-cidentally dethroning the Oedipus complex, and proposed a reformed therapeutic technique based on the overcoming of the birth trauma. Freud's published references to the book seemed at first to be favourable. But the present work shows a complete and final reversal of that opinion. His rejection of Rank's views, however, stimulated him to a reconsideration of his own, and *Inhibitions, Symptoms and Anxiety* was the result.

INHIBITIONS, SYMPTOMS AND
ANXIETY

I

IN the description of pathological phenomena, linguistic usage enables us to distinguish symptoms from inhibitions, without, however, attaching much importance to the distinction. Indeed, we might hardly think it worth while to differentiate exactly between the two, were it not for the fact that we meet with illnesses in which we observe the presence of inhibitions but not of symptoms and are curious to know the reason for this.

The two concepts are not upon the same plane. Inhibition has a special relation to function. It does not necessarily have a pathological implication. One can quite well call a normal restriction of a function an inhibition of it. A symptom, on the other hand, actually denotes the presence of some pathological process. Thus, an inhibition may be a symptom as well. Linguistic usage, then, employs the word *inhibition* when there is a simple lowering of function, and *symptom* when a function has undergone some unusual change or when a new phenomenon has arisen out of it. Very often it seems to be quite an arbitrary matter whether we emphasize the positive side of a pathological process and call its outcome a symptom, or its negative side and call its outcome an inhibition. But all this is really of little interest; and the problem as we have stated it does not carry us very far.

Since the concept of inhibition is so intimately associated with that of function, it might be helpful to examine the various functions of the ego with a view to discovering the forms which any disturbance of those functions assumes in each of the different neurotic affections. Let us pick out for a comparative study of this kind the sexual function and those of eating, of locomotion and of professional work.

(a) The sexual function is liable to a great number of disturbances, most of which exhibit the characteristics of simple inhibitions. These are classed together as psychical impotence. The normal performance of the sexual function can only come about as the result of a very complicated process, and disturbances may appear at any point in it. In men the chief stages at which inhibition occurs are shown by: a turning away of the libido at the very beginning of the process (psychical unpleasure); an absence of the physical preparation for it (lack of erection); an abridgement of the sexual act (*ejaculatio praecox*), an occurrence which might equally well be regarded as a symptom; an arrest of the act before it has reached its natural conclusion (absence of ejaculation); or a non-appearance of the psychical outcome (lack of the feeling of pleasure in orgasm). Other disturbances arise from the sexual function becoming dependent on special conditions of a perverse or fetishist nature.

That there is a relationship between inhibition and anxiety is pretty evident. Some inhibitions obviously represent a relinquishment of a function because its exercise would produce anxiety. Many women are openly afraid of the sexual function. We class this anxiety under hysteria, just as we do the defensive symptom of disgust which, arising originally as a deferred reaction to the experiencing of a passive sexual act, appears later whenever the *idea* of such an act is presented. Furthermore, many obsessional acts turn out to be measures of precaution and security against sexual experiences and are thus of a phobic character.

This is not very illuminating. We can only note that disturbances of the sexual function are brought about by a great variety of means. (1) The libido may simply be turned away (this seems most readily to produce what we regard as an inhibition pure and simple); (2) the function may be less well carried out; (3) it may be hampered by having conditions attached to it, or modified by being diverted to other aims; (4) it may be prevented by security measures; (5) if it cannot be prevented from starting, it may be immediately interrupted by the appearance of anxiety; and (6), if it is nevertheless carried out, there may be a subsequent reaction of protest against it and an attempt to undo what has been done.

(b) The function of nutrition is most frequently disturbed by a disinclination to eat, brought about by a withdrawal of libido. An increase in the desire to eat is also a not uncommon thing. The compulsion to eat is attributed to a fear of starving; but this is a subject which has been but little studied. The symptoms of vomiting is known to us as a hysterical defence against eating. Refusal to eat owing to anxiety is a concomitant of psychotic states (delusions of being poisoned).

(c) In some neurotic conditions locomotion is inhibited by a disinclination to walk or a weakness in walking. In hysteria there will be a paralysis of the motor apparatus, or this one special function of the apparatus will be abolished (abasia). Especially characteristic are the increased difficulties that appear in locomotion owing to the introduction of certain stipulations whose non-observance results in anxiety (phobia).

(d) In inhibition in work – a thing which we so often have to deal with as an isolated symptom in our therapeutic work – the subject feels a decrease in his pleasure in it or becomes less able to do it well; or he has certain reactions to it, like fatigue, giddiness or sickness, if he is obliged to go on with it. If he is a hysteric he will have to give up his work owing to the appearance of organic and functional paralyses which make it impossible for him to carry it on. If he is an obsessional neurotic he will be perpetually being distracted from his work or losing time over it through the introduction of delays and repetitions.

Our survey might be extended to other functions as well; but there would be nothing more to be learnt by doing so. For we should not penetrate below the surface of the phenomena presented to us. Let us then proceed to describe inhibition in such a way as to leave very little doubt about what is meant by it, and say that inhibition is the expression of a *restriction of an ego-function*. A restriction of this kind can itself have very different causes. Some of the mechanisms involved in this renunciation of function are well known to us, as is a certain general purpose which governs it.

This purpose is more easily recognizable in the *specific* inhibition. Analysis shows that when activities like playing the piano, writing or even walking are subjected to neurotic inhibitions it is because the physical organs brought into play – the fingers or the legs – have become too strongly erotized. It has been discovered as a general fact that the ego-function of an organ is impaired if its erotogenicity – its sexual significance – is increased. It behaves, if I may be allowed a rather absurd analogy, like a maid-servant who refuses to go on cooking because her master has started a love-affair with her. As soon as writing, which entails making a liquid flow out of a tube on to a piece of white paper, assumes the significance of copulation, or as soon as walking becomes a symbolic substitute for treading upon the body of mother earth, both writing and walking are stopped because they represent the performance of a forbidden sexual act. The ego renounces these functions, which are within its sphere, in order not to have to undertake fresh measures of repression – *in order to avoid a conflict with the id*.

There are clearly also inhibitions which serve the purpose of self-punishment. This is often the case in inhibitions of professional activities. The ego is not allowed to carry on those activities, because they would bring success and gain, and these are things which the severe super-ego has forbidden. So the ego gives them up too, *in order to avoid coming into conflict with the super-ego.*

The more *generalized* inhibitions of the ego obey a different mechanism of a simple kind. When the ego is involved in a particularly difficult psychical task, as occurs in mourning, or when there is some tremendous suppression of affect or when a continual flood of sexual phantasies has to be kept down, it loses so much of the energy at its disposal that it has to cut down the expenditure of it at many points at once. It is in the position of a speculator whose money has become tied up in his various enterprises. I came across an instructive example of this kind of intense, though short-lived, general inhibition. The patient, an obsessional neurotic, used to be overcome by a paralysing fatigue which lasted for one or more days whenever something occurred which should obviously have thrown him into a rage. We have here a point from which it should be possible to reach an understanding of the condition of general inhibition which characterizes states of depression, including the gravest form of them, melancholia.

As regards inhibitions, then, we may say in conclusion that they are restrictions of the functions of the ego which have been either imposed as a measure of precaution or brought about as a result of an impoverishment of energy; and we can see without difficulty in what respect an inhibition differs from a symptom: for a symptom cannot any longer be described as a process that takes place within, or acts upon, the ego.

THE main characteristics of the formation of symptoms have long since been studied and, I hope, established beyond dispute.[1] A symptom is a sign of, and a substitute for, an instinctual satisfaction which has remained in abeyance; it is a consequence of the process of repression. Repression proceeds from the ego when the latter – it may be at the behest of the superego – refuses to associate itself with an instinctual cathexis which has been aroused in the id. The ego is able by means of repression to keep the idea which is the vehicle of the reprehensible impulse from becoming conscious. Analysis shows that the idea often persists as an unconscious formation.

So far everything seems clear; but we soon come upon difficulties which have not as yet been solved. Up till now our account of what occurs in repression has laid great stress on this point of exclusion from consciousness.[2] But it has left other points open to uncertainty. One question that arose was, what happened to the instinctual impulse which has been activated in the id and which sought satisfaction? The answer was an indirect one. It was that owing to the process of repression the pleasure that would have been expected from satisfaction had been transformed into unpleasure. But we were then faced with the problem of how the satisfaction of an instinct could produce unpleasure. The whole matter can be clarified, I think, if we commit ourselves to the definite statement that as a result of repression the intended course of the excitatory process in the id does not occur at all; the ego succeeds in inhibiting or deflecting it. If this is so the problem of 'transformation of affect' under repression disappears.[3] At the same time this view

1. [See, for instance, the *Three Essays* (1905*d*), P.F.L., **7**, 78.]
2. [Cf. the statement very near the beginning of 'Repression' (1915*d*).]
3. [The question was discussed by Freud in the 'Dora' case history

implies a concession to the ego that it can exert a very extensive influence over processes in the id, and we shall have to find out in what way it is able to develop such surprising powers.

It seems to me that the ego obtains this influence in virtue of its intimate connections with the perceptual system – connections which, as we know, constitute its essence and provide the basis of its differentiation from the id. The function of this system, which we have called *Pcpt.-Cs.*, is bound up with the phenomenon of consciousness.[1] It receives excitations not only from outside but from within, and endeavours, by means of the sensations of pleasure and unpleasure which reach it from these quarters, to direct the course of mental events in accordance with the pleasure principle. We are very apt to think of the ego as powerless against the id; but when it is opposed to an instinctual process in the id it has only to give a '*signal of unpleasure*'[2] in order to attain its object with the aid of that almost omnipotent institution, the pleasure principle. To take this situation by itself for a moment, we can illustrate it by an example from another field. Let us imagine a country in which a certain small faction objects to a proposed measure the passage of which would have the support of the masses. This minority obtains command of the press and by its help manipulates the supreme arbiter, 'public opinion', and so succeeds in preventing the measure from being passed.

But this explanation opens up fresh problems. Where does the energy come from which is employed for giving the signal of unpleasure? Here we may be assisted by the idea that a defence against an unwelcome *internal* process will be modelled upon the defence adopted against an *external* stimulus, that the ego wards off internal and external dangers alike along identical

---

(1905*e*), *P.F.L.*, **8**, 59, where an Editor's footnote gives a number of other references to the subject.]

1. [Cf. the beginning of Chapter IV of *Beyond the Pleasure Principle* (1920*g*).]

2. [See Editor's Introduction, p. 234 above.]

lines. In the case of external danger the organism has recourse to attempts at flight. The first thing it does is to withdraw cathexis from the perception of the dangerous object; later on it discovers that it is a better plan to perform muscular movements of such a sort as will render perception of the dangerous object impossible even in the absence of any refusal to perceive it – that it is a better plan, that is, to remove itself from the sphere of danger. Repression is an equivalent of this attempt at flight. The ego withdraws its (preconscious) cathexis from the instinctual representative[1] that is to be repressed and uses that cathexis for the purpose of releasing unpleasure (anxiety). The problem of how anxiety arises in connection with repression may be no simple one; but we may legitimately hold firmly to the idea that the ego is the actual seat of anxiety and give up our earlier view that the cathectic energy of the repressed impulse is automatically turned into anxiety. If I expressed myself earlier in the latter sense, I was giving a phenomenological description and not a metapsychological account of what was occurring.

This brings us to a further question: how is it possible, from an economic point of view, for a mere process of withdrawal and discharge, like the withdrawing of a preconscious ego-cathexis, to produce unpleasure or anxiety, seeing that, according to our assumptions, unpleasure and anxiety can only arise as a result of an *increase* in cathexis? The reply is that this causal sequence should not be explained from an economic point of view. Anxiety is not newly created in repression; it is reproduced as an affective state in accordance with an already existing mnemic image. If we go further and enquire into the origin of that anxiety – and of affects in general – we shall be leaving the realm of pure psychology and entering the borderland of physiology. Affective states have become incorporated in the mind as precipitates of primaeval traumatic experiences, and when a similar situation occurs they are revived like mnemic

1. [i.e. what represents the instinct in the mind.]

symbols.[1] I do not think I have been wrong in likening them to the more recent and individually acquired hysterical attack and in regarding them as its normal prototypes.[2] In man and the higher animals it would seem that the act of birth, as the individual's first experience of anxiety, has given the affect of anxiety certain characteristic forms of expression. But, while acknowledging this connection, we must not lay undue stress on it nor overlook the fact that biological necessity demands that a situation of danger should have an affective symbol, so that a symbol of this kind would have to be created in any case. Moreover, I do not think that we are justified in assuming that whenever there is an outbreak of anxiety something like a reproduction of the situation of birth goes on in the mind. It is not even certain whether hysterical attacks, though they were originally traumatic reproductions of this sort, retain that character permanently.

As I have shown elsewhere, most of the repressions with which we have to deal in our therapeutic work are cases of *after*-pressure.[3] They presuppose the operation of earlier, *primal repressions* which exert an attraction on the more recent situation. Far too little is known as yet about the background and preliminary stages of repression. There is a danger of over-estimating the part played in repression by the super-ego. We cannot at present say whether it is perhaps the emergence of the super-ego which provides the line of demarcation between primal repression and after-pressure. At any rate, the earliest outbreaks of anxiety, which are of a very intense kind, occur before the super-ego has become differentiated. It is highly probable that the immediate precipitating causes of primal repressions are quantitative factors such as an excessive force

1. [Cf. a footnote to the paper on 'Hysterical Phantasies (1908a), p. 91 *n.* 2 above.]

2. [See the Editor's Introduction, p. 235 and also below, pp. 289-90.]

3. [This is discussed near the beginning of 'Repression' (1915d).]

of excitation and the breaking through of the protective shield against stimuli.[1]

This mention of the protective shield sounds a note which recalls to us the fact that repression occurs in two different situations – namely, when an undesirable instinctual impulse is aroused by some external perception, and when it arises internally without any such provocation. We shall return to this difference later [p. 314 f.]. But the protective shield exists only in regard to external stimuli, not in regard to internal instinctual demands.

So long as we direct our attention to the ego's attempt at flight we shall get no nearer to the subject of symptom-form-ation. A symptom arises from an instinctual impulse which has been detrimentally affected by repression. If the ego, by making use of the signal of unpleasure, attains its object of completely suppressing the instinctual impulse, we learn nothing of how this has happened. We can only find out about it from those cases in which repression must be described as having to a greater or lesser extent failed. In this event the position, generally speak-ing, is that the instinctual impulse has found a substitute in spite of repression, but a substitute which is very much reduced, displaced and inhibited and which is no longer recognizable as a satisfaction. And when the substitutive impulse is carried out there is no sensation of pleasure; its carrying out has, instead, the quality of a compulsion.

In thus degrading a process of satisfaction to a symptom, repression displays its power in a further respect. The sub-stitutive process is prevented, if possible, from finding discharge through motility; and even if this cannot be done, the process is forced to expend itself in making alterations in the subject's own body and is not permitted to impinge upon the external world. It must not be transformed into action. For, as we know, in repression the ego is operating under the influence of

1. [Cf. *Beyond the Pleasure Principle* (1920g), Chapter IV.]

external reality and therefore it debars the substitutive process from having any effect upon that reality.

Just as the ego controls the path to action in regard to the external world, so it controls access to consciousness. In repression it exercises its power in both directions, acting in the one manner upon the instinctual impulse itself and in the other upon the [psychical] representative of that impulse. At this point it is relevant to ask how I can reconcile this acknowledgement of the might of the ego with the description of its position which I gave in *The Ego and the Id*. In that book I drew a picture of its dependent relationship to the id and to the super-ego and revealed how powerless and apprehensive it was in regard to both and with what an effort it maintained its show of superiority over them.[1] This view has been widely echoed in psychoanalytic literature. Many writers have laid much stress on the weakness of the ego in relation to the id and of our rational elements in the face of the daemonic forces within us; and they display a strong tendency to make what I have said into a corner-stone of a psychoanalytic *Weltanschauung*. Yet surely the psychoanalyst, with his knowledge of the way in which repression works, should, of all people, be restrained from adopting such an extreme and one-sided view.

I must confess that I am not at all partial to the fabrication of *Weltanschauungen*.[2] Such activities may be left to philosophers, who avowedly find it impossible to make their journey through life without a Baedeker of that kind to give them information on every subject. Let us humbly accept the contempt with which they look down on us from the vantage-ground of their superior needs. But since *we* cannot forgo our narcissistic pride either, we will draw comfort from the reflection that such 'Handbooks to Life' soon grow out of date and that it is pre-

---

1. [*The Ego and the Id* (1923b), Chapter V.]

2. [Cf. a prolonged discussion of this in the last of Freud's *New Introductory Lectures* (1933a).]

cisely our short-sighted, narrow and finicky work which obliges them to appear in new editions, and that even the most up-to-date of them are nothing but attempts to find a substitute for the ancient, useful and all-sufficient Church Catechism. We know well enough how little light science has so far been able to throw on the problems that surround us. But however much ado the philosophers may make, they cannot alter the situation. Only patient, persevering research, in which everything is subordinated to the one requirement of certainty, can gradually bring about a change. The benighted traveller may sing aloud in the dark to deny his own fears; but, for all that, he will not see an inch further beyond his nose.

III

To return to the problem of the ego.[1] The apparent contradiction is due to our having taken abstractions too rigidly and attended exclusively now to the one side and now to the other of what is in fact a complicated state of affairs. We were justified, I think, in dividing the ego from the id, for there are certain considerations which necessitate that step. On the other hand the ego is identical with the id, and is merely a specially differentiated part of it. If we think of this part by itself in contradistinction to the whole, or if a real split has occurred between the two, the weakness of the ego becomes apparent. But if the ego remains bound up with the id and indistinguishable from it, then it displays its strength. The same is true of the relation between the ego and the super-ego. In many situations the two are merged; and as a rule we can only distinguish one from the other when there is a tension or conflict between them. In repression the decisive fact is that the ego is an organization and the id is not. The ego is, indeed, the organized portion of the id. We should be quite wrong if we pictured the ego and the id as two opposing camps and if we supposed that, when the ego tries to suppress a part of the id by means of repression, the remainder of the id comes to the rescue of the endangered part and measures its strength with the ego. This may often be what happens, but it is certainly not the initial situation in repression. As a rule the instinctual impulse which is to be repressed remains isolated. Although the act of repression demonstrates the strength of the ego, in one particular it reveals the ego's powerlessness and how impervious to influence are the separate instinctual impulses of the id. For the mental process which has been turned into a symptom owing to repression

1. [i.e. the contrast between its strength and weakness in relation to the id.]

now maintains its existence outside the organization of the ego and independently of it. Indeed, it is not that process alone but all its derivatives which enjoy, as it were, this same privilege of extra-territoriality; and whenever they come into associative contact with a part of the ego-organization, it is not at all certain that they will not draw that part over to themselves and thus enlarge themselves at the expense of the ego. An analogy with which we have long been familiar compared a symptom to a foreign body which was keeping up a constant succession of stimuli and reactions in the tissue in which it was embedded.[1] It does sometimes happen that the defensive struggle against an unwelcome instinctual impulse is brought to an end with the formation of a symptom. As far as can be seen, this is most often possible in hysterical conversion. But usually the outcome is different. The initial act of repression is followed by a tedious interminable sequel in which the struggle against the instinctual impulse is prolonged into a struggle against the symptom.

In this secondary defensive struggle the ego presents two faces with contradictory expressions. The one line of behaviour it adopts springs from the fact that its very nature obliges it to make what must be regarded as an attempt at restoration or reconciliation. The ego is an organization. It is based on the maintenance of free intercourse and of the possibility of reciprocal influence between all its parts. Its desexualized energy still shows traces of its origin in its impulsion to bind together and unify, and this necessity to synthesize grows stronger in proportion as the strength of the ego increases. It is therefore only natural that the ego should try to prevent symptoms from remaining isolated and alien by using every possible method to bind them to itself in one way or another, and to incorporate them into its organization by means of those bonds. As we

1. [This analogy is discussed and criticized in Freud's contribution to *Studies on Hysteria* (1895*d*), P.F.L., **3**, 376–7. It appeared originally in the 'Preliminary Communication' (1893*a*), ibid., 56–7.]

know, a tendency of this kind is already operative in the very act of forming a symptom. A classical instance of this are those hysterical symptoms which have been shown to be a compromise between the need for satisfaction and the need for punishment.[1] Such symptoms participate in the ego from the very beginning, since they fulfil a requirement of the super-ego, while on the other hand they represent positions occupied by the repressed and points at which an irruption has been made by it into the ego-organization. They are a kind of frontier-station with a mixed garrison.[2] (Whether all primary hysterical symptoms are constructed on these lines would be worth enquiring into very carefully.) The ego now proceeds to behave as though it recognized that the symptom had come to stay and that the only thing to do was to accept the situation in good part and draw as much advantage from it as possible. It makes an adaptation to the symptom – to this piece of the internal world which is alien to it – just as it normally does to the real external world. It can always find plenty of opportunities for doing so. The presence of a symptom may entail a certain impairment of capacity, and this can be exploited to appease some demand on the part of the super-ego or to refuse some claim from the external world. In this way the symptom gradually comes to be the representative of important interests; it is found to be useful in asserting the position of the self and becomes more and more closely merged with the ego and more and more indispensable to it. It is only very rarely that the physical process of 'healing' round a foreign body follows such a course as this. There is a danger, too, of exaggerating the importance of a secondary adaptation of this kind to a symptom, and of saying that the ego has created the symptom merely in order to enjoy its advantages. It would be equally true to say that a man who

1. [This idea was foreshadowed in Section II of Freud's second paper on 'The Neuro-Psychoses of Defence' (1896b).]

2. [There is an allusion in this metaphor to the fact that '*Besetzung*', the German word for 'cathexis', can also have the sense of 'garrison'.]

had lost his leg in the war had got it shot away so that he might thenceforward live on his pension without having to do any more work.

In obsessional neurosis and paranoia the forms which the symptoms assume become very valuable to the ego because they obtain for it, not certain advantages, but a narcissistic satisfaction which it would otherwise be without. The systems which the obsessional neurotic constructs flatter his self-love by making him feel that he is better than other people because he is specially clean or specially conscientious. The delusional constructions of the paranoic offer to his acute perceptive and imaginative powers a field of activity which he could not easily find elsewhere.

All of this results in what is familiar to us as the '(secondary) gain from illness' which follows a neurosis.[1] This gain comes to the assistance of the ego in its endeavour to incorporate the symptom and increases the symptom's fixation. When the analyst tries subsequently to help the ego in its struggle against the symptom, he finds that these conciliatory bonds between ego and symptom operate on the side of the resistances and that they are not easy to loosen.

The two lines of behaviour which the ego adopts towards the symptom are in fact directly opposed to each other. For the other line is less friendly in character, since it continues in the direction of repression. Nevertheless the ego, it appears, cannot be accused of inconsistency. Being of a peaceable disposition it would like to incorporate the symptom and make it part of itself. It is from the symptom itself that the trouble comes. For the symptom, being the true substitute for and derivative of the repressed impulse, carries on the role of the latter; it continually renews its demands for satisfaction and thus obliges the ego in its turn to give the signal of unpleasure and put itself in a posture of defence.

1. [Cf. a discussion of this in a footnote to the paper on 'Hysterical Attacks' (1909a) p. 100 n. 2 above.]

The secondary defensive struggle against the symptom takes many shapes. It is fought out on different fields and makes use of a variety of methods. We shall not be able to say much about it until we have made an enquiry into the various different instances of symptom-formation. In doing this we shall have an opportunity of going into the problem of anxiety – a problem which has long been looming in the background. The wisest plan will be to start from the symptoms produced by the hysterical neurosis; for we are not as yet in a position to consider the conditions in which the symptoms of obsessional neurosis, paranoia and other neuroses are formed.

IV

Let us start with an infantile hysterical phobia of animals – for instance, the case of 'Little Hans' [1909b], whose phobia of horses was undoubtedly typical in all its main features.[1] The first thing that becomes apparent is that in a concrete case of neurotic illness the state of affairs is much more complex than one would suppose so long as one was dealing with abstractions. It takes a little time to find one's bearings and to decide which the repressed impulse is, what substitutive symptom it has found and where the motive for repression lies.

'Little Hans' refused to go out into the street because he was afraid of horses. This was the raw material of the case. Which part of it constituted the symptom? Was it his having the fear? Was it his choice of an object for his fear? Was it his giving up of his freedom of movement? Or was it more than one of these combined? What was the satisfaction which he renounced? And why did he have to renounce it?

At a first glance one is tempted to reply that the case is not so very obscure. 'Little Hans's' unaccountable fear of horses was the symptom and his inability to go out into the streets was an inhibition, a restriction which his ego had imposed on itself so as not to arouse the anxiety-symptom. The second point is clearly correct; and in the discussion which follows I shall not concern myself any further with this inhibition. But as regards the alleged symptom, a superficial acquaintance with the case does not even disclose its true formulation. For further investigation shows that what he was suffering from was not a vague fear of horses but a quite definite apprehension that a horse was going to bite him.[2] This idea, indeed, was endeavouring to withdraw from consciousness and get itself replaced by

1. [Cf. the case history in *P.F.L.*, **8**, 169 ff.]
2. [Ibid., 187.]

an undefined phobia in which only the anxiety and its object still appeared. Was it perhaps this idea that was the nucleus of his symptom?

We shall not make any headway until we have reviewed the little boy's psychical situation as a whole as it came to light in the course of the analytic treatment. He was at the time in the jealous and hostile Oedipus attitude towards his father, whom nevertheless – except in so far as his mother was the cause of estrangement – he dearly loved. Here, then, we have a conflict due to ambivalence: a well-grounded love and a no less justifiable hatred directed towards one and the same person. 'Little Hans's' phobia must have been an attempt to solve this conflict. Conflicts of this kind due to ambivalence are very frequent and they can have another typical outcome, in which one of the two conflicting feelings (usually that of affection) becomes enormously intensified and the other vanishes. The exaggerated degree and compulsive character of the affection alone betray the fact that it is not the only one present but is continually on the alert to keep the opposite feeling under suppression, and enable us to postulate the operation of a process which we call repression by means of *reaction-formation* (in the ego). Cases like 'Little Hans's' show no traces of a reaction-formation of this kind. There are clearly different ways of egress from a conflict due to ambivalence.

Meanwhile we have been able to establish another point with certainty. The instinctual impulse which underwent repression in 'Little Hans' was a hostile one against his father. Proof of this was obtained in his analysis while the idea of the biting horse was being followed up. He had seen a horse fall down and he had also seen a playmate, with whom he was playing at horses, fall down and hurt himself.[1] Analysis justified the inference that he had a wishful impulse that his father should fall down and hurt himself as his playmate and the horse had done. Moreover, his attitude towards someone's departure on

1. [Ibid., 211–12 and 242.]

a certain occasion[1] makes it probable that his wish that his father should be out of the way also found less hesitating expression. But a wish of this sort is tantamount to an intention of putting one's father out of the way oneself – is tantamount, that is, to the murderous impulse of the Oedipus complex.

So far there seem to be no connecting links between 'Little Hans's' repressed instinctual impulse and the substitute for it which we suspect is to be seen in his phobia of horses. Let us simplify his psychical situation by setting on one side the infantile factor and the ambivalence. Let us imagine that he is a young servant who is in love with the mistress of the house and has received some tokens of her favour. He hates his master, who is more powerful than he is, and he would like to have him out of the way. It would then be eminently natural for him to dread his master's vengeance and to develop a fear of him – just as 'Little Hans' developed a phobia of horses. We cannot, therefore, describe the fear belonging to this phobia as a symptom. If 'Little Hans', being in love with his mother, had shown fear of his father, we should have no right to say that he had a neurosis or a phobia. His emotional reaction would have been entirely comprehensible. What made it a neurosis was one thing alone: the replacement of his father by a horse. It is this displacement, then, which has a claim to be called a symptom, and which, incidentally, constitutes the alternative mechanism which enables a conflict due to ambivalence to be resolved without the aid of a reaction-formation. [Cf. above, p. 255.] Such a displacement is made possible or facilitated at 'Little Hans's' early age because the inborn traces of totemic thought can still be easily revived. Children do not as yet recognize or, at any rate, lay such exaggerated stress upon the gulf that separates human beings from the animal world. In their eyes the grown man, the object of their fear and admiration, still belongs to the same category as the big animal who has so many enviable attributes but against whom

1. [Ibid., 192.]

they have been warned because he may become dangerous. As we see, the conflict due to ambivalence is not dealt with in relation to one and the same person: it is circumvented, as it were, by one of the pair of conflicting impulses being directed to another person as a substitutive object.

So far everything is clear. But the analysis of 'Hans's' phobia has been a complete disappointment in one respect. The distortion which constituted the symptom-formation was not applied to the [psychical] representative (the ideational content) of the instinctual impulse that was to be repressed; it was applied to a quite different representative and one which only corresponded to a *reaction* to the disagreeable instinct. It would be more in accordance with our expectations if 'Little Hans' had developed, instead of a fear of horses, an inclination to ill-treat them and to beat them or if he had expressed in plain terms a wish to see them fall down or be hurt or even die in convulsions ('make a row with their feet').[1] Something of the sort did in fact emerge in his analysis, but it was not by any means in the forefront of his neurosis. And, curiously enough, if he really had produced a hostility of this sort not against his father but against horses as his main symptom, we should not have said that he was suffering from a neurosis. There must be something wrong either with our view of repression or with our definition of a symptom. One thing, of course, strikes us at once: if 'Little Hans' had really behaved like that to horses, it would mean that repression had in no way altered the character of his objectionable and aggressive instinctual impulse itself but only the object towards which it was directed.

Undoubtedly there are cases in which this is all that repression does. But more than this happened in the development of 'Little Hans's' phobia – how much more can be guessed from a part of another analysis.

As we know, 'Little Hans' alleged that what he was afraid of was that a horse would bite him. Now some time later I was

1. [Ibid., 211-12.]

able to learn something about the origin of another animal phobia. In this instance the dreaded animal was a wolf; it, too, had the significance of a father-substitute. As a boy the patient in question – a Russian whom I did not analyse till he was in his twenties – had had a dream (whose meaning was revealed in analysis) and, immediately after it, had developed a fear of being devoured by a wolf, like the seven little goats in the fairy tale.[1] In the case of 'Little Hans' the ascertained fact that his father used to play at horses with him[2] doubtless determined his choice of a horse as his anxiety-animal. In the same way it appeared at least highly probable that the father of my Russian patient used, when playing with him, to pretend to be a wolf and jokingly threaten to gobble him up.[3] Since then I have come across a third instance. The patient was a young American who came to me for analysis. He did not, it is true, develop an animal phobia, but it is precisely because of this omission that his case helps to throw light upon the other two. As a child he had been sexually excited by a fantastic children's story which had been read aloud to him about an Arab chief who pursued a 'ginger-bread man'[4] so as to eat him up. He identified himself with this edible person, and the Arab chief was easily recognizable as a father-substitute. This phantasy formed the earliest substratum of his auto-erotic phantasies.

The idea of being devoured by the father is typical age-old childhood material. It has familiar parallels in mythology (e.g. the myth of Kronos) and in the animal kingdom. Yet in spite of this confirmation the idea is so strange to us that we can hardly credit its existence in a child. Nor do we know whether it really means what it seems to say, and we cannot understand how it can have become the subject of a phobia. Analytic observation supplies the requisite information. It shows that the idea of being

1. 'From the History of an Infantile Neurosis' (1918b) [P.F.L., 9, 259 ff.]

2. [P.F.L., 8, 284.]

3. [P.F.L., 9, 263.]

4. [In English in the original.]

devoured by the father gives expression, in a form that has undergone regressive degradation, to a passive, tender impulse to be loved by him in a genital-erotic sense. Further investigation of the case history[1] leaves no doubt of the correctness of this explanation. The genital impulse, it is true, betrays no sign of its tender purpose when it is expressed in the language belonging to the superseded transitional phase between the oral and sadistic organizations of the libido. Is it, moreover, a question merely of the replacement of the [psychical] representative by a regressive form of expression or is it a question of a genuine regressive degradation of the genitally-directed impulse in the id? It is not at all easy to make certain. The case history of the Russian 'Wolf Man' gives very definite support to the second, more serious, view; for, from the time of the decisive dream onward, the boy became naughty, tormenting and sadistic, and soon afterwards developed a regular obsessional neurosis. At any rate, we can see that repression is not the only means which the ego can employ for the purpose of defence against an unwelcome instinctual impulse. If it succeeds in making an instinct regress, it will actually have done it more injury than it could have by repressing it. Sometimes, indeed, after forcing an instinct to regress in this way, it goes on to repress it.

The case of the 'Wolf Man' and the somewhat less complicated one of 'Little Hans' raise a number of further considerations. But we have already made two unexpected discoveries. There can be no doubt that the instinctual impulse which was repressed in both phobias was a hostile one against the father. One might say that that impulse had been repressed by the process of being transformed into its opposite. Instead of aggressiveness on the part of the subject towards his father, there appeared aggressiveness (in the shape of revenge) on the part of his father towards the subject. Since this aggressiveness is in any case rooted in the sadistic phase of the libido, only a

1. [Of the Russian patient.]

certain amount of degradation is needed to reduce it to the oral stage. This stage, while only hinted at in 'Little Hans's' fear of being bitten, was blatantly exhibited in the 'Wolf Man's' terror of being devoured. But, besides this, the analysis has demonstrated, beyond a shadow of doubt, the presence of another instinctual impulse of an opposite nature which had succumbed to repression. This was a tender, passive impulse directed towards the father, which had already reached the genital (phallic) level of libidinal organization. As regards the final outcome of the process of repression, this impulse seems, indeed, to have been the more important of the two; it underwent a more far-reaching regression and had a decisive influence upon the content of the phobia. In following up a *single* instinctual repression we have thus had to recognize a convergence of *two* such processes. The two instinctual impulses that have been overtaken by repression – sadistic aggressiveness towards the father and a tender passive attitude to him – form a pair of opposites. Furthermore, a full appreciation of 'Little Hans's case shows that the formation of his phobia had had the effect of abolishing his affectionate object-cathexis of his mother as well, though the actual content of his phobia betrayed no sign of this. The process of repression had attacked almost all the components of his Oedipus complex – both his hostile and his tender impulses towards his father and his tender impulses towards his mother. In my Russian patient this state of affairs was much less obvious.

These are unwelcome complications, considering that we only set out to study simple cases of symptom-formation due to repression, and with that intention selected the earliest and, to all appearances, most transparent neuroses of childhood. Instead of a single repression we have found a collection of them and have become involved with regression into the bargain. Perhaps we have added to the confusion by treating the two cases of animal phobia at our disposal – 'Little Hans' and the 'Wolf Man' – as though they were cast in the same mould. As a matter of fact, certain differences between them stand out. It is only with regard to 'Little Hans' that we can say with certainty that what his phobia disposed of were the two main impulses of the Oedipus complex – his aggressiveness towards his father and his over-fondness for his mother. A tender feeling for his father was undoubtedly there too and played a part in repressing the opposite feeling; but we can prove neither that it was strong enough to draw repression upon itself nor that it disappeared afterwards. 'Hans' seems, in fact, to have been a normal boy with what is called a 'positive' Oedipus complex. It is possible that the factors which we do not find were actually at work in him, but we cannot demonstrate their existence. Even the most exhaustive analysis has gaps in its data and is insufficiently documented. In the case of the Russian the deficiency lies elsewhere. His attitude to female objects had been disturbed by an early seduction[1] and his passive, feminine side was strongly developed. The analysis of his wolf-dream revealed very little intentional aggressiveness towards his father, but it brought forward unmistakable proof that what repression overtook was his passive tender attitude to his father. In his case, too, the other factors may have been operative as well; but they were not in evidence. How is it that, in spite of these differences in the two cases, almost amounting to an antithesis, the final outcome – a phobia – was approximately the same? The answer must be sought in another quarter. I think it will be found in the second fact which emerges from our brief comparative examination. It seems to me that in both cases we can detect what the motive force of the repression was and can substantiate our view of its nature from the line of development which the two children subsequently pursued. This motive force was the same in both of them. It was the fear of impending castration. 'Little Hans' gave up his aggressiveness towards his father from fear of being castrated. His fear that a horse would bite him can, without any forcing,

1. [*P.F.L.*, **9**, 248 ff.]

be given the full sense of a fear that a horse would bite off his genitals, would castrate him. But it was from fear of being castrated, too, that the little Russian relinquished his wish to be loved by his father, for he thought that a relation of that sort presupposed a sacrifice of his genitals – of the organ which distinguished him from a female. As we see, both forms of the Oedipus complex, the normal, active form and the inverted one, came to grief through the castration complex. The Russian boy's anxiety-idea of being devoured by a wolf contained, it is true, no suggestion of castration, for the oral regression it had undergone had removed it too far from the phallic stage. But the analysis of his dream rendered further proof superfluous. It was a triumph of repression that the form in which his phobia was expressed should no longer have contained any allusion to castration.

Here, then, is our unexpected finding: in both patients the motive force of the repression was fear of castration. The ideas contained in their anxiety – being bitten by a horse and being devoured by a wolf – were substitutes by distortion for the idea of being castrated by their father. This was the idea which had undergone repression. In the Russian boy the idea was an expression of a wish which was not able to subsist in the face of his masculine revolt; in 'Little Hans' it was the expression of a reaction in him which had turned his aggressiveness into its opposite. But the *affect* of anxiety, which was the essence of the phobia, came, not from the process of repression, not from the libidinal cathexes of the repressed impulses, but from the repressing agency itself. The anxiety belonging to the animal phobias was an untransformed fear of castration. It was therefore a realistic fear,[1] a fear of a danger which was

1. ['*Realangst*' in the German. The adjective 'realistic' has, throughout the *Standard Edition*, been preferred to the impossible 'real' and to 'objective' which has been used elsewhere, but which gives rise to evident ambiguities. On the other hand, for '*Realgefahr*' we have 'real danger'.]

actually impending or was judged to be a real one. It was anxiety which produced repression and not, as I formerly believed, repression which produced anxiety.

It is no use denying the fact, though it is not pleasant to recall it, that I have on many occasions asserted that in repression the instinctual representative is distorted, displaced, and so on, while the libido belonging to the instinctual impulse is transformed into anxiety.[1] But now an examination of phobias, which should be best able to provide confirmatory evidence, fails to bear out my assertion; it seems, rather, to contradict it directly. The anxiety felt in animal phobias is the ego's fear of castration; while the anxiety felt in agoraphobia (a subject that has been less thoroughly studied) seems to be its fear of sexual temptation – a fear which, after all, must be connected in its origins with the fear of castration. As far as can be seen at present, the majority of phobias go back to an anxiety of this kind felt by the ego in regard to the demands of the libido. It is always the ego's attitude of anxiety which is the primary thing and which sets repression going. Anxiety never arises from repressed libido. If I had contented myself earlier with saying that after the occurrence of repression a certain amount of anxiety appeared in place of the manifestation of libido that was to be expected, I should have nothing to retract to-day. The description would be correct; and there does undoubtedly exist a correspondence of the kind asserted between the strength of the impulse that has to be repressed and the intensity of the resultant anxiety. But I must admit that I thought I was giving more than a mere description. I believed I had put my finger on a metapsychological process of direct transformation of libido into anxiety. I can now no longer maintain this view. And, indeed, I found it impossible

1. [See, for instance, Freud's paper on repression (1915*d*), some three pages before the end, where the case of the 'Wolf Man' is also considered. A further discussion will be found in Addendum A(*b*), p. 320 ff., below, as well as in the Editor's Introduction, p. 230 ff.]

at the time to explain how a transformation of that kind was carried out.

It may be asked how I arrived at this idea of transformation in the first instance. It was while I was studying the 'actual neuroses', at a time when analysis was still a very long way from distinguishing between processes in the ego and processes in the id.[1] I found that outbreaks of anxiety and a general state of preparedness for anxiety were produced by certain sexual practices such as *coitus interruptus*, undischarged sexual excitation or enforced abstinence – that is, whenever sexual excitation was inhibited, arrested or deflected in its progress towards satisfaction. Since sexual excitation was an expression of libidinal instinctual impulses it did not seem too rash to assume that the libido was turned into anxiety through the agency of these disturbances. The observations which I made at the time still hold good. Moreover, it cannot be denied that the libido belonging to the id-processes is subjected to disturbance at the instigation of repression. It might still be true, therefore, that in repression anxiety is produced from the libidinal cathexis of the instinctual impulses. But how can we reconcile this conclusion with our other conclusion that the anxiety felt in phobias is an ego anxiety and arises in the ego, and that it does not proceed out of repression but, on the contrary, sets repression in motion? There seems to be a contradiction here which it is not at all a simple matter to solve. It will not be easy to reduce the two sources of anxiety to a single one. We might attempt to do so by supposing that, when coitus is disturbed or sexual excitation interrupted or abstinence enforced, the ego scents certain dangers to which it reacts with anxiety. But this takes us nowhere. On the other hand, our analysis of the phobias seems to admit of no correction. *Non liquet.*[2]

1. [See Freud's first paper on anxiety neurosis (1895*b*) p. 35 ff. above.]
2. ['It is not clear.' An old legal verdict used when the evidence was inconclusive; compare the Scottish 'not proven'.]

V

We set out to study the formation of symptoms and the secondary struggle waged by the ego against symptoms. But in picking on the phobias for this purpose we have clearly made an unlucky choice. The anxiety which predominates in the picture of these disorders is now seen as a complication which obscures the situation. There are plenty of neuroses which exhibit no anxiety whatever. True conversion hysteria is one of these. Even in its most severe symptoms no admixture of anxiety is found. This fact alone ought to warn us against making too close a connection between anxiety and symptom-formation. The phobias are so closely akin to conversion hysteria in every other respect that I have felt justified in classing them alongside of it under the name of 'anxiety hysteria'. But no one has as yet been able to say what it is that determines whether any given case shall take the form of a conversion hysteria or a phobia – has been able, that is to say, to establish what determines the generating of anxiety in hysteria.

The commonest symptoms of conversion hysteria – motor paralyses, contractures, involuntary actions or discharges, pains and hallucinations – are cathectic processes which are either permanently maintained or intermittent. But this puts fresh difficulties in the way. Not much is actually known about these symptoms. Analysis can show what the disturbed excitatory process is which the symptoms replace. It usually turns out that they themselves have a share in that process. It is as though the whole energy of the process had been concentrated in this one part of it. For instance, it will be found that the pains from which a patient suffers were present in the situation in which the repression occurred; or that his hallucination was, at that time, a perception; or that his motor paralysis is a defence against an action which should have been performed in that situation but was inhibited; or that his contracture is usually a displacement of an intended innervation of the muscles in some other part of his body; or that his convulsions are the expression of an outburst of affect which has been withdrawn from the normal control of the ego. The sensation of unpleasure which accompanies the appearance of the symptoms varies in a striking degree. In chronic symptoms which have been displaced on to motility, like paralyses and contractures, it is almost always entirely absent; the ego behaves towards the symptoms as though it had nothing to do with them. In intermittent symptoms and in those concerned with the sensory sphere, sensations of unpleasure are as a rule distinctly felt; and in symptoms of pain these may reach an extreme degree. The picture presented is so manifold that it is difficult to discover the factor which permits of all these variations and yet allows a uniform explanation of them. There is, moreover, little to be seen in conversion hysteria of the ego's struggle against the symptom after it has been formed. It is only when sensitivity to pain in some part of the body constitutes the symptom that that symptom is in a position to play a dual role. The symptom of pain will appear no less regularly whenever the part of the body concerned is touched from outside than when the pathogenic situation which it represents is associatively activated from within; and the ego will take precautions to prevent the symptom from being aroused through external perceptions. Why the formation of symptoms in conversion hysteria should be such a peculiarly obscure thing I cannot tell; but the fact affords us a good reason for quitting such an unproductive field of enquiry without delay.

Let us turn to the obsessional neuroses in the hope of learning more about the formation of symptoms. The symptoms belonging to this neurosis fall, in general, into two groups, each having an opposite trend. They are either prohibitions, precautions and expiations – that is, negative in character – or they are, on the contrary, substitutive satisfactions which often appear in symbolic disguise. The negative, defensive group of symptoms is the older of the two; but as illness is prolonged, the satisfactions, which scoff at all defensive measures, gain the upper hand. The symptom-formation scores a triumph if it succeeds in combining the prohibition with satisfaction so that what was originally a defensive command or prohibition acquires the significance of a satisfaction as well; and in order to achieve this end it will often make use of the most ingenious associative paths. Such an achievement demonstrates the tendency of the ego to synthesize, which we have already observed [p. 250]. In extreme cases the patient manages to make most of his symptoms acquire, in addition to their original meaning, a directly contrary one. This is a tribute to the power of ambivalence, which, for some unknown reason, plays such a large part in obsessional neuroses. In the crudest instance the symptom is diphasic:[1] an action which carries out a certain injunction is immediately succeeded by another action which stops or undoes the first one even if it does not go quite so far as to carry out its opposite.

Two impressions at once emerge from this brief survey of obsessional symptoms. The first is that a ceaseless struggle is being waged against the repressed, in which the repressing forces steadily lose ground; the second is that the ego and the super-ego have a specially large share in the formation of the symptoms.

Obsessional neurosis is unquestionably the most interesting and repaying subject of analytic research. But as a problem it has not yet been mastered. It must be confessed that, if we endeavour to penetrate more deeply into its nature, we still have to rely upon doubtful assumptions and unconfirmed suppositions. Obsessional neurosis originates, no doubt, in the same situation as hysteria, namely, the necessity of fending off the libidinal demands of the Oedipus complex. Indeed,

1. [i.e. occurs in two instalments. See below, p. 274.]

every obsessional neurosis seems to have a substratum of hysterical symptoms that have been formed at a very early stage.[1] But it is subsequently shaped along quite different lines owing to a constitutional factor. The genital organization of the libido turns out to be feeble and insufficiently resistant, so that when the ego begins its defensive efforts the first thing it succeeds in doing is to throw back the genital organization (of the phallic phase), in whole or in part, to the earlier sadistic-anal level. This fact of regression is decisive for all that follows.

Another possibility has to be considered. Perhaps regression is the result not of a constitutional factor but of a time-factor. It may be that regression is rendered possible not because the genital organization of the libido is too feeble but because the opposition of the ego begins too early, while the sadistic phase is at its height. I am not prepared to express a definite opinion on this point, but I may say that analytic observation does not speak in favour of such an assumption. It shows rather that, by the time an obsessional neurosis is entered upon, the phallic stage has already been reached. Moreover, the onset of this neurosis belongs to a later time of life than that of hysteria – to the second period of childhood, after the latency period has set in. In a woman patient whose case I was able to study and who was overtaken by this disorder at a very late date, it became clear that the determining cause of her regression and of the emergence of her obsessional neurosis was a real occurrence through which her genital life, which had up till then been intact, lost all its value.[2]

As regards the metapsychological explanation of regression, I am inclined to find it in a 'defusion of instinct', in a detachment of the erotic components which, with the onset of the genital

1. [An example occurs in the 'Wolf Man' analysis (1918*b*), P.F.L., 9, 312.]

2. See my paper on 'The Disposition to Obsessional Neurosis' (1913*i*) [p. 136 f. above.]

stage, had joined the destructive cathexes belonging to the sadistic phase.[1]

In enforcing regression, the ego scores its first success in its defensive struggle against the demands of the libido. (In this connection it is of advantage to distinguish the more general notion of 'defence' from 'repression'.[2] Repression is only one of the mechanisms which defence makes use of.) It is perhaps in obsessional cases more than in normal or hysterical ones that we can most clearly recognize that the motive force of defence is the castration complex and that what is being fended off are the trends of the Oedipus complex. We are at present dealing with the beginning of the latency period, a period which is characterized by the dissolution of the Oedipus complex, the creation or consolidation of the super-ego and the erection of ethical and aesthetic barriers in the ego. In obsessional neuroses these processes are carried further than is normal. In addition to the destruction of the Oedipus complex a regressive degradation of the libido takes place, the super-ego becomes exceptionally severe and unkind, and the ego, in obedience to the super-ego, produces strong reaction-formations in the shape of conscientiousness, pity and cleanliness. Implacable, though not always on that account successful, severity is shown in condemning the temptation to continue early infantile masturbation, which now attaches itself to regressive (sadistic-anal) ideas but which nevertheless represents the unsubjugated part of the phallic organization. There is an inherent contradiction about this state of affairs, in which, precisely in the interests of masculinity (that is to say, from fear of castration), every activity belonging to masculinity is stopped. But here, too, obsessional neurosis is only overdoing the normal method of

1. [Towards the beginning of Chapter IV of *The Ego and the Id* (1923*b*), Freud had suggested that the advance from the sadistic-anal to the genital phase is conditioned by an accession of erotic components.]

2. [This is discussed at length below, in Addendum A(*c*), p. 322 ff.]

getting rid of the Oedipus complex. We once more find here an illustration of the truth that every exaggeration contains the seed of its own undoing. For, under the guise of obsessional acts, the masturbation that has been suppressed approaches ever more closely to satisfaction.

The reaction-formations in the ego of the obsessional neurotic, which we recognize as exaggerations of normal character-formation, should be regarded, I think, as yet another mechanism of defence and placed alongside of regression and repression. They seem to be absent or very much weaker in hysteria. Looking back, we can now get an idea of what is peculiar to the defensive process in hysteria. It seems that in it the process is limited to repression alone. The ego turns away from the disagreeable instinctual impulse, leaves it to pursue its course in the unconscious, and takes no further part in its fortunes. This view cannot be absolutely correct, for we are acquainted with the case in which a hysterical symptom is at the same time a fulfilment of a penalty imposed by the super-ego; but it may describe a general characteristic of the behaviour of the ego in hysteria.

We can either simply accept it as a fact that in obsessional neurosis a super-ego of this severe kind emerges, or we can take the regression of the libido as the fundamental characteristic of the affection and attempt to relate the severity of the super-ego to it. And indeed the super-ego, originating as it does from the id, cannot dissociate itself from the regression and defusion of instinct which have taken place there. We cannot be surprised if it becomes harsher, unkinder and more tormenting than where development has been normal.

The chief task during the latency period seems to be the fending-off of the temptation to masturbate. This struggle produces a series of symptoms which appear in a typical fashion in the most different individuals and which in general have the character of a ceremonial. It is a great pity that no one has as yet collected them and systematically analysed them. Being the earliest products of the neurosis they should best be able to shed light on the mechanisms employed in its symptom-formation. They already exhibit the features which will emerge so disastrously if a serious illness follows. They tend to become attached to activities (which would later be carried out almost automatically) such as going to sleep, washing, dressing and walking about; and they tend also to repetition and waste of time. Why this should be so is at present not at all clear; but the sublimation of anal-erotic components plays an unmistakable part in it.

The advent of puberty opens a decisive chapter in the history of an obsessional neurosis. The genital organization which has been broken off in childhood starts again with great vigour. But, as we know, the sexual development in childhood determines what direction this new start at puberty will take. Not only will the early aggressive impulses be re-awakened; but a greater or lesser proportion of the new libidinal impulses – in bad cases the whole of them – will have to follow the course prescribed for them by regression and will emerge as aggressive and destructive tendencies. In consequence of the erotic trends being disguised in this way and owing to the powerful reaction-formations in the ego, the struggle against sexuality will henceforward be carried on under the banner of ethical principles. The ego will recoil with astonishment from promptings to cruelty and violence which enter consciousness from the id, and it has no notion that in them it is combating erotic wishes, including some to which it would not otherwise have taken exception. The overstrict super-ego insists all the more strongly on the suppression of sexuality, since this has assumed such repellent forms. Thus in obsessional neurosis the conflict is aggravated in two directions: the defensive forces become more intolerant and the forces that are to be fended off become more intolerable. Both effects are due to a single factor, namely, regression of the libido.

A good deal of what has been said may be objected to on

the ground that the unpleasant obsessive ideas are themselves quite conscious. But there is no doubt that before becoming conscious they have been through the process of repression. In most of them the actual wording of the aggressive instinctual impulse is altogether unknown to the ego, and it requires a good deal of analytic work to make it conscious. What does penetrate into consciousness is usually only a distorted substitute which is either of a vague, dream-like and indeterminate nature or so travestied as to be unrecognizable. Even where repression has not encroached upon the content of the aggressive impulse it has certainly got rid of its accompanying affective character. As a result, the aggressiveness appears to the ego not to be an impulsion, but, as the patients themselves say, merely a 'thought' which awakens no feeling.[1] But the remarkable thing is that this is not the case. What happens is that the affect left out when the obsessional idea is perceived appears in a different place. The super-ego behaves as though repression had not occurred and as though it knew the real wording and full affective character of the aggressive impulse, and it treats the ego accordingly. The ego which, on the one hand, knows that it is innocent is obliged, on the other hand, to be aware of a sense of guilt and to carry a responsibility which it cannot account for. This state of affairs is, however, not so puzzling as it would seem at first sight. The behaviour of the super-ego is perfectly intelligible, and the contradiction in the ego merely shows that it has shut out the id by means of repression, while remaining fully accessible to the influence of the super-ego.[2] If it is asked why the ego does not also attempt to withdraw from the tormenting criticism of the super-ego, the answer is that it *does* manage to do so in a great number of instances. There are obsessional neuroses in which no sense of guilt whatever is present. In them, as far as can be seen, the ego has avoided be-

1. [For all of this, see the 'Rat Man' case history (1909*d*), *P.F.L.*, **9**, 101 ff. and 48 *n*.]

2. Cf. Theodor Reik, 1925, 51.

coming aware of it by instituting a fresh set of symptoms, penances or restrictions of a self-punishing kind. These symptoms, however, represent at the same time a satisfaction of masochistic impulses which, in their turn, have been reinforced by regression.

Obsessional neurosis presents such a vast multiplicity of phenomena that no efforts have yet succeeded in making a coherent synthesis of all its variations. All we can do is to pick out certain typical correlations; but there is always the risk that we may have overlooked other uniformities of a now less important kind.

I have already described the general tendency of symptom-formation in obsessional neurosis. It is to give ever greater room to substitutive satisfaction at the expense of frustration. Symptoms which once stood for a restriction of the ego come later on to represent satisfactions as well, thanks to the ego's inclination to synthesis, and it is quite clear that this second meaning gradually becomes the more important of the two. The result of this process, which approximates more and more to a complete failure of the original purpose of defence, is an extremely restricted ego which is reduced to seeking satisfaction in the symptoms. The displacement of the distribution of forces in favour of satisfaction may have the dreaded final outcome of paralysing the will of the ego, which in every decision it has to make is almost as strongly impelled from the one side as from the other. The over-acute conflict between id and super-ego which has dominated the illness from the very beginning may assume such extensive proportions that the ego, unable to carry out its office of mediator, can undertake nothing which is not drawn into the sphere of that conflict.

VI

IN the course of these struggles we come across two activities of the ego which form symptoms and which deserve special attention because they are obviously surrogates of repression and therefore well calculated to illustrate its purpose and technique. The fact that such auxiliary and substitutive techniques emerge may argue that true repression has met with difficulties in its functioning. If one considers how much more the ego is the scene of action of symptom-formation in obsessional neurosis than it is in hysteria and with what tenacity the ego clings to its relations to reality and to consciousness, employing all its intellectual faculties to that end – and indeed how the very process of thinking becomes hypercathected and erotized – then one may perhaps come to a better understanding of these variations of repression.

The two techniques I refer to are *undoing what has been done* and *isolating*.[1] The first of these has a wide range of application and goes back very far. It is, as it were, negative magic, and endeavours, by means of motor symbolism, to 'blow away' not merely the *consequences* of some event (or experience or impression) but the event itself. I choose the term 'blow away' advisedly, so as to remind the reader of the part played by this technique not only in neuroses but in magical acts, popular customs and religious ceremonies as well. In obsessional neurosis the technique of undoing what has been done is first met with in the 'diphasic' symptoms [p. 267], in which one action is cancelled out by a second, so that it is as though neither action had taken place, whereas, in reality, both have. This aim of undoing is the second underlying motive of

1. [Both these techniques are referred to in the 'Rat Man' analysis (1909*d*), *P.F.L.*, **9**, 115 and 122. The first of them, in German '*ungeschehenmachen*', means literally 'making unhappened'.]

obsessional ceremonials, the first being to take precautions in order to prevent the occurrence or recurrence of some particular event. The difference between the two is easily seen: the precautionary measures are rational, while trying to get rid of something by 'making it not to have happened' is irrational and in the nature of magic. It is of course to be suspected that the latter is the earlier motive of the two and proceeds from the animistic attitude towards the environment. This endeavour to undo shades off into normal behaviour in the case in which a person decides to regard an event as not having happened.[1] But whereas he will take no direct steps against the event, and will simply pay no further attention to it or its consequences, the neurotic person will try to make the past itself non-existent. He will try to repress it by motor means. The same purpose may perhaps account for the obsession for *repeating* which is so frequently met with in this neurosis and the carrying out of which serves a number of contradictory intentions at once. When anything has not happened in the desired way it is undone by being repeated in a different way; and thereupon all the motives that exist for lingering over such repetitions come into play as well. As the neurosis proceeds, we often find that the endeavour to undo a traumatic experience is a motive of first-rate importance in the formation of symptoms. We thus unexpectedly discover a new, motor technique of defence, or (as we may say in this case with less inaccuracy) of repression.

The second of these techniques which we are setting out to describe for the first time, that of *isolation*, is peculiar to obsessional neurosis. It, too, takes place in the motor sphere. When something unpleasant has happened to the subject or when he himself has done something which has a significance for his neurosis, he interpolates an interval during which nothing further must happen – during which he must perceive nothing and do nothing.[2] This behaviour, which seems strange

1. [In the original: 'as "*non arrivé*"'.]
2. [Cf. the 'Rat Man', *P.F.L.*, **9**, 126.]

at first sight, is soon seen to have a relation to repression. We know that in hysteria it is possible to cause a traumatic experience to be overtaken by amnesia. In obsessional neurosis, this can often not be achieved: the experience is not forgotten, but, instead, it is deprived of its affect, and its associative connections are suppressed or interrupted so that it remains as though isolated and is not reproduced in the ordinary processes of thought. The effect of this isolation is the same as the effect of repression with amnesia. This technique, then, is reproduced in the isolations of obsessional neurosis; and it is at the same time given motor reinforcement for magical purposes. The elements that are held apart in this way are precisely those which belong together associatively. The motor isolation is meant to ensure an interruption of the connection in thought. The normal phenomenon of concentration provides a pretext for this kind of neurotic procedure: what seems to us important in the way of an impression or a piece of work must not be interfered with by the simultaneous claims of any other mental processes or activities. But even a normal person uses concentration to keep away not only what is irrelevant or unimportant, but, above all, what is unsuitable because it is contradictory. He is most disturbed by those elements which once belonged together but which have been torn apart in the course of his development – as, for instance, by manifestations of the ambivalence of his father-complex in his relation to God, or by impulses attached to his excretory organs in his emotions of love. Thus, in the normal course of things, the ego has a great deal of isolating work to do in its function of directing the current of thought. And, as we know, we are obliged, in carrying out our analytic technique, to train it to relinquish that function for the time being, eminently justified as it usually is.

We have all found by experience that it is especially difficult for an obsessional neurotic to carry out the fundamental rule of psychoanalysis. His ego is more watchful and makes sharper isolations, probably because of the high degree of tension due to conflict that exists between his super-ego and his id. While he is engaged in thinking, his ego has to keep off too much – the intrusion of unconscious phantasies and the manifestation of ambivalent trends. It must not relax, but is constantly prepared for a struggle. It fortifies this compulsion to concentrate and to isolate by the help of the magical acts of isolation, which, in the form of symptoms, grow to be so noticeable and to have so much practical importance for the patient, but which are, of course, useless in themselves and are in the nature of ceremonials.

But in this endeavouring to prevent associations and connections of thought, the ego is obeying one of the oldest and most fundamental commands of obsessional neurosis, the taboo on *touching*. If we ask ourselves why the avoidance of touching, contact or contagion should play such a large part in this neurosis and should become the subject-matter of complicated systems, the answer is that touching and physical contact are the immediate aim of the aggressive as well as the loving object-cathexes.[1] Eros desires contact because it strives to make the ego and the loved object one, to abolish all spatial barriers between them. But destructiveness, too, which (before the invention of long-range weapons) could only take effect at close quarters, must presuppose physical contact, a coming to grips. To 'touch' a woman has become a euphemism for using her as a sexual object. Not to 'touch' one's genitals is the phrase employed for forbidding auto-erotic satisfaction. Since obsessional neurosis begins by persecuting erotic touching and then, after regression has taken place, goes on to persecute touching in the guise of aggressiveness, it follows that nothing is so strongly proscribed in that illness as touching nor so well suited to become the central point of a system of prohibitions. But isolating is removing the possibility of contact; it is a method of withdrawing a thing from being touched in any way. And when a

1. [Cf. several passages in the second essay in *Totem and Taboo* (1912–13).]

neurotic isolates an impression or an activity by interpolating an interval, he is letting it be understood symbolically that he will not allow his thoughts about that impression or activity to come into associative contact with other thoughts.

This is as far as our investigations into the formation of symptoms take us. It is hardly worth while summing them up, for the results they have yielded are scanty and incomplete and tell us scarcely anything that we do not already know. It would be fruitless to turn our attention to symptom-formation in other disorders besides phobias, conversion hysteria and obsessional neurosis, for too little is known about them. But in reviewing those three neuroses together we are brought up against a very serious problem the consideration of which can no longer be put off. All three have as their outcome the destruction of the Oedipus complex; and in all three the motive force of the ego's opposition is, we believe, the fear of castration. Yet it is only in the phobias that this fear comes to the surface and is acknowledged. What has become of it in the other two neuroses? How has the ego spared itself this fear? The problem becomes accentuated when we recall the possibility, already referred to, that anxiety arises directly, by a kind of fermentation, from a libidinal cathexis whose processes have been disturbed. Furthermore, is it absolutely certain that fear of castration is the only motive force of repression (or defence)? If we think of neuroses in women we are bound to doubt it. For though we can with certainty establish in them the presence of a castration *complex*, we can hardly speak with propriety of castration *anxiety* where castration has already taken place.

VII

LET us go back again to infantile phobias of animals; for, when all is said and done, we understand them better than any other cases. In animal phobias, then, the ego has to oppose a libidinal object-cathexis coming from the id – a cathexis that belongs either to the positive or the negative Oedipus complex – because it believes that to give way to it would entail the danger of castration. This question has already been discussed, but there still remains a doubtful point to clear up. In 'Little Hans's' case – that is, in the case of a positive Oedipus complex – was it his fondness for his mother or was it his aggressiveness towards his father which called out the defence by the ego? In practice it seems to make no difference, especially as each set of feelings implies the other; but the question has a theoretical interest, since it is only the feeling of affection for the mother which can count as a purely erotic one. The aggressive impulse flows mainly from the destructive instinct; and we have always believed that in a neurosis it is against the demands of the libido and not against those of any other instinct that the ego is defending itself. In point of fact we know that after 'Hans's' phobia had been formed, his tender attachment to his mother seemed to disappear, having been completely disposed of by repression, while the formation of the symptom (the substitutive formation) took place in relation to his aggressive impulses. In the 'Wolf Man' the situation was simpler. The impulse that was repressed – his feminine attitude towards his father – was a genuinely erotic one; and it was in relation to that impulse that the formation of his symptoms took place.

It is almost humiliating that, after working so long, we should still be having difficulty in understanding the most fundamental facts. But we have made up our minds to simplify nothing and to hide nothing. If we cannot see things clearly we will at least see clearly what the obscurities are. What is hampering us here is evidently some hitch in the development of our theory of the instincts. We began by tracing the organization of the libido through its successive stages – from the oral through the sadistic-anal to the genital – and in doing so placed all the components of the sexual instinct on the same footing. Later it appeared that sadism was the representative of another instinct, which was opposed to Eros. This new view, that the instincts fall into two groups, seems to explode the earlier construction of the successive stages of libidinal organization. But we do not have to break fresh ground in order to find a way out of the difficulty. The solution has been at hand for a long time and lies in the fact that what we are concerned with are scarcely ever pure instinctual impulses but mixtures in various proportions of the two groups of instincts. If this is so, there is no need to revise our view of the organizations of the libido. A sadistic cathexis of an object may also legitimately claim to be treated as a libidinal one; and an aggressive impulse against the father can just as well be subjected to repression as a tender impulse towards the mother. Nevertheless we shall bear in mind for future consideration the possibility that repression is a process which has a special relation to the *genital* organization of the libido and that the ego resorts to other methods of defence when it has to secure itself against the libido on other levels of organization. To continue: a case like 'Little Hans's' does not enable us to come to any clear conclusion. It is true that in him an aggressive impulse was disposed of by repression, but this happened after the genital organization had been reached.

This time we will not lose sight of the part played by anxiety. We have said that as soon as the ego recognizes the danger of castration it gives the signal of anxiety and inhibits through the pleasure-unpleasure agency (in a way which we cannot as yet understand) the impending cathectic process in the id. At the same time the phobia is formed. And now the castration anxiety is directed to a different object and expressed in a distorted form, so that the patient is afraid, not of being castrated by his father, but of being bitten by a horse or devoured by a wolf. This substitutive formation has two obvious advantages. In the first place it avoids a conflict due to ambivalence (for the father was a loved object too), and in the second place it enables the ego to cease generating anxiety. For the anxiety belonging to a phobia is conditional; it only emerges when the object of it is perceived – and rightly so, since it is only then that the danger-situation is present. There is no need to be afraid of being castrated by a father who is not there. On the other hand one cannot get rid of a father; he can appear whenever he chooses. But if he is replaced by an animal, all one has to do is to avoid the sight of it – that is, its presence – in order to be free from danger and anxiety. 'Little Hans', therefore, imposed a restriction upon his ego. He produced the inhibition of not leaving the house, so as not to come across any horses. The young Russian had an even easier time of it, for it was hardly a privation for him not to look at a particular picture-book any more. If his naughty sister had not kept on showing him the book with the picture of the wolf standing upright in it, he would have been able to feel safe from his fear.[1]

On a previous occasion I have stated that phobias have the character of a projection in that they replace an internal, instinctual danger by an external, perceptual one. The advantage of this is that the subject can protect himself against an external danger by fleeing from it and avoiding the perception of it, whereas it is useless to flee from dangers that arise from within.[2] This statement of mine was not incorrect, but it did not go below the surface of things. For an instinctual demand

1. [*P.F.L.*, 9, 243.]

2. [See the account of phobias given in Section IV of Freud's metapsychological paper on 'The Unconscious' (1915*e*). See also Editor's Introduction, p. 232 above.]

is, after all, not dangerous in itself; it only becomes so inasmuch as it entails a real external danger, the danger of castration. Thus what happens in a phobia in the last resort is merely that one external danger is replaced by another. The view that in a phobia the ego is able to escape anxiety by means of avoidance or of inhibitory symptoms fits in very well with the theory that that anxiety is only an affective signal and that no alteration has taken place in the economic situation.

The anxiety felt in animal phobias is, therefore, an affective reaction on the part of the ego to danger; and the danger which is being signalled in this way is the danger of castration. This anxiety differs in no respect from the realistic anxiety which the ego normally feels in situations of danger, except that its content remains unconscious and only becomes conscious in the form of a distortion.

The same will prove true, I think, of the phobias of adults, although the material which their neuroses work over is much more abundant and there are some additional factors in the formation of the symptoms. Fundamentally the position is identical. The agoraphobic patient imposes a restriction on his ego so as to escape a certain instinctual danger – namely, the danger of giving way to his erotic desires. For if he did so the danger of being castrated, or some similar danger, would once more be conjured up as it was in his childhood. I may cite as an instance the case of a young man who became agoraphobic because he was afraid of yielding to the solicitations of prostitutes and of contracting a syphilitic infection from them as a punishment.

I am well aware that a number of cases exhibit a more complicated structure and that many other repressed instinctual impulses can enter into a phobia. But they are only tributary streams which have for the most part joined the main current of the neurosis at a later stage. The symptomatology of agoraphobia is complicated by the fact that the ego does not confine itself to making a renunciation. In order to rob the situation of danger it does more: it usually effects a temporal regression to infancy (in extreme cases, to a time when the subject was in his mother's womb and protected against the dangers which threaten him in the present). Such a regression now becomes a condition whose fulfilment exempts the ego from making its renunciation. For instance, an agoraphobic patient may be able to walk in the street provided he is accompanied, like a small child, by someone he knows and trusts; or, for the same reason, he may be able to go out alone provided he remains within a certain distance of his own house and does not go to places which are not familiar to him or where people do not know him. What these stipulations are will depend in each case on the infantile factors which dominate him through his neurosis. The phobia of being alone is unambiguous in its meaning, irrespective of any infantile regression: it is, ultimately, an endeavour to avoid the temptation to indulge in solitary masturbation. Infantile regression can, of course, only take place when the subject is no longer a child.

A phobia generally sets in after a first anxiety attack has been experienced in specific circumstances, such as in the street or in a train or in solitude. Thereafter the anxiety is held in ban by the phobia, but it re-emerges whenever the protective condition cannot be fulfilled. The mechanism of phobia does good service as a means of defence and tends to be very stable. A continuation of the defensive struggle, in the shape of a struggle against the symptom, occurs frequently but not invariably.

What we have learnt about anxiety in phobias is applicable to obsessional neuroses as well. In this respect it is not difficult for us to put obsessional neuroses on all fours with phobias. In the former, the mainspring of all later symptom-formation is clearly the ego's fear of its super-ego. The danger-situation from which the ego must get away is the hostility of the super-ego. There is no trace of projection here; the danger is completely internalized. But if we ask ourselves what it is that the ego fears from the super-ego, we cannot but think that the punishment threatened by the latter must be an extension of the punishment of castration. Just as the father has become depersonalized in the shape of the super-ego, so has the fear of castration at his hands become transformed into an undefined social or moral anxiety.[1] But this anxiety is concealed. The ego escapes it by obediently carrying out the commands, precautions and penances that have been enjoined on it. If it is impeded in doing so, it is at once overtaken by an extremely distressing feeling of discomfort which may be regarded as an equivalent of anxiety and which the patients themselves liken to anxiety.

The conclusion we have come to, then, is this. Anxiety is a reaction to a situation of danger. It is obviated by the ego's doing something to avoid that situation or to withdraw from it. It might be said that symptoms are created so as to avoid the generating of anxiety. But this does not go deep enough. It would be truer to say that symptoms are created so as to avoid a *danger-situation* whose presence has been signalled by the generation of anxiety. In the cases that we have discussed, the danger concerned was the danger of castration or of something traceable back to castration.

If anxiety is a reaction of the ego to danger, we shall be tempted to regard the traumatic neuroses, which so often follow upon a narrow escape from death, as a direct result of a fear of death (or fear *for* life) and to dismiss from our minds the question of castration and the dependent relationships of the ego [p. 247]. Most of those who observed the traumatic neuroses that

1. ['*Gewissensangst*', literally 'conscience anxiety'. This word is a cause of constant trouble to the translator. In ordinary usage it means no more than 'qualms of conscience'. But often in Freud, as in the present passage, stress is laid on the factor of anxiety in the concept. Sometimes, even, it might be rendered 'fear of conscience' where the distinction between 'conscience' and 'super-ego' is not sharply drawn. The fullest discussion of these questions will be found in Chapters VII and VIII of *Civilization and its Discontents* (1930a). Cf also above, p. 38 and *n*. 2.]

occurred during the last war[1] took this line, and triumphantly announced that proof was now forthcoming that a threat to the instinct of self-preservation could by itself produce a neurosis without any admixture of sexual factors and without requiring any of the complicated hypotheses of psychoanalysis. It is in fact greatly to be regretted that not a single analysis of a traumatic neurosis of any value is extant.[2] And it is to be regretted, not because such an analysis would contradict the aetiological importance of sexuality – for any such contradiction has long since been disposed of by the introduction of the concept of narcissism, which brings the libidinal cathexis of the ego into line with the cathexes of objects and emphasizes the libidinal character of the instinct of self-preservation – but because, in the absence of any analyses of this kind, we have lost a most precious opportunity of drawing decisive conclusions about the relations between anxiety and the formation of symptoms. In view of all that we know about the structure of the comparatively simple neuroses of everyday life, it would seem highly improbable that a neurosis could come into being merely because of the objective presence of danger, without any participation of the deeper levels of the mental apparatus. But the unconscious seems to contain nothing that could give any content to our concept of the annihilation of life. Castration can be pictured on the basis of the daily experience of the faeces being separated from the body or on the basis of losing the mother's breast at weaning.[3] But nothing resembling death can ever have been experienced; or if it has, as in fainting, it has left no observable traces behind. I am therefore inclined to adhere to the view that the fear of death should be regarded as analogous to the fear of castration and that the situation to

1. [The First World War.]
2. [See Freud's discussion of the war neuroses (1919d).]
3. [See a footnote added in 1923 to the 'Little Hans' case history, P.F.L., 8, 172 n. 2.]

which the ego is reacting is one of being abandoned by the protecting super-ego – the powers of destiny – so that it has no longer any safeguard against all the dangers that surround it.[1] In addition, it must be remembered that in the experiences which lead to a traumatic neurosis the protective shield against external stimuli is broken through and excessive amounts of excitation impinge upon the mental apparatus [cf. p. 245 f.]; so that we have here a second possibility – that anxiety is not only being signalled as an affect but is also being freshly created out of the economic conditions of the situation.

The statement I have just made, to the effect that the ego has been prepared to expect castration by having undergone constantly repeated object-losses, places the question of anxiety in a new light. We have hitherto regarded it as an affective signal of danger; but now, since the danger is so often one of castration, it appears to us as a reaction to a loss, a separation. Even though a number of considerations immediately arise which make against this view, we cannot but be struck by one very remarkable correlation. The first experience of anxiety which an individual goes through (in the case of human beings, at all events) is birth, and, objectively speaking, birth is a separation from the mother. It could be compared to a castration of the mother (by equating the child with a penis). Now it would be very satisfactory if anxiety, as a symbol of a separation, were to be repeated on every subsequent occasion on which a separation took place. But unfortunately we are prevented from making use of this correlation by the fact that birth is not experienced subjectively as a separation from the mother, since the foetus, being a completely narcissistic creature, is totally unaware of her existence as an object. Another adverse argument is that we know what the affective reactions to a separation are: they are pain and mourning, not anxiety. Incidentally, it may be remembered that in discussing the

1. [Cf. the last few paragraphs of *The Ego and the Id* (1923b). See also below, p. 297.]

question of mourning we also failed to discover why it should be such a painful thing.[1]

1. [See 'Mourning and Melancholia' (1917*e*). Freud returns to this subject in Addendum C, p. 329 ff. below.]

VIII

THE time has come to pause and consider. What we clearly want is to find something that will tell us what anxiety really is, some criterion that will enable us to distinguish true statements about it from false ones. But this is not easy to get. Anxiety is not so simple a matter. Up till now we have arrived at nothing but contradictory views about it, none of which can, to the unprejudiced eye, be given preference over the others. I therefore propose to adopt a different procedure. I propose to assemble, quite impartially, all the facts that we know about anxiety without expecting to arrive at a fresh synthesis.

Anxiety, then, is in the first place something that is felt. We call it an affective state, although we are also ignorant of what an affect is. As a feeling, anxiety has a very marked character of unpleasure. But that is not the whole of its quality. Not every unpleasure can be called anxiety, for there are other feelings, such as tension, pain or mourning, which have the character of unpleasure. Thus anxiety must have other distinctive features besides this quality of unpleasure. Can we succeed in understanding the differences between these various unpleasurable affects?

We can at any rate note one or two things about the feeling of anxiety. Its unpleasurable character seems to have a note of its own – something not very obvious, whose presence is difficult to prove yet which is in all likelihood there. But besides having this special feature which is difficult to isolate, we notice that anxiety is accompanied by fairly definite physical sensations which can be referred to particular organs of the body. As we are not concerned here with the physiology of anxiety, we shall content ourselves with mentioning a few representatives of these sensations. The clearest and most frequent ones are those connected with the respiratory organs and with the heart.[1] They provide evidence that motor innervations – that is, processes of discharge – play a part in the general phenomenon of anxiety.

Analysis of anxiety-states therefore reveals the existence of (1) a specific character of unpleasure, (2) acts of discharge and (3) perceptions of those acts. The two last points indicate at once a difference between states of anxiety and other similar states, like those of mourning and pain. The latter do not have any motor manifestation; or if they have, the manifestation is not an integral part of the whole state but is distinct from it as being a result of it or a reaction to it. Anxiety, then, is a special state of unpleasure with acts of discharge along particular paths. In accordance with our general views[2] we should be inclined to think that anxiety is based upon an increase of excitation which on the one hand produces the character of unpleasure and on the other finds relief through the acts of discharge already mentioned. But a purely physiological account of this sort will scarcely satisfy us. We are tempted to assume the presence of a historical factor which binds the sensations of anxiety and its innervations firmly together. We assume, in other words, that an anxiety-state is the reproduction of some experience which contained the necessary conditions for such an increase of excitation and a discharge along particular paths, and that from this circumstance the unpleasure of anxiety receives its specific character. In man, birth provides a prototypic experience of this kind, and we are therefore inclined to regard anxiety-states as a reproduction of the trauma of birth. [See above, p. 245.]

This does not imply that anxiety occupies an exceptional position among the affective states. In my opinion the other affects are also reproductions of very early, perhaps even pre-individual, experiences of vital importance; and I should be

1. [Cf. Freud's first paper on anxiety neurosis (1895b), p. 39 above.]
2. [As expressed, for instance, in the opening pages of *Beyond the Pleasure Principle* (1920g).]

inclined to regard them as universal, typical and innate hysterical attacks, as compared to the recently and individually acquired attacks which occur in hysterical neuroses and whose origin and significance as mnemic symbols have been revealed by analysis. It would be very desirable, of course, to be able to demonstrate the truth of this view in a number of such affects – a thing which is still very far from being the case.[1]

The view that anxiety goes back to the event of birth raises immediate objections which have to be met. It may be argued that anxiety is a reaction which, in all probability, is common to every organism, certainly every organism of a higher order, whereas birth is only experienced by the mammals; and it is doubtful whether in all of them, even, birth has the significance of a trauma. Therefore there can be anxiety without the prototype of birth. But this objection takes us beyond the barrier that divides psychology from biology. It may be that, precisely because anxiety has an indispensable biological function to fulfil as a reaction to a state of danger, it is differently contrived in different organisms. We do not know, besides, whether anxiety involves the same sensations and innervations in organisms far removed from man as it does in man himself. Thus there is no good argument here against the view that, in man, anxiety is modelled upon the process of birth.

If the structure and origin of anxiety are as described, the next question is: what is the function of anxiety and on what occasions is it reproduced? The answer seems to be obvious and convincing: anxiety arose originally as a reaction to a state of *danger* and it is reproduced whenever a state of that kind recurs.

This answer, however, raises further considerations. The innervations involved in the original state of anxiety probably

1. [This notion is probably derived from Darwin's *Expression of the Emotions* (1872), which was quoted by Freud in a similar connection in *Studies on Hysteria* (1895*d*), P.F.L., **3**, 254. See Editor's Introduction, p. 235 above.]

had a meaning and purpose, in just the same way as the muscular movements which accompany a first hysterical attack. In order to understand a hysterical attack, all one has to do is to look for the situation in which the movements in question formed part of an appropriate and expedient action. Thus at birth it is probable that the innervation, in being directed to the respiratory organs, is preparing the way for the activity of the lungs, and, in accelerating the heartbeat, is helping to keep the blood free from toxic substances. Naturally, when the anxiety-state is reproduced later as an affect it will be lacking in any such expediency, just as are the repetitions of a hysterical attack. When the individual is placed in a new situation of danger it may well be quite inexpedient for him to respond with an anxiety-state (which is a reaction to an earlier danger) instead of initiating a reaction appropriate to the current danger. But his behaviour may become expedient once more if the danger-situation is recognized as it approaches and is signalled by an outbreak of anxiety. In that case he can at once get rid of his anxiety by having recourse to more suitable measures. Thus we see that there are two ways in which anxiety can emerge: in an inexpedient way, when a new situation of danger has occurred, or in an expedient way in order to give a signal and prevent such a situation from occurring.

But what is a 'danger'? In the act of birth there is a real danger to life. We know what this means objectively; but in a psychological sense it says nothing at all to us. The danger of birth has as yet no psychical content. We cannot possibly suppose that the foetus has any sort of knowledge that there is a possibility of its life being destroyed. It can only be aware of some vast disturbance in the economy of its narcissistic libido. Large sums of excitation crowd in upon it, giving rise to new kinds of feelings of unpleasure, and some organs acquire an increased cathexis, thus foreshadowing the object-cathexis which will soon set in. What elements in all this will be made use of as the sign of a 'danger-situation'?

Unfortunately far too little is known about the mental make-up of a new-born baby to make a direct answer possible. I cannot even vouch for the validity of the description I have just given. It is easy to say that the baby will repeat its affect of anxiety in every situation which recalls the event of birth. The important thing to know is what recalls the event and what it is that is recalled.

All we can do is to examine the occasions on which infants in arms or somewhat older children show readiness to produce anxiety. In his book on the trauma of birth, Rank (1924) has made a determined attempt to establish a relationship between the earliest phobias of children and the impressions made on them by the event of birth. But I do not think he has been successful. His theory is open to two objections. In the first place, he assumes that the infant has received certain sensory impressions, in particular of a visual kind, at the time of birth, the renewal of which can recall to its memory the trauma of birth and thus evoke a reaction of anxiety. This assumption is quite unfounded and extremely improbable. It is not credible that a child should retain any but tactile and general sensations relating to the process of birth. If, later on, children show fear of small animals that disappear into holes or emerge from them, this reaction, according to Rank, is due to their perceiving an analogy. But it is an analogy of which they cannot be aware. In the second place, in considering these later anxiety-situations Rank dwells, as suits him best, now on the child's recollection of its happy intra-uterine existence, now on its recollection of the traumatic disturbance which interrupted that existence – which leaves the door wide open for arbitrary interpretation. There are, moreover, certain examples of childhood anxiety which directly traverse his theory. When, for instance, a child is left alone in the dark one would expect it, according to his view, to welcome the re-establishment of the intra-uterine situation; yet it is precisely on such occasions that the child reacts with anxiety. And if this is explained by saying that the child is being reminded of the interruption which the event of birth made in its intra-uterine happiness, it becomes impossible to shut one's eyes any longer to the far-fetched character of such explanations.[1]

I am driven to the conclusion that the earliest phobias of infancy cannot be directly traced back to impressions of the act of birth and that so far they have not been explained. A certain preparedness for anxiety is undoubtedly present in the infant in arms. But this preparedness for anxiety, instead of being at its maximum immediately after birth and then slowly decreasing, does not emerge till later, as mental development proceeds, and lasts over a certain period of childhood. If these early phobias persist beyond that period one is inclined to suspect the presence of a neurotic disturbance, although it is not at all clear what their relation is to the undoubted neuroses that appear later on in childhood.

Only a few of the manifestations of anxiety in children are comprehensible to us, and we must confine our attention to them. They occur, for instance, when a child is alone, or in the dark,[2] or when it finds itself with an unknown person instead of one to whom it is used – such as its mother. These three instances can be reduced to a single condition – namely, that of missing someone who is loved and longed for. But here, I think, we have the key to an understanding of anxiety and to a reconciliation of the contradictions that seem to beset it.

The child's mnemic image of the person longed for is no doubt intensely cathected, probably in a hallucinatory way at first. But this has no effect; and now it seems as though the longing turns into anxiety. This anxiety has all the appearance of being an expression of the child's feeling at its wits' end, as though in its still very undeveloped state it did not know how better to cope with its cathexis of longing. Here anxiety appears

1. [Rank's theory is further discussed below, p. 308 ff.]
2. [Cf. a footnote to Section 5 of the third of Freud's *Three Essays* (1905*d*), *P.F.L.*, **7**, 147.]

as a reaction to the felt loss of the object; and we are at once reminded of the fact that castration anxiety, too, is a fear of being separated from a highly valued object, and that the earliest anxiety of all – the 'primal anxiety' of birth – is brought about on the occasion of a separation from the mother.

But a moment's reflection takes us beyond this question of loss of object. The reason why the infant in arms wants to perceive the presence of its mother is only because it already knows by experience that she satisfies all its needs without delay. The situation, then, which it regards as a 'danger' and against which it wants to be safeguarded is that of non-satisfaction, of a *growing tension due to need*, against which it is helpless. I think that if we adopt this view all the facts fall into place. The situation of non-satisfaction in which the amounts of stimulation rise to an unpleasurable height without its being possible for them to be mastered psychically or discharged must for the infant be analogous to the experience of being born – must be a repetition of the situation of danger. What both situations have in common is the economic disturbance caused by an accumulation of amounts of stimulation which require to be disposed of. It is this factor, then, which is the real essence of the 'danger'. In both cases the reaction of anxiety sets in. (This reaction is still an expedient one in the infant in arms, for the discharge, being directed into the respiratory and vocal muscular apparatus, now calls its mother to it, just as it activated the lungs of the new-born baby to get rid of the internal stimuli.) It is unnecessary to suppose that the child carries anything more with it from the time of its birth than this way of indicating the presence of danger.

When the infant has found out by experience that an external, perceptible object can put an end to the dangerous situation which is reminiscent of birth, the content of the danger it fears is displaced from the economic situation on to the condition which determined that situation, viz., the loss of object. It is the absence of the mother that is now the danger;

and as soon as that danger arises the infant gives the signal of anxiety, before the dreaded economic situation has set in. This change constitutes a first great step forward in the provision made by the infant for its self-preservation, and at the same time represents a transition from the automatic and involuntary fresh appearance of anxiety to the intentional reproduction of anxiety as a signal of danger.

In these two aspects, as an automatic phenomenon and as a rescuing signal, anxiety is seen to be a product of the infant's mental helplessness which is a natural counterpart of its biological helplessness. The striking coincidence by which the anxiety of the new-born baby and the anxiety of the infant in arms are both conditioned by separation from the mother does not need to be explained on psychological lines. It can be accounted for simply enough biologically; for, just as the mother originally satisfied all the needs of the foetus through the apparatus of her own body, so now, after its birth, she continues to do so, though partly by other means. There is much more continuity between intra-uterine life and earliest infancy than the impressive caesura[1] of the act of birth would have us believe. What happens is that the child's biological situation as a foetus is replaced for it by a psychical object-relation to its mother. But we must not forget that during its intra-uterine life the mother was not an object for the foetus, and that at that time there were no objects at all. It is obvious that in this scheme of things there is no place for the abreaction of the birth-trauma. We cannot find that anxiety has any function other than that of being a signal for the avoidance of a danger-situation.

The significance of the loss of object as a determinant of anxiety extends considerably further. For the next transformation of anxiety, viz. the castration anxiety belonging to the phallic phase, is also a fear of separation and is thus attached

1. [The word 'caesura' is a term derived from classical prosody, and means a particular kind of break in a line of verse.]

to the same determinant. In this case the danger is of being separated from one's genitals. Ferenczi [1925] has traced, quite correctly, I think, a clear line of connection between this fear and the fears contained in the earlier situations of danger. The high degree of narcissistic value which the penis possesses can appeal to the fact that that organ is a guarantee to its owner that he can be once more united to his mother – i.e. to a substitute for her – in the act of copulation. Being deprived of it amounts to a renewed separation from her, and this in its turn means being helplessly exposed to an unpleasurable tension due to instinctual need, as was the case at birth. But the need whose increase is feared is now a specific one belonging to the genital libido and is no longer an indeterminate one, as it was in the period of infancy. It may be added that for a man who is impotent (that is, who is inhibited by the threat of castration) the substitute for copulation is a phantasy of returning into his mother's womb. Following Ferenczi's line of thought, we might say that the man in question, having tried to bring about his return into his mother's womb by using his genital organ to represent him, is now [in this phantasy] replacing that organ regressively by his whole person.[1]

The progress which the child makes in its development – its growing independence, the sharper division of its mental apparatus into several agencies, the advent of new needs – cannot fail to exert an influence upon the content of the danger-situation. We have already traced the change of that content from loss of the mother as an object to castration. The next change is caused by the power of the super-ego. With the depersonalization of the parental agency from which castration was feared, the danger becomes less defined. Castration anxiety develops into moral anxiety – social anxiety – and it is not so easy now to know what the anxiety is about. The formula, 'separation and expulsion from the horde', only applies to that

1. [Freud had already discussed this phantasy in the 'Wolf Man' analysis (1918b), P.F.L., 9, 340 –43.]

later portion of the super-ego which has been formed on the basis of social prototypes, not to the nucleus of the super-ego, which corresponds to the introjected parental agency. Putting it more generally, what the ego regards as the danger and responds to with an anxiety-signal is that the super-ego should be angry with it or punish it or cease to love it. The final transformation which the fear of the super-ego undergoes is, it seems to me, the fear of death (or fear for life) which is a fear of the super-ego projected on to the powers of destiny.[1]

At one time I attached some importance to the view that what was used as a discharge of anxiety was the cathexis which had been withdrawn in the process of repression.[2] To-day this seems to me of scarcely any interest. The reason for this is that whereas I formerly believed that anxiety invariably arose automatically by an economic process, my present conception of anxiety as a signal given by the ego in order to affect the pleasure-unpleasure agency does away with the necessity of considering the economic factor. Of course there is nothing to be said against the idea that it is precisely the energy that has been liberated by being withdrawn through repression which is used by the ego to arouse the affect; but it is no longer of any importance which portion of energy is employed for this purpose. [Cf. Editor's Introduction, p. 232.]

This new view of things calls for an examination of another assertion of mine – namely, that the ego is the actual seat of anxiety.[3] I think this proposition still holds good. There is no reason to assign any manifestation of anxiety to the super-ego; while the expression 'anxiety of the id' would stand in need of correction, though rather as to its form than its substance. Anxiety is an affective state and as such can, of course, only be

1. [Cf. above, pp. 285–6.]
2. [See, for instance, Section IV of Freud's metapsychological paper on 'The Unconscious' (1915e).]
3. [This will be found a couple of pages before the end of *The Ego and the Id* (1923b).]

felt by the ego. The id cannot have anxiety as the ego can; for it is not an organization and cannot make a judgement about situations of danger. On the other hand it very often happens that processes take place or begin to take place in the id which cause the ego to produce anxiety. Indeed, it is probable that the earliest repressions as well as most of the later ones are motivated by an ego-anxiety of this sort in regard to particular processes in the id. Here again we are rightly distinguishing between two cases: the case in which something occurs in the id which activates one of the danger-situations for the ego and induces the latter to give the anxiety-signal for inhibition to take place, and the case in which a situation analogous to the trauma of birth is established in the id and an automatic reaction of anxiety ensues. The two cases may be brought closer together if it is pointed out that the second case corresponds to the earliest and original danger-situation, while the first case corresponds to any one of the later determinants of anxiety that have been derived from it; or, as applied to the disorders which we in fact come across, that the second case is operative in the aetiology of the 'actual' neuroses, while the first remains typical for that of the psychoneuroses.

We see, then, that it is not so much a question of taking back our earlier findings as of bringing them into line with more recent discoveries. It is still an undeniable fact that in sexual abstinence, in improper interference with the course of sexual excitation or if the latter is diverted from being worked over psychically,[1] anxiety arises directly out of libido; in other words, that the ego is reduced to a state of helplessness in the face of an excessive tension due to need, as it was in the situation of birth, and that anxiety is then generated. Here once more, though the matter is of little importance, it is very possible that what finds discharge in the generating of anxiety is precisely

1. [The phrase will be found in Section III of Freud's first paper on anxiety neurosis (1895b), of which the whole of the present passage is an echo. Cf. pp. 55–7 above.]

the surplus of unutilized libido.[1] As we know, a psychoneurosis is especially liable to develop on the basis of an 'actual' neurosis. This looks as though the ego were attempting to save itself from anxiety, which it has learned to keep in suspension for a while, and to bind it by the formation of symptoms. Analysis of the traumatic war neuroses – a term which, incidentally, covers a great variety of disorders – would probably have shown that a number of them possess some characteristics of the 'actual' neuroses. [Cf. above, pp. 284–5.]

In describing the evolution of the various danger-situations from their prototype, the act of birth, I have had no intention of asserting that every later determinant of anxiety completely invalidates the preceding one. It is true that, as the development of the ego goes on, the earlier danger-situations tend to lose their force and to be set aside, so that we might say that each period of the individual's life has its appropriate determinant of anxiety. Thus the danger of psychical helplessness is appropriate to the period of life when his ego is immature; the danger of loss of object, to early childhood when he is still dependent on others; the danger of castration, to the phallic phase; and the fear of his super-ego, to the latency period. Nevertheless, all these danger-situations and determinants of anxiety can persist side by side and cause the ego to react to them with anxiety at a period later than the appropriate one; or, again, several of them can come into operation at the same time. It is possible, moreover, that there is a fairly close relationship between the danger-situation that is operative and the form taken by the ensuing neurosis.[2]

1. [Cf. the similar remark at the end of the last paragraph but one, but see also the Editor's Introduction, p. 232 above.]

2. Since the differentiation of the ego and the id, our interest in the problems of repression, too, was bound to receive a fresh impetus. Up till then we had been content to confine our interest to those aspects of repression which concerned the ego – the keeping away from consciousness and from motility, and the formation of substitutes (symptoms). With regard to the repressed instinctual impulses themselves, we

When, in an earlier part of this discussion, we found that the danger of castration was of importance in more than one neurotic illness, we put ourselves on guard against over-estimating that factor, since it could not be a decisive one for the female sex, who are undoubtedly more subject to neuroses than men. [See p. 278.] We now see that there is no danger of our regarding castration anxiety as the sole motive force of the defensive processes which lead to neurosis. I have shown elsewhere[1] how little girls, in the course of their development, are led into making a tender object-cathexis by their castration complex. It is precisely in women that the danger-situation of loss of object seems to have remained the most effective. All

---

assumed that they remained unaltered in the unconscious for an in-definite length of time. But now our interest is turned to the vicissitudes of the repressed and we begin to suspect that it is not self-evident, perhaps not even usual, that those impulses should remain unaltered and unalterable in this way. There is no doubt that the original impulses have been inhibited and deflected from their aim through repression. But has the portion of them in the unconscious maintained itself and been proof against the influences of life that tend to alter and depreciate them? In other words, do the old wishes, about whose former existence analysis tells us, still exist? The answer seems ready to hand and certain. It is that the old, repressed wishes must still be present in the uncon-scious since we still find their derivatives, the symptoms, in operation. But this answer is not sufficient. It does not enable us to decide between two possibilities: either that the old wish is now operating only through its derivatives, having transferred the whole of its cathectic energy to them, or that it is itself still in existence too. If its fate has been to exhaust itself in cathecting its derivatives, there is yet a third possibility. In the course of the neurosis it may have become re-animated by regression, anachronistic though it may now be. These are no idle speculations. There are many things about mental life, both normal and pathological, which seem to call for the raising of such questions. In my paper, 'The Dissolution of the Oedipus Complex' [1924*d*], I had occasion to notice the difference between the mere repression and the real removal of an old wishful impulse. [Cf. *P.F.L.*, **7**, 314 ff. and in particular p. 319.]

1. [See the second half of the paper on the consequences of the anatomical distinction between the sexes (1925*j*), *P.F.L.*, **7**, 334 ff.]

we need to do is to make a slight modification in our description of their determinant of anxiety, in the sense that it is no longer a matter of feeling the want of, or actually losing the object itself, but of losing the object's love. Since there is no doubt that hysteria has a strong affinity with femininity, just as obsessional neurosis has with masculinity, it appears probable that, as a determinant of anxiety, loss of love plays much the same part in hysteria as the threat of castration does in phobias and fear of the super-ego in obsessional neurosis.

IX

WHAT is now left for us is to consider the relationship between the formation of symptoms and the generating of anxiety.

There seem to be two very widely held opinions on this subject. One is that anxiety is itself a symptom of neurosis. The other is that there is a much more intimate relation between the two.[1] According to the second opinion, symptoms are only formed in order to avoid anxiety: they bind the psychical energy which would otherwise be discharged as anxiety. Thus anxiety would be the fundamental phenomenon and main problem of neurosis.

That this latter opinion is at least in part true is shown by some striking examples. If an agoraphobic patient who has been accompanied into the street is left alone there, he will produce an anxiety attack. Or if an obsessional neurotic is prevented from washing his hands after having touched something, he will become a prey to almost unbearable anxiety. It is plain, then, that the purpose and the result of the imposed condition of being accompanied in the street and the obsessional act of washing the hands were to obviate outbreaks of anxiety of this kind. In this sense every inhibition which the ego imposes on itself can be called a symptom.

Since we have traced back the generating of anxiety to a situation of danger, we shall prefer to say that symptoms are created in order to remove the ego from a situation of danger. If the symptoms are prevented from being formed, the danger does in fact materialize; that is, a situation analogous to birth is established in which the ego is helpless in the face of a constantly increasing instinctual demand – the earliest and original determinant of anxiety. Thus in our view the relation between anxiety and symptom is less close than was supposed, for we

1. [i.e. between anxiety and neurosis.]

have inserted the factor of the danger-situation between them. We can also add that the generating of anxiety sets symptom-formation going and is, indeed, a necessary prerequisite of it. For if the ego did not arouse the pleasure-unpleasure agency by generating anxiety, it would not obtain the power to arrest the process which is preparing in the id and which threatens danger. There is in all this an evident inclination to limit to a minimum the amount of anxiety generated and to employ it only as a signal; for to do otherwise would only result in feeling in another place the unpleasure which the instinctual process was threatening to produce, and that would not be a success from the standpoint of the pleasure principle, although it is one that occurs often enough in the neuroses.

Symptom-formation, then, does in fact put an end to the danger-situation. It has two aspects: one, hidden from view, brings about the alteration in the id in virtue of which the ego is removed from danger; the other, presented openly, shows what has been created in place of the instinctual process that has been affected – namely, the substitutive formation.

It would, however, be more correct to ascribe to the *defensive process* what we have just said about symptom-formation and to use the latter term as synonymous with substitute-formation. It will then be clear that the defensive process is analogous to the flight by means of which the ego removes itself from a danger that threatens it from outside. The defensive process is an attempt at flight from an instinctual danger. An examination of the weak points in this comparison will make things clearer.

One objection to it is that loss of an object (or loss of love on the part of the object) and the threat of castration are just as much dangers coming from outside as, let us say, a ferocious animal would be; they are not instinctual dangers. Neverthe-less, the two cases are not the same. A wolf would probably attack us irrespectively of our behaviour towards it; but the loved person would not cease to love us nor should we be threatened with castration if we did not entertain certain feelings and intentions within us. Thus such instinctual impulses are determinants of external dangers and so become dangerous in themselves; and we can now proceed against the external danger by taking measures against the internal ones. In phobias of animals the danger seems to be still felt entirely as an external one, just as it has undergone an external displacement in the symptom. In obsessional neuroses the danger is much more internalized. That portion of anxiety in regard to the super-ego which constitutes *social* anxiety, still represents an internal substitute for an external danger, while the other portion – *moral* anxiety – is already completely endopsychic.[1]

Another objection is that in an attempt at flight from an impending external danger all that the subject is doing is to increase the distance between himself and what is threatening him. He is not preparing to defend himself against it or attempting to alter anything about it, as would be the case if he attacked the wolf with a stick or shot at it with a gun. But the defensive process seems to do something more than would correspond to an attempt at flight. It joins issue with the threatening instinctual process and somehow suppresses it or deflects it from its aims and thus renders it innocuous. This objection seems unimpeachable and must be given due weight. I think it is probable that there are some defensive processes which can truly be likened to an attempt at flight, while in others the ego takes a much more active line of self-protection and initiates vigorous counter-measures. But perhaps the whole analogy between defence and flight is invalidated by the fact that both the ego and the instinct in the id are parts of the same organization, not separate entities like the wolf and the child, so that any kind of

1. [Much of the present discussion is a reassessment of the arguments which Freud had used in his metapsychological papers on 'Repression' (1915*d*) and 'The Unconscious' (1915*e*), in particular, Section IV. – For 'moral anxiety' cf. footnote, p. 284 above.]

behaviour on the part of the ego will result in an alteration in the instinctual process as well.

This study of the determinants of anxiety has, as it were, shown the defensive behaviour of the ego transfigured in a rational light. Each situation of danger corresponds to a particular period of life or a particular developmental phase of the mental apparatus and appears to be justifiable for it. In early infancy the individual is really not equipped to master psychically the large sums of excitation that reach him whether from without or from within. Again, at a certain period of life his most important interest really is that the people he is dependent on should not withdraw their loving care of him. Later on in his boyhood, when he feels that his father is a powerful rival in regard to his mother and becomes aware of his own aggressive inclinations towards him and of his sexual intentions towards his mother, he really is justified in being afraid of his father; and his fear of being punished by him can find expression through phylogenetic reinforcement in the fear of being castrated. Finally, as he enters into social relationships, it really is necessary for him to be afraid of his super-ego, to have a conscience; and the absence of that factor would give rise to severe conflicts, dangers and so on.

But this last point raises a fresh problem. Instead of the affect of anxiety let us take, for a moment, another affect – that of pain, for instance. It seems quite normal that at four years of age a girl should weep painfully if her doll is broken; or at six, if her governess reproves her; or at sixteen, if she is slighted by her young man; or at twenty-five, perhaps, if a child of her own dies. Each of these determinants of pain has its own time and each passes away when that time is over. Only the final and definitive determinants remain throughout life. We should think it strange if this same girl, after she had grown to be a wife and mother, were to cry over some worthless trinket that had been damaged. Yet that is how the neurotic behaves. Although all the agencies for mastering stimuli have long ago been developed within wide limits in his mental apparatus, and although he is sufficiently grown-up to satisfy most of his needs for himself and has long ago learnt that castration is no longer practised as a punishment, he nevertheless behaves as though the old danger-situations still existed, and keeps hold of all the earlier determinants of anxiety.

Why this should be so calls for a rather long reply. First of all, we must sift the facts. In a great number of cases the old determinants of anxiety do really lapse, after having produced neurotic reactions. The phobias of very young children, fears of being alone or in the dark or with strangers – phobias which can almost be called normal – usually pass off later on; the child 'grows out of them', as we say about some other disturbances of childhood. Animal phobias, which are of such frequent occurrence, undergo the same fate and many conversion hysterias of early years find no continuation in later life. Ceremonial actions appear extremely often in the latency period, but only a very small percentage of them develop later into a full obsessional neurosis. In general, so far as we can tell from our observations of town children belonging to the white races and living according to fairly high cultural standards, the neuroses of childhood are in the nature of regular episodes in a child's development, although too little attention is still being paid to them. Signs of childhood neuroses can be detected in *all* adult neurotics without exception; but by no means all children who show those signs become neurotic in later life. It must be, therefore, that certain determinants of anxiety are relinquished and certain danger-situations lose their significance as the individual becomes more mature. Moreover, some of these danger-situations manage to survive into later times by modifying their determinants of anxiety so as to bring them up to date. Thus, for instance, a man may retain his fear of castration in the guise of a syphilidophobia, after he has come to know that it is no longer customary to castrate people for indulging their sexual lusts, but that, on the other hand, severe diseases may overtake anyone who thus gives way to his instincts. Other determinants of anxiety, such as fear of the super-ego, are destined not to disappear at all but to accompany people throughout their lives. In that case the neurotic will differ from the normal person in that his reactions to the dangers in question will be unduly strong. Finally, being grown-up affords no absolute protection against a return of the original traumatic anxiety-situation. Each individual has in all probability a limit beyond which his mental apparatus fails in its function of mastering the quantities of excitation which require to be disposed of.

These minor rectifications cannot in any way alter the fact which is here under discussion, that a great many people remain infantile in their behaviour in regard to danger and do not overcome determinants of anxiety which have grown out of date. To deny this would be to deny the existence of neurosis, for it is precisely such people whom we call neurotics. But how is this possible? Why are not all neuroses episodes in the development of the individual which come to a close when the next phase is reached? Whence comes the element of persistence in these reactions to danger? Why does the affect of anxiety alone seem to enjoy the advantage over all other affects of evoking reactions which are distinguished from the rest in being abnormal and which, through their inexpediency, run counter to the movement of life? In other words, we have once more come unawares upon the riddle which has so often confronted us: whence does neurosis come – what is its ultimate, its own peculiar *raison d'être*? After tens of years of psycho-analytic labours, we are as much in the dark about this problem as we were at the start.

X

ANXIETY is the reaction to danger. One cannot, after all, help suspecting that the reason why the affect of anxiety occupies a unique position in the economy of the mind has something to do with the essential nature of danger. Yet dangers are the common lot of humanity; they are the same for everyone. What we need and cannot lay our finger on is some factor which will explain why some people are able to subject the affect of anxiety, in spite of its peculiar quality, to the normal workings of the mind, or which decides who is doomed to come to grief over that task. Two attempts to find a factor of this kind have been made; and it is natural that such efforts should meet with a sympathetic reception, since they promise help to meet a tormenting need. The two attempts in question are mutually complementary; they approach the problem at opposite ends. The first was made by Alfred Adler more than ten years ago.[1] His contention, reduced to its essence, was that the people who came to grief over the task set them by danger were those who were too greatly impeded by some organic inferiority. If it were true that *simplex sigillum veri*,[2] we should welcome such a solution [*Lösung*] as a deliverance [*Erlösung*]. But on the contrary, our critical studies of the last ten years have effectively demonstrated the total inadequacy of such an explanation – an explanation, moreover, which sets aside the whole wealth of material that has been discovered by psychoanalysis.

The second attempt was made by Otto Rank in 1923 in his book, *The Trauma of Birth*. [See pp. 236 and 292f.] It would be unjust to put his attempt on the same level as Adler's except in this single point which concerns us here, for it remains on

1. [See for instance, Adler, 1907].
2. [i.e., simplicity is the seal of truth.]

psychoanalytic ground and pursues a psychoanalytic line of thought, so that it may be accepted as a legitimate endeavour to solve the problems of analysis. In this matter of the relation of the individual to danger Rank moves away from the question of organic defect in the individual and concentrates on the variable degree of intensity of the danger. The process of birth is the first situation of danger, and the economic upheaval which it produces becomes the prototype of the reaction of anxiety. We have already [p. 293 ff.] traced the line of development which connects this first danger-situation and determinant of anxiety with all the later ones, and we have seen that they all retain a common quality in so far as they signify in a certain sense a separation from the mother – at first only in a biological sense, next as a direct loss of object and later as a loss of object incurred indirectly. The discovery of this extensive concatenation is an undoubted merit of Rank's construction. Now the trauma of birth overtakes each individual with a different degree of intensity, and the violence of his anxiety-reaction varies with the strength of the trauma; and it is the initial amount of anxiety generated in him which, according to Rank, decides whether he will ever learn to control it – whether he will become neurotic or normal.

It is not our business to criticize Rank's hypothesis in detail here. We have only to consider whether it helps to solve our particular problem. His formula – that those people become neurotic in whom the trauma of birth was so strong that they have never been able completely to abreact it – is highly disputable from a theoretical point of view. We do not rightly know what is meant by abreacting the trauma. Taken literally, it implies that the more frequently and the more intensely a neurotic person reproduces the affect of anxiety the more closely will he approach to mental health – an untenable conclusion. It was because it did not tally with the facts that I gave up the theory of abreaction which had played such a large part in the cathartic method. To lay so much stress, too, on the variability in the strength of the birth trauma is to leave no room for the legitimate claims of hereditary constitution as an aetiological factor. For this variability is an organic factor which operates in an accidental fashion in relation to the constitution and is itself dependent on many influences which might be called accidental – as, for instance, on timely assistance in child-birth. Rank's theory completely ignores constitutional factors as well as phylogenetic ones. If, however, we were to try to find a place for the constitutional factor by qualifying his statement with the proviso, let us say, that what is really important is the extent to which the individual reacts to the variable intensity of the trauma of birth, we should be depriving his theory of its significance and should be relegating the new factor introduced by him to a position of minor importance: the factor which decided whether a neurosis should supervene or not would lie in a different, and once more in an unknown, field.

Moreover, the fact that while man shares the process of birth with the other mammals he alone has the privilege over them of possessing a special disposition to neurosis is hardly favourable to Rank's theory. But the main objection to it is that it floats in the air instead of being based upon ascertained observations. No body of evidence has been collected to show that difficult and protracted birth does in fact coincide with the development of a neurosis, or even that children so born exhibit the phenomena of early infantile apprehensiveness more strongly and over a longer period than other children. It might be rejoined that induced labour and births that are easy for the mother may possibly involve a severe trauma for the child. But we can still point out that births which lead to asphyxia would be bound to give clear evidence of the results which are supposed to follow. It should be one of the advantages of Rank's aetiological theory that it postulates a factor whose existence can be verified by observation. And so long as no such attempt at verification has been made it is impossible to assess the theory's value.

On the other hand I cannot identify myself with the view that Rank's theory contradicts the aetiological importance of the sexual instincts as hitherto recognized by psychoanalysis. For his theory only has reference to the individual's relation to the danger-situation, so that it leaves it perfectly open to us to assume that if a person has not been able to master his first dangers he is bound to come to grief as well in later situations involving sexual danger and thus be driven into a neurosis.

I do not believe, therefore, that Rank's attempt has solved the problem of the causation of neurosis; nor do I believe that we can say as yet how much it may nevertheless have *contributed* to such a solution. If an investigation into the effects of difficult birth on the disposition to neurosis should yield negative results, we shall rate the value of his contribution low. It is to be feared that our need to find a single, tangible 'ultimate cause' of neurotic illness will remain unsatisfied. The ideal solution, which medical men no doubt still yearn for, would be to discover some bacillus which could be isolated and bred in a pure culture and which, when injected into anyone, would invariably produce the same illness; or, to put it rather less extravagantly, to demonstrate the existence of certain chemical substances the administration of which would bring about or cure particular neuroses. But the probability of a solution of this kind seems slight.

Psychoanalysis leads to less simple and satisfactory conclusions. What I have to say in this connection has long been familiar and I have nothing new to add. If the ego succeeds in protecting itself from a dangerous instinctual impulse, through, for instance, the process of repression, it has certainly inhibited and damaged the particular part of the id concerned; but it has at the same time given it some independence and has renounced some of its own sovereignty. This is inevitable from the nature of repression, which is, fundamentally, an attempt at flight. The repressed is now, as it were, an outlaw; it is excluded from the great organization of the ego and is subject only to the laws which govern the realm of the unconscious. If, now, the danger-situation changes so that the ego has no reason for fending off a new instinctual impulse analogous to the repressed one, the consequence of the restriction of the ego which has taken place will become manifest. The new impulse will run its course, under an automatic influence – or, as I should prefer to say, under the influence of the compulsion to repeat. It will follow the same path as the earlier, repressed impulse, as though the danger-situation that had been overcome still existed. The fixating factor in repression, then, is the unconscious id's compulsion to repeat – a compulsion which in normal circumstances is only done away with by the freely mobile function of the ego. The ego may occasionally manage to break down the barriers of repression which it has itself put up and to recover its influence over the instinctual impulse and direct the course of the new impulse in accordance with the changed danger-situation. But in point of fact the ego very seldom succeeds in doing this: it cannot undo its repressions. It is possible that the way the struggle will go depends upon quantitative relations. In some cases one has the impression that the outcome is an enforced one: the regressive attraction exerted by the repressed impulse and the strength of the repression are so great that the new impulse has no choice but to obey the compulsion to repeat. In other cases we perceive a contribution from another play of forces: the attraction exerted by the repressed prototype is reinforced by a repulsion coming from the direction of difficulties in real life which stand in the way of any different course that might be taken by the new instinctual impulse.

That this is a correct account of fixation upon repression and of the retention of danger-situations that are no longer present-day ones is confirmed by the fact of analytic therapy – a fact which is modest enough in itself but which can hardly be overrated from a theoretical point of view. When, in analysis, we have given the ego assistance which is able to put it in a position to lift its repressions, it recovers its power over the repressed id and can allow the instinctual impulses to run their course as though the old situations of danger no longer existed. What we can do in this way tallies with what can be achieved in other fields of medicine; for as a rule our therapy must be content with bringing about more quickly, more reliably and with less expenditure of energy than would otherwise be the case the good result which in favourable circumstances would have occurred of itself.

We see from what has been said that *quantitative* relations – relations which are not directly observable but which can only be inferred – are what determine whether or not old situations of danger shall be preserved, repressions on the part of the ego maintained and childhood neuroses find a continuation. Among the factors that play a part in the causation of neuroses and that have created the conditions under which the forces of the mind are pitted against one another, three emerge into prominence: a biological, a phylogenetic and a purely psychological factor.

The biological factor is the long period of time during which the young of the human species is in a condition of helplessness and dependence. Its intra-uterine existence seems to be short in comparison with that of most animals, and it is sent into the world in a less finished state. As a result, the influence of the real external world upon it is intensified and an early differentiation between the ego and the id is promoted. Moreover, the dangers of the external world have a greater importance for it, so that the value of the object which can alone protect it against them and take the place of its former intra-uterine life is enormously enhanced. The biological factor, then, establishes the earliest situations of danger and creates the need to be loved which will accompany the child through the rest of its life.

The existence of the second, phylogenetic, factor, is based only upon inference. We have been led to assume its existence by a remarkable feature in the development of the libido. We have found that the sexual life of man, unlike that of most of the animals nearly related to him, does not make a steady advance from birth to maturity, but that, after an early efflorescence up till the fifth year, it undergoes a very decided interruption; and that it then starts on its course once more at puberty, taking up again the beginnings broken off in early childhood. This has led us to suppose that something momentous must have occurred in the vicissitudes of the human species[1] which has left behind this interruption in the sexual development of the individual as a historical precipitate. This factor owes its pathogenic significance to the fact that the majority of the instinctual demands of this infantile sexuality are treated by the ego as dangers and fended off as such, so that the later sexual impulses of puberty, which in the natural course of things would be ego-syntonic, run the risk of succumbing to the attraction of their infantile prototypes and following them into repression. It is here that we come upon the most direct aetiology of the neuroses. It is a curious thing that early contact with the demands of sexuality should have a similar effect on the ego to that produced by premature contact with the external world.

The third, psychological, factor resides in a defect of our mental apparatus which has to do precisely with its differentiation into an id and an ego, and which is therefore also attributable ultimately to the influence of the external world. In view of the dangers of [external] reality, the ego is obliged to guard against certain instinctual impulses in the id and to treat them as dangers. But it cannot protect itself from internal instinctual dangers as effectively as it can from some piece of reality that is not part of itself. Intimately bound up with the id as it is, it can only fend off an instinctual danger by restricting its own organization and by acquiescing in the formation of symptoms

1. [In Chapter III of *The Ego and the Id* (1923*b*), Freud makes it clear that he has the geological glacial epoch in mind. The idea had been put forward earlier by Ferenczi (1913).]

in exchange for having impaired the instinct. If the rejected instinct renews its attack, the ego is overtaken by all those difficulties which are known to us as neurotic ailments.

Further than this, I believe, our knowledge of the nature and causes of neurosis has not as yet been able to go.

XI
ADDENDA

IN the course of this discussion various themes have had to be put aside before they had been fully dealt with. I have brought them together in this chapter so that they may receive the attention they deserve.

(A) MODIFICATIONS OF EARLIER VIEWS

(a) *Resistance and Anticathexis*

An important element in the theory of repression is the view that repression is not an event that occurs once but that it requires a permanent expenditure [of force]. If this expenditure were to cease, the repressed impulse, which is being fed all the time from its sources, would on the next occasion flow along the channels from which it had been forced away, and the repression would either fail in its purpose or would have to be repeated an indefinite number of times.[1] Thus it is because instincts are continuous in their nature that the ego has to make its defensive action secure by a permanent expenditure [of force]. This action undertaken to protect repression is observable in analytic treatment as *resistance*. Resistance presupposes the existence of what I have called *anticathexis*. An anticathexis of this kind is clearly seen in obsessional neurosis. It appears there in the form of an alteration of the ego, as a reaction-formation in the ego, and is effected by the reinforcement of the attitude which is the opposite of the instinctual trend that has to be repressed – as,

1. [Cf. a passage near the middle of the paper on 'Repression' (1915*d*), *P. F. L.* **11**]

for instance, in pity, conscientiousness and cleanliness. These reaction-formations of obsessional neurosis are essentially exaggerations of the normal traits of character which develop during the latency period. The presence of an anticathexis in hysteria is much more difficult to detect, though theoretically it is equally indispensable. In hysteria, too, a certain amount of alteration of the ego through reaction-formation is unmistakable and in some circumstances becomes so marked that it forces itself on our attention as the principle symptom. The conflict due to ambivalence, for instance, is resolved in hysteria by this means. The subject's hatred of a person whom he loves is kept down by an exaggerated amount of tenderness for him and apprehensiveness about him. But the difference between reaction-formations in obsessional neurosis and in hysteria is that in the latter they do not have the universality of a character-trait but are confined to particular relationships. A hysterical woman, for instance, may be specially affectionate with her own children whom at bottom she hates; but she will not on that account be more loving in general than other women or even more affectionate to other children. The reaction-formation of hysteria clings tenaciously to a particular object and never spreads over into a general disposition of the ego, whereas what is characteristic of obsessional neurosis is precisely a spreading-over of this kind – a loosening of relations to the object and a facilitation of displacement in the choice of object.

There is another kind of anticathexis, however, which seems more suited to the peculiar character of hysteria. A repressed instinctual impulse can be activated (newly cathected) from two directions: from within, through reinforcement from its internal sources of excitation, and from without, through the perception of an object that it desires. The hysterical anticathexis is mainly directed outwards, against dangerous perceptions. It takes the form of a special kind of vigilance which, by means of restrictions of the ego, causes situations to be avoided that would entail such perceptions, or, if they do occur, manages to withdraw the subject's attention from them. Some French analysts, in particular Laforgue [1926], have recently given this action of hysteria the special name of 'scotomization'.[1] This technique of anticathexis is still more noticeable in the phobias, whose interest is concentrated on removing the subject ever further from the possibility of the occurrence of the feared perception. The fact that anticathexis has an opposite direction in hysteria and the phobias from what it has in obsessional neurosis – though the distinction is not an absolute one – seems to be significant. It suggests that there is an intimate connection between repression and external anticathexis on the one hand and between regression and internal anticathexis (i.e. alteration of the ego through reaction-formation) on the other. The task of defence against a dangerous perception is, incidentally, common to all neuroses. Various commands and prohibitions in obsessional neurosis have the same end in view.

We showed on an earlier occasion[2] that the resistance that has to be overcome in analysis proceeds from the ego, which clings to its anticathexes. It is hard for the ego to direct its attention to perceptions and ideas which it has up till now made a rule of avoiding, or to acknowledge as belonging to itself impulses that are the complete opposite of those which it knows as its own. Our fight against resistance in analysis is based upon this view of the facts. If the resistance is itself unconscious, as so often happens owing to its connection with the repressed material, we make it conscious. If it is conscious, or when it has become conscious, we bring forward logical arguments against it; we promise the ego rewards and advantages if it will give up its resistance. There can be no doubt or mistake about the

1. [Freud discussed this term at some length in his later paper on 'Fetishism' (1927e) in connection with the concept of disavowal (*Verleugnung*). Cf. P.F.L., **7**, 352 ff.]

2. [Towards the end of Chapter I of *The Ego and the Id* (1923b).]

existence of this resistance on the part of the ego. But we have to ask ourselves whether it covers the whole state of affairs in analysis. For we find that even after the ego has decided to relinquish its resistances it still has difficulty in undoing the repressions; and we have called the period of strenuous effort which follows after its praiseworthy decision, the phase of 'working-through'. The dynamic factor which makes a working-through of this kind necessary and comprehensible is not far to seek. It must be that after the ego-resistance has been removed the power of the compulsion to repeat – the attraction exerted by the unconscious prototypes upon the repressed instinctual process – has still to be overcome. There is nothing to be said against describing this factor as the *resistance of the unconscious*. There is no need to be discouraged by these emendations. They are to be welcomed if they add something to our knowledge, and they are no disgrace to us so long as they enrich rather than invalidate our earlier views – by limiting some statement, perhaps, that was too general or by enlarging some idea that was too narrowly formulated.

It must not be supposed that these emendations provide us with a complete survey of all the kinds of resistance that are met with in analysis. Further investigation of the subject shows that the analyst has to combat no less than five kinds of resistance, emanating from three directions – the ego, the id and the super-ego. The ego is the source of three of these, each differing in its dynamic nature. The first of these three ego-resistances is the *repression* resistance, which we have already discussed above [p. 316 ff.] and about which there is least new to be added. Next there is the *transference* resistance, which is of the same nature but which has different and much clearer effects in analysis, since it succeeds in establishing a relation to the analytic situation or the analyst himself and thus re-animating a repression which should only have been recollected. The third resistance, though also an ego-resistance, is of quite a different nature. It proceeds from the *gain from illness* and is based upon an assimilation of the symptom into the ego. [See above, p. 252.] It represents an unwillingness to renounce any satisfaction or relief that has been obtained. The fourth variety, arising from the *id*, is the resistance which, as we have just seen, necessitates 'working-through'. The fifth, coming from the *super-ego* and the last to be discovered, is also the most obscure though not always the least powerful one. It seems to originate from the sense of guilt or the need for punishment; and it opposes every move towards success, including, therefore, the patient's own recovery through analysis.[1]

(b) Anxiety from Transformation of Libido

The view of anxiety which I have put forward in these pages diverges somewhat from the one I have hitherto thought correct. Formerly I regarded anxiety as a general reaction of the ego under conditions of unpleasure. I always sought to justify its appearance on economic grounds and I assumed, on the strength of my investigations into the 'actual' neuroses, that libido (sexual excitation) which was rejected or not utilized by the ego found direct discharge in the form of anxiety. It cannot be denied that these various assertions did not go very well together, or at any rate did not necessarily follow from one another. Moreover, they gave the impression of there being a specially intimate connection between anxiety and libido and this did not accord with the general character of anxiety as a reaction to unpleasure.

The objection to this view arose from our coming to regard the ego as the sole seat of anxiety. It was one of the results of the attempt at a structural division of the mental apparatus which I made in *The Ego and the Id*. Whereas the old view made it natural to suppose that anxiety arose from the libido belonging to the repressed instinctual impulses, the new one, on the contrary, made the ego the source of anxiety. Thus it is a question

1. [This was discussed in the earlier part of Chapter V of *The Ego and the Id*.]

of instinctual (id-) anxiety or ego-anxiety. Since the energy which the ego employs is desexualized, the new view also tended to weaken the close connection between anxiety and libido. I hope I have at least succeeded in making the contradiction plain and in giving a clear idea of the point in doubt.

Rank's contention – which was originally my own[1] – , that the affect of anxiety is a consequence of the event of birth and a repetition of the situation then experienced, obliged me to review the problem of anxiety once more. But I could make no headway with his idea that birth is a trauma, states of anxiety a reaction of discharge to it and all subsequent affects of anxiety an attempt to 'abreact' it more and more completely. I was obliged to go back from the anxiety reaction to the *situation of danger* that lay behind it. The introduction of this element opened up new aspects of the question. Birth was seen to be the prototype of all later situations of danger which overtook the individual under the new conditions arising from a changed mode of life and a growing mental development. On the other hand its own significance was reduced to this prototypic relationship to danger. The anxiety felt at birth became the prototype of an affective state which had to undergo the same vicissitudes as the other affects. Either the state of anxiety reproduced itself *automatically* in situations analogous to the original situation and was thus an inexpedient form of reaction instead of an expedient one as it had been in the first situation of danger; or the ego acquired power over this affect, reproduced it on its own initiative, and employed it as a warning of danger and as a means of setting the pleasure-unpleasure mechanism in motion. We thus gave the biological aspect of the anxiety affect its due importance by recognizing anxiety as the general reaction to situations of danger; while we endorsed the part played by the ego as the seat of anxiety by allocating to it the function of producing the anxiety affect according to its needs. Thus we attributed two modes of origin to anxiety in later

1. [See Editor's Introduction, p. 235–6 above.]

life. One was involuntary, automatic and always justified on economic grounds, and arose whenever a danger-situation analogous to birth had established itself. The other was produced by the ego as soon as a situation of this kind merely threatened to occur, in order to call for its avoidance. In the second case the ego subjects itself to anxiety as a sort of inoculation, submitting to a slight attack of the illness in order to escape its full strength. It vividly imagines the danger-situation, as it were, with the unmistakable purpose of restricting that distressing experience to a mere indication, a signal. We have already seen in detail [pp. 393–7] how the various situations of danger arise one after the other, retaining at the same time a genetic connection.

We shall perhaps be able to proceed a little further in our understanding of anxiety when we turn to the problem of the relation between neurotic anxiety and realistic anxiety [p. 324 ff.].

Our former hypothesis of a direct transformation of libido into anxiety possesses less interest for us now than it did. But if we do nevertheless consider it, we shall have to distinguish different cases. As regards anxiety evoked by the ego as a signal, it does not come into consideration; nor does it, therefore, in any of those danger-situations which move the ego to bring on repression. The libidinal cathexis of the repressed instinctual impulse is employed otherwise than in being transformed into anxiety and discharged as such – as is most clearly seen in conversion hysteria. On the other hand, further enquiry into the question of the danger-situation will bring to our notice an instance of the production of anxiety which will, I think, have to be accounted for in a different way [p. 328 f.].

(c) Repression and Defence

In the course of discussing the problem of anxiety I have revived a concept or, to put it more modestly, a term, of which I made exclusive use thirty years ago when I first began to study the subject but which I later abandoned. I refer to the term 'defensive process'.[1] I afterwards replaced it by the word 'repression', but the relation between the two remained uncertain. It will be an undoubted advantage, I think, to revert to the old concept of 'defence', provided we employ it explicitly as a general designation for all the techniques which the ego makes use of in conflicts which may lead to a neurosis, while we retain the word 'repression' for the special method of defence which the line of approach taken by our investigations made us better acquainted with in the first instance.

Even a purely terminological innovation ought to justify its adoption; it ought to reflect some new point of view or some extension of knowledge. The revival of the concept of defence and the restriction of that of repression takes into account a fact which has long since been known but which has received added importance owing to some new discoveries. Our first observations of repression and of the formation of symptoms were made in connection with hysteria. We found that the perceptual content of exciting experiences and the ideational content of pathogenic structures of thought were forgotten and debarred from being reproduced in memory, and we therefore concluded that the keeping away from consciousness was a main characteristic of hysterical repression. Later on, when we came to study the obsessional neuroses, we found that in that illness pathogenic occurrences are not forgotten. They remain conscious but they are 'isolated' in some way that we cannot as yet grasp, so that much the same result is obtained as in hysterical amnesia. Nevertheless the difference is great enough to justify the belief that the process by which instinctual demands are set aside in obsessional neurosis cannot be the same as in hysteria. Further investigations have shown that in obsessional neurosis a regression of the instinctual impulses to

1. Cf. 'The Neuro-Psychoses of Defence' [1894a]. [The account which Freud gives here of the history of these two terms is a little misleading. Cf. his paper on sexuality in the neuroses (1906a) and the information in an Editor's footnote, p. 77 and n. above.]

an earlier libidinal stage is brought about through the oppo-sition of the ego, and that this regression, although it does not make repression unnecessary, clearly works in the same sense as repression. We have seen, too, that in obsessional neurosis anticathexis, which is also presumably present in hysteria, plays a specially large part in protecting the ego by effecting a reactive alteration in it. Our attention has, moreover, been drawn to a process of 'isolation' (whose technique cannot as yet be elucidated), which finds direct symptomatic manifest-ation, and to a procedure, that may be called magical, of 'undoing' what has been done – a procedure about whose defensive purpose there can be no doubt, but which has no longer any resemblance to the process of 'repression'. These observations provide good enough grounds for re-introducing the old concept of *defence*, which can cover all these processes that have the same purpose – namely, the protection of the ego against instinctual demands – and for subsuming repression under it as a special case. The importance of this nomenclature is heightened if we consider the possibility that further in-vestigations may show that there is an intimate connection between special forms of defence and particular illness, as, for instance, between repression and hysteria. In addition we may look forward to the possible discovery of yet another important correlation. It may well be that before its sharp cleavage into an ego and an id, and before the formation of a super-ego, the mental apparatus makes use of different methods of defence from those which it employs after it has reached these stages of organization.

(B) SUPPLEMENTARY REMARKS ON ANXIETY

The affect of anxiety exhibits one or two features the study of which promises to throw further light on the subject. Anxiety [*Angst*] has an unmistakable relation to *expectation*: it is anxiety about[1] something. It has a quality of *indefiniteness and lack of object*. In precise speech we use the word 'fear' [*Furcht*] rather than 'anxiety' [*Angst*] if it has found an object. Moreover, in addition to its relation to danger, anxiety has a relation to neurosis which we have long been trying to elucidate. The question arises: why are not all reactions of anxiety neurotic – why do we accept so many of them as normal? And finally the problem of the difference between realistic anxiety and neurotic anxiety awaits a thorough examination.

To begin with the last problem. The advance we have made is that we have gone behind reactions of anxiety to situations of danger. If we do the same thing with realistic anxiety we shall have no difficulty in solving the question. Real danger is a danger that is known, and realistic anxiety is anxiety about a known danger of this sort. Neurotic anxiety is anxiety about an unknown danger. Neurotic danger is thus a danger that has still to be discovered. Analysis has shown that it is an instinctual danger. By bringing this danger which is not known to the ego into consciousness, the analyst makes neurotic anxiety no different from realistic anxiety, so that it can be dealt with in the same way.

There are two reactions to real danger. One is an affective reaction, an outbreak of anxiety. The other is a protective action. The same will presumably be true of instinctual danger. We know how the two reactions can co-operate in an expedient way, the one giving the signal for the other to appear. But we also know that they can behave in an inexpedient way: paralysis from anxiety may set in, and the one reaction spread at the cost of the other.

In some cases the characteristics of realistic anxiety and neurotic anxiety are mingled. The danger is known and real but the anxiety in regard to it is over-great, greater than seems

---

1. [In German '*vor*', literally 'before'. See an Editor's Appendix on the use of the term '*Angst*', at the end of Freud's early paper on anxiety neurosis (1895*b*), pp. 64–5 above.]

proper to us. It is this surplus of anxiety which betrays the presence of a neurotic element. Such cases, however, introduce no new principle; for analysis shows that to the known real danger an unknown instinctual one is attached.

We can find out still more about this if, not content with tracing anxiety back to danger, we go on to enquire what the essence and meaning of a danger-situation is. Clearly, it consists in the subject's estimation of his own strength compared to the magnitude of the danger and in his admission of helplessness in the face of it – physical helplessness if the danger is real and psychical helplessness if it is instinctual. In doing this he will be guided by the actual experiences he has had. (Whether he is wrong in his estimation or not is immaterial for the outcome.) Let us call a situation of helplessness of this kind that has been actually experienced a *traumatic situation*. We shall then have good grounds for distinguishing a traumatic situation from a *danger-situation*.

The individual will have made an important advance in his capacity for self-preservation if he can foresee and expect a traumatic situation of this kind which entails helplessness, instead of simply waiting for it to happen. Let us call a situation which contains the determinant for such an expectation a danger-situation. It is in this situation that the signal of anxiety is given. The signal announces: 'I am expecting a situation of helplessness to set in', or: 'The present situation reminds me of one of the traumatic experiences I have had before. Therefore I will anticipate the trauma and behave as though it had already come, while there is yet time to turn it aside.' Anxiety is therefore on the one hand an expectation of a trauma, and on the other a repetition of it in a mitigated form. Thus the two features of anxiety which we have noted have a different origin. Its connection with expectation belongs to the danger-situation, whereas its indefiniteness and lack of object belong to the traumatic situation of helplessness – the situation which is anticipated in the danger-situation.

Taking this sequence, anxiety – danger – helplessness (trauma), we can now summarize what has been said. A danger-situation is a recognized, remembered, expected situation of helplessness. Anxiety is the original reaction to helplessness in the trauma and is reproduced later on in the danger-situation as a signal for help. The ego, which experienced the trauma passively, now repeats it actively in a weakened version, in the hope of being able itself to direct its course. It is certain that children behave in this fashion towards every distressing impression they receive, by reproducing it in their play. In thus changing from passivity to activity they attempt to master their experiences psychically.[1] If this is what is meant by 'abreacting a trauma' we can no longer have anything to urge against the phrase. [See p. 309.] But what is of decisive importance is the first displacement of the anxiety-reaction from its origin in the situation of helplessness to an expectation of that situation, that is, to the danger-situation. After that come the later displacements, from the danger to the determinant of the danger – loss of the object and the modifications of that loss with which we are already acquainted.

The undesirable result of 'spoiling' a small child is to magnify the importance of the danger of losing the object (the object being a protection against every situation of helplessness) in comparison with every other danger. It therefore encourages the individual to remain in the state of childhood, the period of life which is characterized by motor and psychical helplessness.

So far we have had no occasion to regard realistic anxiety in any different light from neurotic anxiety. We know what the distinction is. A real danger is a danger which threatens a person from an external object, and a neurotic danger is one which threatens him from an instinctual demand. In so far as the instinctual demand is something real, his neurotic anxiety, too, can be admitted to have a realistic basis. We have seen that

1. [Cf. the end of the second chapter in *Beyond the Pleasure Principle*, (1920g).]

the reason why there seems to be a specially close connection between anxiety and neurosis is that the ego defends itself against an instinctual danger with the help of the anxiety re-action just as it does against an external real danger, but that this line of defensive activity eventuates in a neurosis owing to an imperfection of the mental apparatus. We have also come to the conclusion that an instinctual demand often only be-comes an (internal) danger because its satisfaction would bring on an external danger – that is, because the internal danger represents an external one.

On the other hand, the external (real) danger must also have managed to become internalized if it is to be significant for the ego. It must have been recognized as related to some situation of helplessness that has been experienced.[1] Man seems not to have been endowed, or to have been endowed to only a very small degree, with an instinctive recognition of the dangers that threaten him from without. Small children are constantly doing things which endanger their lives, and that is precisely why they cannot afford to be without a protecting object. In relation to the traumatic situation, in which the subject is helpless, external and internal dangers, real dangers and instinctual demands converge. Whether the ego is suffering from a pain which will not stop or experiencing an accumula-tion of instinctual needs which cannot obtain satisfaction, the economic situation is the same, and the motor helplessness of the ego finds expression in psychical helplessness.

In this connection the puzzling phobias of early childhood

[1]. It may quite often happen that although a danger-situation is correctly estimated in itself, a certain amount of instinctual anxiety is added to the realistic anxiety. In that case the instinctual demand before whose satisfaction the ego recoils is a masochistic one: the instinct of destruction directed against the subject himself. Perhaps an addition of this kind explains cases in which reactions of anxiety are exaggerated, inexpedient or paralysing. Phobias of heights (windows, towers, preci-pices and so on) may have some such origin. Their hidden feminine significance is closely connected with masochism.

deserve to be mentioned once again. [Cf. p. 293.] We have been able to explain some of them, such as the fear of being alone or in the dark or with strangers, as reactions to the danger of losing the object. Others, like the fear of small animals, thunderstorms, etc., might perhaps be accounted for as vestigial traces of the congenital preparedness to meet real dangers which is so strongly developed in other animals. In man, only that part of this archaic heritage is appropriate which has reference to the loss of the object. If childhood phobias become fixated and grow stronger and persist into later years, analysis shows that their content has become associated with instinctual demands and has come to stand for internal dangers as well.

(C) ANXIETY, PAIN AND MOURNING

So little is known about the psychology of emotional processes that the tentative remarks I am about to make on the subject may claim a very lenient judgement. The problem before us arises out of the conclusion we have reached that anxiety comes to be a reaction to the danger of a loss of an object. Now we already know one reaction to the loss of an object, and that is mourning. The question therefore is, when does that loss lead to anxiety and when to mourning? In discussing the subject of mourning on a previous occasion I found that there was one feature about it which remained quite unexplained. This was its peculiar painfulness. [Cf. p. 286 f.][1] And yet it seems self-evident that separation from an object should be painful. Thus the problem becomes more complicated: when does separating from an object produce anxiety, when does it produce mourning and when does it produce, it may be, only pain?

Let me say at once that there is no prospect in sight of answer-

[1]. 'Mourning and Melancholia' [1917e]. [See in particular a passage fairly near the beginning of the paper.]

ing these questions. We must content ourselves with drawing certain distinctions and adumbrating certain possibilities.

Our starting-point will again be the one situation which we believe we understand – the situation of the infant when it is presented with a stranger instead of its mother. It will exhibit the anxiety which we have attributed to the danger of loss of object. But its anxiety is undoubtedly more complicated than this and merits a more thorough discussion. That it does have anxiety there can be no doubt; but the expression of its face and its reaction of crying indicate that it is feeling pain as well. Certain things seem to be joined together in it which will later on be separated out. It cannot as yet distinguish between temporary absence and permanent loss. As soon as it loses sight of its mother it behaves as if it were never going to see her again; and repeated consoling experiences to the contrary are necessary before it learns that her disappearance is usually followed by her re-appearance. Its mother encourages this piece of knowledge which is so vital to it by playing the familiar game of hiding her face from it with her hands and then, to its joy, uncovering it again.[1] In these circumstances it can, as it were, feel longing unaccompanied by despair.

In consequence of the infant's misunderstanding of the facts, the situation of missing its mother is not a danger-situation but a traumatic one. Or, to put it more correctly, it is a traumatic situation if the infant happens at the time to be feeling a need which its mother should be the one to satisfy. It turns into a danger-situation if this need is not present at the moment. Thus, the first determinant of anxiety, which the ego itself introduces, is loss of perception of the object (which is equated with loss of the object itself). There is as yet no question of loss of love. Later on, experience teaches the child that the object can be present but angry with it; and then loss of love from the

1. [Cf. the child's game described in the second half of Chapter II of *Beyond the Pleasure Principle.*]

object becomes a new and much more enduring danger and determinant of anxiety.

The traumatic situation of missing the mother differs in one important respect from the traumatic situation of birth. At birth no object existed and so no object could be missed. Anxiety was the only reaction that occurred. Since then repeated situations of satisfaction have created an object out of the mother; and this object, whenever the infant feels a need, receives an intense cathexis which might be described as a 'longing' one. It is to this new aspect of things that the reaction of pain is referable. Pain is thus the actual reaction to loss of object, while anxiety is the reaction to the danger which that loss entails and, by a further displacement, a reaction to the danger of the loss of object itself.

We know very little about pain either. The only fact we are certain of is that pain occurs in the first instance and as a regular thing whenever a stimulus which impinges on the periphery breaks through the devices of the protective shield against stimuli and proceeds to act like a continuous instinctual stimulus, against which muscular action, which is as a rule effective because it withdraws the place that is being stimulated from the stimulus, is powerless[1]. If the pain proceeds not from a part of the skin but from an internal organ, the situation is still the same. All that has happened is that a portion of the inner periphery has taken the place of the outer periphery. The child obviously has occasion to undergo experiences of pain of this sort, which are independent of its experiences of need. This determinant of the generating of pain seems, however, to have very little similarity with the loss of an object. And besides, the element which is essential to pain, peripheral stimulation, is entirely absent in the child's situation of longing. Yet it cannot be for nothing that the common usage of speech should have created the notion of internal, mental pain and

1. [See the last part of Chapter IV of *Beyond the Pleasure Principle*.]

have treated the feeling of loss of object as equivalent to physical pain.

When there is physical pain, a high degree of what may be termed narcissistic cathexis of the painful place occurs.[1] This cathexis continues to increase and tends, as it were, to empty the ego.[2] It is well known that when internal organs are giving us pain we receive spatial and other presentations of parts of the body which are ordinarily not represented at all in conscious ideation. Again, the remarkable fact that, when there is a psychical diversion brought about by some other interest, even the most intense physical pains fail to arise (I must not say 'remain unconscious' in this case) can be accounted for by there being a concentration of cathexis on the psychical representative of the part of the body which is giving pain. I think it is here that we shall find the point of analogy which has made it possible to carry sensations of pain over to the mental sphere. For the intense cathexis of longing which is concentrated on the missed or lost object (a cathexis which steadily mounts up because it cannot be appeased) creates the same economic conditions as are created by the cathexis of pain which is concentrated on the injured part of the body. Thus the fact of the peripheral causation of physical pain can be left out of account. The transition from physical pain to mental pain corresponds to a change from narcissistic cathexis to object-cathexis. An object-presentation which is highly cathected by instinctual need plays the same role as a part of the body which is cathected by an increase of stimulus. The continuous nature of the cathectic process and the impossibility of inhibiting it produce the same state of mental helplessness. If the feeling of unpleasure which then arises has the specific character of pain (a character which cannot be more exactly described) instead of manifesting itself in the reactive form of anxiety, we may plausibly attribute this to a factor which we have not sufficiently made use of in

1. [Cf. the beginning of Section II of 'On Narcissism' (1914c).]
2. [See *Beyond the Pleasure Principle*, loc. cit.]

our explanations – the high level of cathexis and 'binding' that prevails while these processes which lead to a feeling of unpleasure take place.[1]

We know of yet another emotional reaction to the loss of an object, and that is mourning. But we have no longer any difficulty in accounting for it. Mourning occurs under the influence of reality-testing; for the latter function demands categorically from the bereaved person that he should separate himself from the object, since it no longer exists.[2] Mourning is entrusted with the task of carrying out this retreat from the object in all those situations in which it was the recipient of a high degree of cathexis. That this separation should be painful fits in with what we have just said, in view of the high and unsatisfiable cathexis of longing which is concentrated on the object by the bereaved person during the reproduction of the situations in which he must undo the ties that bind him to it.

1. [See *Beyond the Pleasure Principle*, loc. cit.]
2. ['Mourning and Melancholia' (1917e); cf. a passage near the beginning of the paper.]

BIBLIOGRAPHY
AND AUTHOR INDEX

Titles of books and periodicals are in italics, titles of papers are in inverted commas. Abbreviations are in accordance with the *World List of Scientific Periodicals* (London, 1963–5). Further abbreviations used in this volume will be found in the List at the end of this bibliography. Numerals in bold type refer to volumes, ordinary numerals refer to pages. The figures in round brackets at the end of each entry indicate the page or pages of this volume on which the work in question is mentioned.

In the case of the Freud entries, only English translations are given. The initial dates are those of the German, or other, original publications. (The date of writing is added in square brackets where it differs from the latter.) The letters attached to the dates of publication are in accordance with the corresponding entries in the complete bibliography of Freud's writings included in Volume 24 of the *Standard Edition*. Details of the original publication, including the original German (or other) title, are given in the editorial introduction to each work included in the *Pelican Freud Library*.

For non-technical authors, and for technical authors where no specific work is mentioned, see the General Index.

ABRAHAM, K. and FREUD, S. (1965) *See* FREUD, S. (1965a)

ADLER, A. (1907) *Studie über Minderwertigkeit von Organen*, Berlin and Vienna. (308)

[*Trans.: Study of Organ-Inferiority and its Psychical Compensation*, New York, 1917.]

(1910) 'Der psychische Hermaphroditismus im Leben und in der Neurose', *Fortschr. Med.*, **28**, 486. (189–91)

ANDREAS-SALOMÉ, L. and FREUD, S. (1966) *See* FREUD, S. (1966a)

BEARD, G. M. (1881) *American Nervousness, its Causes and Consequences*, New York. (35)

(1884) *Sexual Neurasthenia (Nervous Exhaustion), Its Hygiene, Causes, Symptoms and Treatment*, New York. (35)

BINET, A. (1888) *Études de psychologie experimentale: le fétichisme dans l'amour*, Paris. (162)

BLEULER, E. (1913) 'Der Sexualwiderstand', *Jb. psychoanalyt. psycho-path. Forsch.*, **5**, 442. (181)

(1916) 'Physisch und Psychisch in der Pathologie', *Z. ges. Neurol. Psychiat.*, **30**, 426. (203–4)

BREUER, J. and FREUD, S. (1893) *See* FREUD, S. (1893a)

(1895) *See* FREUD, S. (1895d)

DARWIN, C. (1872) *The Expression of the Emotions in Man and Animals*, London. (2nd ed., 1890) (235, 290)

ELLIS, HAVELOCK (1898) 'Auto-Erotism: A Psychological Study', *Alien. & Neurol.*, **19**, 260. (133)

(1899) *Studies in the Psychology of Sex*, Vol. I: *The Evolution of Modesty; the Phenomena of Sexual Periodicity; and Auto-Erotism*, 'Leipzig' London. (3rd ed., Philadelphia, 1910.) (87)

FERENCZI, S. (1913) 'Entwicklungsstufen des Wirklichkeitssinnes', *Int. Z. ärztl. Psychoanal.*, **1**, 124. (143, 314)

   [*Trans.*: 'Stages in the Development of the Sense of Reality', *First Contributions to Psycho-Analysis*, London, 1952, Chap. VIII.]

(1919) *Hysterie und Pathoneurosen*, Leipzig and Vienna. (Includes 'Hysterische Materializationsphänomene'.) (224)

   [*Trans: In Further Contributions to the Theory and Technique of Psycho-Analysis*, London, 1926, Chaps. V, VI, IX, X, XI, XV.]

(1925) 'Zur Psychoanalyse von Sexualgewohnheiten', *Int. Z. Psychoanal.*, **11**, 6. (296)

   [*Trans.*: 'Psycho-Analysis of Sexual Habits', *Further Contributions to the Theory and Technique of Psycho-Analysis*, London, 1926, Chap. XXXII.]

FERENCZI, S. and HOLLÓS, S. (1922) *Zur Psychoanalyse der paralyti-schen Geistesstörung*, Vienna. (211–12)

   [*Trans.*: *Psycho-Analysis and the Psychic Disorder of General Paresis*, New York and Washington, 1925.]

FLIESS, W. (1892) *Neue Beiträge und Therapie der nasalen Reflex-neurose*, Vienna. (35)

(1893) 'Die nasale Reflexneurose', *Verhandlungen des Kongresses für innere Medizin*, Wiesbaden, 384. (35)

FREUD, M. (1957) *Glory Reflected*, London. (24)

FREUD, S. (1891b) *On Aphasia*, London and New York, 1953. (16, 28)

(1893*a*) With BREUER, J., 'On the Psychical Mechanism of Hysterical Phenomena: Preliminary Communication', in *Studies on Hysteria, Standard Ed.*, **2**, 3; *P.F.L.*, **3**, 53. (28, 77, 96, 250)

(1894*a*) 'The Neuro-Psychoses of Defence', *Standard Ed.*, **3**, 43. (42, 44, 77, 211, 323)

(1895*b* [1894]) 'On the Grounds for Detaching a Particular Syndrome from Neurasthenia under the description "Anxiety Neurosis"', *Standard Ed.*, **3**, 87; *P.F.L.*, **10**, 31. (72, 181, 230–31, 232, 235, 264, 284, 289, 298, 325)

(1895*c* [1894]) 'Obsessions and Phobias', *Standard Ed.*, **3**, 71. (36, 43)

(1895*d*) With BREUER, J., *Studies on Hysteria*, London, 1956; *Standard Ed.*, **2**; *P.F.L.*, **3**. (28, 38, 46, 53, 77–8, 87, 91, 96, 100, 119, 147, 192, 222, 235, 250, 290)

(1895*f*) 'A Reply to Criticisms of my Paper on Anxiety Neurosis', *Standard Ed.*, **3**, 121. (52)

(1896*b*) 'Further Remarks on the Neuro-Psychoses of Defence', *Standard Ed.*, **3**, 159. (46, 74, 222, 251)

(1896*c*) 'The Aetiology of Hysteria', *Standard Ed.*, **3**, 189. (74)

(1897*b*) *Abstracts of the Scientific Writings of Dr Sigm. Freud* (1877–1897), *Standard Ed.*, **3**, 225. (34)

(1900*a*) *The Interpretation of Dreams*, London and New York, 1955; *Standard Ed.*, **4–5**; *P.F.L.*, **4**. (23, 28, 87, 88, 91, 98, 99, 204, 235)

(1901*b*) *The Psychopathology of Everyday Life*, *Standard Ed.*, **6**; *P.F.L.*, **5**. (23, 28, 196)

(1905*d*) *Three Essays on the Theory of Sexuality*, London, 1962 *Standard Ed.*, **7**, 125; *P.F.L.*, **7**, 31. (28–9, 52, 55, 56, 75, 76–7, 79, 81, 86, 89, 92, 94, 102, 111, 112, 117, 132–3, 158, 162, 166, 181, 193, 231, 242, 293)

(1905*e* [1901]) 'Fragment of an Analysis of a Case of Hysteria', *Standard Ed.*, **7**, 3; *P.F.L.*, **8**, 29. (59, 86, 100, 114, 242–3)

(1906*a* [1905]) 'My Views on the Part played by Sexuality in the Aetiology of the Neuroses', *Standard Ed.*, **7**, 271; *P.F.L.*, **10**, 71. (85–6, 114, 117, 132, 134, 323)

(1907*a*) *Delusions and Dreams in Jensen's 'Gradiva'*, *Standard Ed.*, **9**, 3; *P.F.L.*, **14**. (86)

(1908*a*) 'Hysterical Phantasies and their Relation to Bisexuality', *Standard Ed.*, **9**, 157; *P.F.L.*, **10**, 83. (44, 56, 98, 226, 245)

FREUD S. (*cont.*)

(1908*b*) 'Character and Anal Erotism', *Standard Ed.*, **9**, 169; *P.F.L.*, **7**, 205. (141)

(1908*c*) 'On the Sexual Theories of Children', *Standard Ed.*, **9**, 207; *P.F.L.*, **7**, 183. (86, 192–3)

(1908*d*) '"Civilized" Sexual Morality and Modern Nervous Illness', *Standard Ed.*, **9**, 179; *P.F.L.*, **12**. (118)

(1908*e* [1907]) 'Creative Writers and Day-Dreaming', *Standard Ed.*, **9**, 143; *P.F.L.*, **14**. (86, 88)

(1909*a* [1908]) 'Some General Remarks on Hysterical Attacks', *Standard Ed.*, **9**, 29; *P.F.L.*, **10**, 95. (86, 94, 235, 252)

(1909*b*) 'Analysis of a Phobia in a Five-Year-Old Boy', *Standard Ed.*, **10**, 3; *P.F.L.*, **8**, 165. (29, 233, 254–8, 259–63, 279–81, 285)

(1909*c* [1908]) 'Family Romances', *Standard Ed.*, **9**, 237; *P.F.L.*, **7**, 217. (86)

(1909*d*) 'Notes upon a Case of Obsessional Neurosis', *Standard Ed.*, **10**, 155; *P.F.L.*, **9**, 31. (56, 143, 147, 272, 274, 275)

(1910*a* [1909]) *Five Lectures on Psycho-Analysis*, *Standard Ed.*, **11**, 3; in *Two Short Accounts of Psycho-Analysis*, Penguin Books, Harmondsworth, 1962. (18, 29, 91)

(1910*c*) *Leonardo da Vinci and a Memory of his Childhood*, *Standard Ed.*, **11**, 59; *P.F.L.*, **14**. (205)

(1910*h*) 'A Special Type of Choice of Object made by Men', *Standard Ed.*, **11**, 165; *P.F.L.*, **7**, 227. (193, 235–6)

(1910*i*) 'The Psycho-Analytic View of Psychogenic Disturbance of Vision', *Standard Ed.*, **11**, 211; *P.F.L.*, **10**, 103. (80)

(1911*b*) 'Formulations on the Two Principles of Mental Functioning', *Standard Ed.*, **12**, 215; *P.F.L.*, **11**. (121, 132, 192, 226)

(1911*c* [1910]) 'Psycho-Analytic Notes on an Autobiographical Account of a Case of Paranoia (Dementia Paranoides)', *Standard Ed.*, **12**, 3; *P.F.L.*, **9**, 129. (29, 118, 132, 136, 137, 139, 146, 149, 189, 199, 215, 225)

(1912*c*) 'Types of Onset of Neurosis', *Standard Ed.*, **12**, 229; *P.F.L.*, **10**, 115. (216)

(1912*d*) 'On the Universal Tendency to Debasement in the Sphere of Love', *Standard Ed.*, **11**, 179; *P.F.L.*,. **7**, 243. (118)

(1912–13) *Totem and Taboo*, London, 1950; New York, 1952; *Standard Ed.*, **13**, 1; *P.F.L.*, **13**. (29, 277)

(1913*i*) 'The Disposition to Obsessional Neurosis', *Standard Ed.*, **12**, 313; *P.F.L.*, **10**, 129. (76, 119, 127, 167, 268)

(1914*c*) 'On Narcissism: an Introduction', *Standard Ed.*, **14**, 69; *P.F.L.*, **11**. (38, 139, 181, 225, 342)

(1914*d*) 'On the History of the Psycho-Analytic Movement', *Standard Ed.*, **14**, 3; *P.F.L.*, **15**. (29, 75)

(1915*c*) 'Instincts and their Vicissitudes', *Standard Ed.*, **14**, 111; *P.F.L.*, **11**. (60, 144, 180)

(1915*d*) 'Repression', *Standard Ed.*, **14**, 143; *P.F.L.*, **11**. (99, 162, 242, 245, 263, 304, 316)

(1915*e*) 'The Unconscious', *Standard Ed.*, **14**, 161; *P.F.L.*, **11**. (99, 138, 162, 225, 234, 281, 297, 304)

(1915*f*) 'A Case of Paranoia Running Counter to the Psycho-Analytic Theory of the Disease', *Standard Ed.*, **14**, 263; *P.F.L.*, **10**, 145.

(1916*d*) 'Some Character-Types Met with in Psycho-Analytic Work', *Standard Ed.*, **14**, 311; *P.F.L.*, **14**. (118)

(1916–17 [1915–17]) *Introductory Lectures on Psycho-Analysis*, New York, 1966; London, 1971; *Standard Ed.*, **15–16**; *P.F.L.*, **1**. (29, 64, 100, 118, 120, 134, 154, 156, 158, 180, 232, 234, 235, 236)

(1917*d* [1915]) 'A Metapsychological Supplement to the Theory of Dreams', *Standard Ed.*, **14**, 219; *P.F.L.*, **11**. (215, 225)

(1917*e* [1915]) 'Mourning and Melancholia', *Standard Ed.*, **14**, 239; *P.F.L.*, **11**. (287, 329, 342)

(1918*b* [1914]) 'From the History of an Infantile Neurosis', *Standard Ed.*, **17**, 3; *P.F.L.*, **9**, 225 (29, 118, 154, 158, 162, 186, 189, 257–63, 268, 279–81, 296)

(1919*d*) Introduction to *Psycho-Analysis and the War Neuroses*, London and New York, 1921; *Standard Ed.*, **17**, 207. (285)

(1919*e*) 'A Child is Being Beaten', *Standard Ed.*, **17**, 177; *P.F.L.*, **10**, 159. (56)

(1920*g*) *Beyond the Pleasure Principle*, London, 1961; *Standard Ed.*, **18**, 7; *P.F.L.*, **11**. (29, 64, 180, 243, 245, 289, 327, 330, 331, 332–3)

(1921*c*) *Group Psychology and the Analysis of the Ego*, London and New York, 1959; *Standard Ed.*, **18**, 69; *P.F.L.*, **12**. (29, 207)

(1922*b*) 'Some Neurotic Mechanisms in Jealousy, Paranoia and Homosexuality', *Standard Ed.*, **18**, 223; *P.F.L.*, **10**, 195.

(1923*b*) *The Ego and the Id*, London and New York, 1962; *Standard*

FREUD S. (*cont*)

Ed., **19**, 3; *P.F.L.*, **11**. (29, 166, 181, 211, 213, 234, 236, 247, 269, 286, 297, 314, 318, 320)

(1923*e*) 'The Infantile Genital Organization', *Standard Ed.*, **19**, 141; *P.F.L.*, **7**, 303. (133, 218)

(1924*b*) 'Neurosis and Psychosis', *Standard Ed.*, **19**, 149; *P.F.L.*, **10**, 209. (220, 221, 222)

(1924*c*) 'The Economic Problem of Masochism', *Standard Ed.*, **19**, 157; *P.F.L.*, **11**. (185, 216, 223)

(1924*d*) 'The Dissolution of the Oedipus Complex', *Standard Ed.*, **19**, 173; *P.F.L.*, **7**, 313. (174, 234, 300)

(1924*e*) 'The Loss of Reality in Neurosis and Psychosis', *Standard Ed.*, **19**, 183; *P.F.L.*, **10**, 219. (121, 211)

(1925*d* [1924]) *An Autobiographical Study*, *Standard Ed.*, **20**, 3; *P.F.L.*, **15**. (14, 75)

(1925*j*) 'Some Psychical Consequences of the Anatomical Distinction between the Sexes', *Standard Ed.*, **19**, 243; *P.F.L.*, **7**, 323. (29, 193, 234, 300)

(1926*d* [1925]) *Inhibitions, Symptoms and Anxiety*, London, 1960; *Standard Ed.*, **20**, 77; *P.F.L.*, **10**, 227. (30, 34, 38, 56, 59, 64–5, 78, 80, 100)

(1927*a*) 'Postscript to *The Question of Lay Analysis*', *Standard Ed.*, **20**, 251; *P.F.L.*, **15**. (14)

(1927*c*) *The Future of an Illusion*, London, 1962; *Standard Ed.*, **21**, 3; *P.F.L.*, **12**. (30)

(1927*e*) 'Fetishism', *Standard Ed.*, **21**, 149; *P.F.L.*, **7**, 345. (217, 220, 318)

(1928*b*) Dostoevsky and Parricide', *Standard Ed.*, **21**, 175; *P.F.L.*, **14**. (96, 102)

(1930*a*) *Civilization and its Discontents*, New York, 1961; London, 1963; *Standard Ed.*, **21**, 59; *P.F.L.*, **12**. (30, 158, 184)

(1931*b*) 'Female Sexuality', *Standard Ed.*, **21**, 223; *P.F.L.*, **7**, 367. (75)

(1933*a* [1932]) *New Introductory Lectures on Psycho-Analysis*, New York, 1966; London, 1971; *Standard Ed.*, **22**; *P.F.L.*, **2**. (75, 110, 232, 233, 247)

(1935*a*) Postscript (1935) to *An Autobiographical Study*, new edition, London and New York; *Standard Ed.*, **20**, 71; *P.F.L.*, **15**. (14)

(1936*a*) 'A Disturbance of Memory on the Acropolis', *Standard Ed.*, **22**, 239; *P.F.L.*, **11.** (118)

(1937*c*) 'Analysis Terminable and Interminable', *Standard Ed.*, **23**, 211. (162)

(1939*a* [1934–8]) *Moses and Monotheism*, *Standard Ed.*, **23**, 3; *P.F.L.*, **13.** (30)

(1940*a* [1938]) *An Outline of Psycho-Analysis*, New York, 1968; London, 1969; *Standard Ed.*, **23**, 141; *P.F.L.*, **15.** (30, 158, 215, 217)

(1940*e* [1938]) 'Splitting of the Ego in the Process of Defence', *Standard Ed.*, **23**, 273; *P.F.L.*, **11.** (217)

(1950*a* [1887–1902]) *The Origins of Psycho-Analysis*, London and New York, 1954. (Partly, including 'A Project for a Scientific Psychology', in *Standard Ed.*, **1**, 175.) (18, 26, 27, 28, 34, 56, 75, 85, 131–2, 162, 222, 231–2)

(1960*a*) *Letters 1873–1939* (ed. E. L. Freud) (trans. T. and J. Stern), New York, 1960; London, 1961. (25, 26)

(1963*a* [1909–39]) *Psycho-Analysis and Faith. The Letters of Sigmund Freud and Oskar Pfister* (ed. H. Meng and E. L. Freud) (trans. E. Mosbacher), London and New York, 1963. (26)

(1965*a* [1907–26]) *A Psycho-Analytic Dialogue. The Letters of Sigmund Freud and Karl Abraham* (ed. H. C. Abraham and E. L. Freud) (trans. B. Marsh and H. C. Abraham), London and New York, 1965. (26)

(1966*a* [1912–36]) *Sigmund Freud and Lou Andreas-Salomé: Letters* (ed. E. Pfeiffer) (trans. W. and E. Robson-Scott), London and New York, 1972. (26)

(1968*a* [1927–39]) *The Letters of Sigmund Freud and Arnold Zweig* (ed. E. L. Freud) (trans. W. and E. Robson-Scott), London and New York, 1970. (26)

(1970*a* [1919–35]) *Sigmund Freud as a Consultant. Recollections of a Pioneer in Psychoanalysis* (Letters from Freud to Edoardo Weiss, including a Memoir and Commentaries by Weiss, with Foreword and Introduction by M. Grotjahn), New York, 1970. (26)

(1974*a* [1906–23]) *The Freud/Jung Letters* (ed. W. McGuire) (trans. R. Manheim and R. F. C. Hull), London and Princeton, N.J., 1974. (26)

HECKER, E. (1893) 'Über larvirte und abortive Angstzustänide be Neurasthenie', *Zentbl. Nervenheilk.*, **16**, 565. (36, 40)

HOLLÓS, S. and FERENCZI, S. *See* FERENCZI, S. and HOLLÓS, S. (1922)

JANET, PIERRE (1898) *Névroses et idées fixes* (2 vols), 2nd ed., Paris. (87)

JONES, E. (1913) 'Hass und Analerotik in der Zwangsneurose', *Int. Z. ärztl. Psychoanal.*, **1**, 425. (139)

[*English Text:* 'Hate and Anal Erotism in the Obsessional Neurosis', *Papers on Psycho-Analysis*, 2nd and 3rd eds. only, London and New York, 1918, 1923, Chap. XXXI.]

(1953) *Sigmund Freud: Life and Work*, Vol. 1, London and New York. (26)

(1955) *Sigmund Freud: Life and Work*, Vol. 2, London and New York. (Page reference is to the English edition.) (26, 105)

(1957) *Sigmund Freud: Life and Work*, Vol. 3, London and New York. (Page references are to the English edition.) (26, 196, 230)

JUNG, C. G. (1909) 'Die Bedeutung des Vaters für das Schicksal des Einzelnen', *Jb. psychoanalyt. psychopath. Forsch.*, **1**, 153. (121)

[*Trans.:* 'The Significance of the Father in the Destiny of the Individual', *Collected Papers on Analytical Psychology*, London, 1916 (2nd ed., London, 1917; New York, 1920), Chap. III.]

(1910) 'Über Konflikte der kindlichen Seele', *Jb. psychoanalyt. psychopath. Forsch.*, **2**, 33. (120)

[*English Version (slightly modified):* 'Experiences Concerning the Psychic Life of the Child', *Collected Papers on Analytical Psychology*, London, 1916 (2nd ed., London, 1917; New York, 1920), Chap. II, (iii).]

(1974) With FREUD, S. *See* FREUD, S. (1974a)

KAAN, H. (1893) *Der neurasthenische Angstaffekt bei Zwangsvorstellungen und der primordiale Grübelzwang*, Vienna. (36)

LAFORGUE, R. (1926) 'Verdrängung und Skotomisation', *Int. Z. Psychoanal.*, **12**, 54. (318)

LÖWENFELD, L. (1904) *Die psychischen Zwangserscheinungen*, Wiesbaden. (36, 43)

LÖWENFELD, L. (1906) *Sexualleben und Nervenleiden*, 4th ed., Wiesbaden. (69-70)

MARCINOWSKI, J. (1918) 'Erotische Quellen der Minderwertigkeitsgefühle', *Z. SexWiss.*, Bonn, **4**, 313. (180)

MÖBIUS, P. J. (1894) *Neurologische Beiträge*, Vol. 2, Leipzig. (44)

MOLL, A. (1898) *Untersuchungen über die Libido sexualis*, Vol. 1, Berlin. (48)

OPHUIJSEN, J. H. W. VAN. (1917) 'Beiträge zum Männlichkeitskomplex der Frau', *Int. Z. ärztl. Psychoanal.*, **4**, 241. (177)
[*Trans.:* 'Contributions to the Masculinity Complex in Women', *Int. J. Psycho-Analysis.*, **5** (1924), 39.]

PEYER, A. (1893) 'Die nervösen Affektionen des Darmes bei der Neurasthenie des männlichen Geschlechtes (Darmneurasthenie)', *Vorträge aus der gesamten praktischen Heilkunde*, Vol. I, Vienna. (44)

PFISTER, O. and FREUD, S. (1963) *See* FREUD, S. (1963a)

PICK, A. (1896) 'Über pathologische Träumerei und ihre Beziehung zur Hysterie', *Jb. Psychiat. Neurol.*, **14**, 280. (87)

RANK, O. (1924) *Das Trauma der Geburt*, Vienna. (236, 292–3, 308–11, 321)
[*Trans.: The Trauma of Birth*, London, 1929.]

REIK, T. (1925) *Geständniszwang und Strafbedürfnis*, Leipzig, Vienna and Zurich. (272)

SADGER, I. (1907) 'Die Bedeutung der psychoanalytischen Methode nach Freud', *Zentbl. Nervenheilk. Psychiat.* N.F., **18**, 41. (93)

SILBERER, H. (1910) 'Phantasie und Mythos', *Jb. psychoanalyt. psychopath. Forsch.*, **2**, 541. (181)

STEKEL, W. (1911) *Die Sprache des Traumes*, Wiesbaden. (2nd ed., 1922.) (143–4)

WEISS, E. and FREUD, S. (1970) *See* FREUD, S. (1970a)

WERNICKE, C. (1894) Lecture on Anxiety Psychosis, reported in *Allg. Z. Psychiat.*, **51** (1895), 1020. (36)

ZWEIG, A., and FREUD, S. (1968) *See* FREUD, S. (1968a)

LIST OF ABBREVIATIONS

Gesammelte Schriften	= Freud, *Gesammelte Schriften* (12 vols), Vienna, 1924–34.
Gesammelte Werke	= Freud, *Gesammelte Werke* (18 vols), Vols 1–17 London, 1940–52, Vol. 18 Frankfurt am Main, 1968. From 1960 the whole edition published by S. Fischer Verlag, Frankfurt am Main.
S.K.S.N.	= Freud, *Sammlung kleiner Schriften zur Neurosenlehre* (5 vols), Vienna, 1906–1922.
Neurosenlehre und Technik	= Freud, *Schriften zur Neurosenlehre und zu psychoanalytischen Technik* (1913–1926), Vienna, 1931.
Collected Papers	= Freud, *Collected Papers* (5 vols), London, 1924–50.
Selected Papers on Hysteria	= Freud, *Selected Papers on Hysteria and other Psycho-Neuroses*, New York, 1909; 2nd ed., 1912; 3rd ed., 1920.
Standard Edition	= *The Standard Edition of the Complete Psychological Works of Sigmund Freud* (24 vols), Hogarth Press and The Institute of Psycho-Analysis, London, 1953–74.
P.F.L.	= *Pelican Freud Library* (15 vols), Penguin Books, Harmondsworth, from 1973.

GENERAL INDEX

This index includes the names of non-technical authors. It also includes the names of technical authors where no reference is made in the text to specific works. For reference to specific technical works, the Bibliography should be consulted. The index is based on originals compiled by Mrs R. S. Partridge and Alix Strachey.